CREATING A LEARNING SOCIETY?

Learning careers and policies for lifelong learning

First published in Great Britain in May 2002 by

The Policy Press
34 Tyndall's Park Road
Bristol BS8 1PY
UK

Tel +44 (0)117 954 6800
Fax +44 (0)117 973 7308
e-mail tpp@bristol.ac.uk
www.policypress.org.uk

British Library Cataloguing in Publication Data

A catalogue record for this book is available from the British Library

ISBN 1 86134 286 1 paperback

A hardcover version of this book is also available

Stephen Gorard and **Gareth Rees** are both Professors in the Cardiff University School of Social Sciences.

Cover design by Qube Design Associates, Bristol.

Front cover: photograph kindly supplied by Mark Simmons Photography, Bristol

Printed and bound in Great Britain by Hobbs the Printers Ltd, Southampton.

Contents

List of tables and figures

Tables

Figures

Acknowledgements

The study on which this book is primarily based was funded by the Economic and Social Research Council (grant L123251041) as part of its 'Learning Society' programme. It also received financial support from the then Gwent, Mid Glamorgan, and West Wales Training and Enterprise Councils. None of these organisations has any responsibility for the views expressed, which remain the responsibility of the authors alone. We should like, however, to record our thanks for their financial support of our research.

In carrying out this research, we have been helped by numerous colleagues. We should like to acknowledge the contributions made to the historical aspects of our work by Alan Burge, Hywel Francis and Colin Trotman, in the Department of Adult and Continuing Education at the University of Wales, Swansea. At the Cardiff University School of Social Sciences, we are grateful for the help of See Beng Huat and Jackie Swift in the analysis of interviews; and of Jane Salisbury and Trevor Welland in carrying them out. Sara Williams completed her PhD on young people's transition to higher education as an affiliated study and made a substantial contribution to the wider research project. Paul Chambers and Emma Renold were at various times research associates on the project and they too made a considerable impact on the study. Most importantly, we should like to thank Ralph Fevre and John Furlong, who were our co-researchers and were instrumental in shaping very important aspects of the analysis that our study has produced and that are reported here.

We also draw – albeit less centrally – on research studies supported financially by the Spencer Foundation, the National Assembly for Wales and the Organisation for Economic Co-operation and Development. Again, we should like to thank these organisations for their financial support, while in no way implicating them in our conclusions. We should also like to acknowledge the major contribution that our colleague, Neil Selwyn, has made to a number of these studies.

Preface

Lifelong learning is a topic that is most often addressed by both policy makers and academics using rhetoric and normative critique, rather than empirical evidence and systematic analysis. In this book, we set out to redress the balance by presenting – hopefully in an accessible form – the results of a large-scale study of patterns of lifelong participation in learning, the social and economic determinants of these patterns, and their impacts on social exclusion. This evidence provides us with the basis to evaluate alternative policy strategies for lifelong learning at national, regional and local levels. Rooting policy development in rigorous research seems to us essential if we are to achieve a truly learning society.

Accordingly, this book is based on a wide variety of empirical evidence, mostly stemming from a project entitled *Patterns of participation in adult education and training*, which was completed between 1996-99 as part of the Economic and Social Research Council's (ESRC's) 'Learning Society' programme. This project was based on our previous theoretical and empirical work, in the areas of work-based learning and vocational education and training, transitions from school to work, and the creation of learner identities. The data sources used in the study include: a large-scale household survey of the learning experiences of around 2,500 people aged 16-65; in-depth interviews with a sub-sample of 110 of these respondents; analysis of historical archives; interviews with education and training providers; and analysis of a variety of secondary statistical sources.

The results of this study are supplemented by the findings of further work we have done in separate projects on learning regions, the policy of setting National Targets for Lifelong Learning and the use of information and communications technology to extend participation in adult learning, by means of initiatives such as the University for Industry (UfI).

These various projects have generated a significant number of academic publications, written primarily to present our findings, to develop social scientific theory, or to explain our methodological strategies. However, this book is new in that it brings together and makes explicit for the first time the *policy implications* of our research; and in doing so, uses a large quantity of previously unpublished material. Shorn of complex methodological considerations, the book is therefore aimed at those involved in shaping and working with policies for lifelong learning. There is a growing body of people who are professionally concerned with the development of lifelong learning: in Local Education Authorities (LEAs); the Learning and Skills Councils (LSCs) and their equivalents in Wales, Scotland and Northern Ireland; the further education sector; in adult and continuing education; the voluntary sector; in private-sector training providers; the training divisions of companies; and in trades unions. We hope that what we have to say will be of interest to these groups, as well as to those in the Westminster and devolved governments who have the responsibility of developing effective policies for fostering lifelong learning. In addition, our book will be a useful reference for both undergraduate and postgraduate students who are attempting to understand what the implications of lifelong learning are for educational provision and a wide variety of other social and economic policies.

Much of the previous research evidence concerning adult participation in education and training is concerned with participants in formal settings (schools, colleges, universities and so on), undertaking taught and certificated courses, and there are many understandable and practical reasons for this. However, the cumulative effect of such an approach is to over-represent the views and opinions of existing or recent participants in learning. Despite the growth of further and higher education, and well-documented progress towards achieving the targets for lifelong learning, it remains true that nearly one third of all adults left school as soon as legally possible (or even before) and have never been involved in any formal education or training since then. This book draws on the accounts of this previously 'invisible' third of the population, as well as of those who have participated in various forms of education and training.

This highlights how the issues identified from a study that includes non-participants (in addition to the more commonly researched participants) change our understanding of the nature of a learning society, with enormous implications for policies of social inclusion and economic improvement. For example, our study begins to identify the vast, untapped potential of *informal* learning opportunities, currently largely ignored by official policies. It also shows how the determinants of adult participation in learning are deeply rooted in family background and early educational experiences. Thus, policies aimed at simply multiplying opportunities or removing practical barriers to participation, such as the UfI/learndirect, for instance, face serious problems. A set of policies aimed at creating a truly inclusive learning society would be very different from both existing and indeed planned initiatives in this area.

Creating a genuinely inclusive and effective learning society involves more than breaking down practical barriers to participation, or increasing opportunities for adult learning, or setting national targets for qualifications. There is no simple technical solution to problems of lack of access to adequate learning opportunities. Creating a learning society involves wider social and economic transformations as well. It involves recognition of the value of different forms of learning and, in particular, informal and uncertificated learning, which currently tends to be ignored. It involves the acceptance that the responsibility for ensuring effective learning rests not simply with individual learners themselves, but also with the providers of education and training, and – perhaps most controversially in the British case – with employers of all kinds. Above all, it involves abandoning a limited 'human capital' model of investment in learning, which reduces the benefits of lifelong learning to a simplistic economic calculus. Participation in learning during adult life reflects profound social and cultural attitudes towards education and learning more widely; attitudes that themselves are shaped by the social experience of learning during the early stages of the life course, within families, communities and formal educational settings such as schools.

In what follows, then, we set out to argue the case for a significant reorientation of approaches to the fostering of lifelong learning. We do this, however, on the basis of what we believe is a clearly argued and systematic analysis of our research findings. Certainly, we hope that our critics will address not simply our policy prescriptions, but equally the research from which they are derived.

Stephen Gorard
Gareth Rees
January 2002

ONE

Contemporary policies for a learning society

The principal purpose of this book is to present the results of research in an accessible form and thereby contribute to the development of more effective policies for fostering lifelong learning and creating a learning society. However, it is important to acknowledge that lifelong learning is an intensely political issue in Britain and elsewhere. There are conflicting views as to the nature of a learning society, the benefits that derive from lifelong learning, as well as the most effective ways of bringing these about.

Accordingly, this first chapter examines the notion of a learning society by outlining some of the chief arguments currently being used to advocate the establishment of such a society, and the policies that these have entailed. These arguments have two main strands. The first is that standards of education and training have a direct impact on the economy, and therefore expenditure on lifelong learning is an investment that will be recouped. The second is the claim that a lack of fairness exists in the distribution of education and its rewards in Britain today, and that widening participation will bring about an increase in social justice. It is important to note that, at this stage, we are talking about the *vision* that underlies the policies rather than the reality. We begin by considering what lifelong learning and a learning society are.

What is a learning society?

Frank Coffield, the Director of the ESRC's Learning Society Research Programme, has described a learning society as one:

> ... in which all citizens acquire a high quality general education, appropriate vocational training and a job ... while continuing to participate in education and training throughout their lives.... Citizens of a learning society would ... be able to engage in critical dialogue and action to improve the quality of life of the whole community. (Coffield, 1994, p 1)

On this view, therefore, a learning society involves a comprehensive post-school education and training system, in which everyone has access to suitable opportunities for lifelong learning.

Although it remains a contested notion (Ranson, 1992), this is a fair summary of what a learning society is deemed to be in the official discourse of contemporary British policy. For example, as the Skills Task Force (2000a) recently put it:

> Too many of our workforce, raised in the routine 'jobs for life' culture of the 1950s, 60s and 70s, left school with few qualifications if any. They lack the basic skills, aspirations, self-belief – and frequently the opportunity – to broaden their horizons through the power of learning. They have become trapped in the decreasing number of low-skill jobs, unable to grasp new opportunities and contribute their latent talents to our increasingly knowledge-based economy. At the same time, failing to utilise the full potential of our whole workforce clearly puts UK businesses and the UK economy at a significant competitive disadvantage. This is a situation we must tackle now if we are to strengthen our position as a world-class economy and create an inclusive society in which everyone has an increasing stake. (p 6)

Within this society, provision of education would be both excellent and fair, leading to national economic prosperity and social integration. It therefore involves action to improve the condition of life for the whole community. Mass participation in such a system is seen by some as necessary to provide a fulfilled life for individuals, a successful and developing economy, and a genuinely participative democracy (NIACE, 1994). This is because successful education transforms people's lives, enhances their confidence, and raises their ambitions (FEU, 1993); while equal opportunities in learning are a valuable precursor to equality of opportunity in employment and citizenship. A true learning society would have opportunities for lifelong learning, formal education for all ages, and support and recognition of informal education and self-directed study (Husen, 1986). A learning society could be seen as the target of the vocational educational strategy of the Employment Department Group (1994): investing in the skills needed for individuals and businesses to succeed, helping those at a disadvantage in the labour market, preparing youngsters for entry to the workforce, and making the labour market more responsive to changing economic needs. Equally, it appears in the Royal Society of Arts' (RSA's) National Campaign for Learning, which seeks to build a society in which all adults have a formal, monitored learning blueprint, every organisation is attempting to convert into a learning organisation (such as those in the Investors in People (IiP) programme), and a university is within reach of every part of the country (Keep, 1997).

Lifelong learning itself is a combination of initial education and adult education, in a way that questions the distinction between the child who learns and the adult who produces (Furter, 1977). School can therefore be seen as providing the basis for adult education, and lifelong learning becomes the embodiment of the contradictory goal of all education, the ability to teach oneself. As a policy objective, it is supported both by those who wish everyone to have the power that education brings, and those in industry who wish employees to have had a more practical education, perhaps one that reduces the likely cost to the employer of any further training (Whitfield and Bourlakis, 1991).

Lifelong learning, it is argued, deals more effectively with the problem of obsolete knowledge than an educational system that is front-loaded, emphasising the learning that takes place in the earlier phases of people's lives. If the notion of a job for life, with a planned career structure and associated company training, has gone (DfEE, 1996), career transitions are becoming more frequent and the knowledge gained at induction or through apprenticeship becomes obsolete more quickly (Rees, 1997). In these circumstances, rote knowledge is of little use, and higher-level cognitive skills such as problem solving are required instead (Downs, 1993); flexibility in the face of change becomes a priority (Edwards, 1997).

There are many good social and economic reasons for children to go to school and it used to be the case that so few continued their education into adulthood that the timing of this continuation was not important to most people (CERI, 1975). But it is not clear why educational expansion has focused on compulsory and continuing initial education in Britain, and why, despite all the rhetoric, it continues to do so. Schools have sucked in almost all the available resources, and this has been justified, in part, by the ensuing greater equity of provision, and appeals to economic progress. Nevertheless, students may stay in education well into adulthood for very negative reasons; while more enthusiastic adults may be excluded from learning opportunities by their age or evidence of early, immature 'failure'. Moreover, traditional forms of adult education have always exhibited a kind of 'second creaming' of attainment, such that only those who do well earlier in their educational careers tend to return to learning later on (Cropley, 1977). Lifelong learning, on the other hand, can be seen as universal rather than elitist, allowing genuine equality of later access, even if an individual lacks interest in school during childhood (Dave, 1976). Therefore, a learning society may also provide a chance to limit the amount spent on initial schooling, in order to put money into the education of adults, who form the majority of the population.

Of course, and as becomes apparent in the evidence presented in this book, everyone is already involved in some form of lifelong learning process: changes at work, meeting new people, and leisure interests, including television, mean that everyone 'learns' something new every day. At the other extreme to this 'loose' definition, "much of the policy interest in lifelong learning is in fact preoccupied with the development of a more productive and efficient workforce" (Field, 2000, p viii). Considerable analytical confusion in this area stems from these varied uses of the same term. Even the term 'learning' has a range of meanings (Bloomer, 2001).

While government policies, such as those detailed in the *Learning Age* (DfEE, 1998), espouse systemic change to encourage social inclusion and lifelong learning, underlying all proposals is an appeal to individuals. Individuals must take responsibility for their learning throughout their life, to become better equipped for employment in the 'information future'. Typical of the policies that this approach entails was the (now discontinued) Individual

Learning Accounts programme (Holden and Hamblett, 2001). 'Employability' is the key notion here, purportedly tying together the two policy elements of lifelong learning: the economic imperative; and the drive for social inclusion. For an individual, increasing their employability is good for them and their vocational prospects; but it is also good for the country and its economic competitiveness. We examine each of these claims separately.

The economic imperative

> Learning is the key to prosperity – for each of us as individuals, as well as a whole. Investment in human capital will be the foundation of success in the knowledge-based global economy of the twenty-first century. (DfEE, 1998, p 7)

One strand of argument behind the current push for a new learning society is based on the relationship between educational outcomes and economic performance. During the 1980s and 1990s, it was frequently argued that Britain's relatively poor economic performance was attributable to failures in education and skills development. Typically, Sir Geoffrey Holland, a former Permanent Secretary at the Department of Employment and a key figure in shaping official approaches to lifelong learning, claimed at the North of England Education Conference in 1995 that while Britain had slipped from 14th to 18th place in a league-table of global economic competitiveness, and from 21st to 24th in terms of the skills levels of the workforce, the quality of education was now rated *35th* in the world.

Certainly, it has become a commonplace of academic analysis that slow economic growth is primarily due to the inadequacy of the education and training system (McNabb and Whitfield, 1994). Much of the blame for this has been laid at the feet of the education and training system (Bosworth, 1992; Haskel and Martin, 1993; IFF, 1994), whose inadequate performance leads to problems for individuals seeking work (Greenhalgh and Stewart, 1987; Main and Shelly, 1990) and for industry as a whole (Keep, 1993). Despite the strong demand for multi-skilled, intermediate occupations, such as craft and technician grades in industry, it is argued that Britain is failing to train adequately (Cutler, 1992); and this is leading to skills shortages, especially in particular sectors and occupational categories (Green and Ashton, 1992). A major problem has been seen as the increasing demand for new skills, especially numerate ones, for multi-skilled workers. "We are hurtling towards a 21st century in which the jobs available will be jobs that robots cannot do and where our survival, both economically and socially, depends on applied intelligence, enterprise, initiative, flexibility and ability to survive rapid change" (Sir Geoffrey Holland at the North of England Education Conference, 1995).

A 'job for life' and a 'career company' are now seemingly obsolete concepts (Ashley and Walkley, 1996) and continuous re-education is needed if people are to lead fruitful and enjoyable lives. "The blunt truth is that there will be no work for the unskilled in the future" (Jones, 1996, p 29). Workers may face the possibility of more part-time and more short-term employment, with brief periods of unemployment and earlier retirement. They therefore need to be educated for 'employability', to have flexible attitudes towards work and an individual responsibility for training, and to realise that suitability for employment is a continuous requirement and not a one-off event.

A modern economy and the creation of wealth therefore needs high levels of skills in the workforce, not just in manufacturing, but also in service industries, and at all occupational levels (Scottish Office, 1991). A poor standard of vocational education and training leads to managers having a poor level of technical education, who find it difficult to see the advantages of new technology, making them conservative in the use of new equipment (Keep, 1993). Lack of skills also means that machinery in Britain is poorly maintained, leading to a high proportion of down time. Low skill levels in the workforce can also trap companies in low-cost, high-volume production: a 'low-skill equilibrium', from which it is difficult to escape, even where the motivation exists to do so (Finegold and Soskice, 1988).

In addition, the acquisition of skills is seen as a key determinant of career success. If occupational status is estimated by payment per hour, those in the lowest paid occupations show far higher mobility if they have had training; while in one study 65% of those with no training were still in the lowest paid category after 10 years (Greenhalgh and Stewart, 1987). Similarly, in another study, 18 months after leaving school, those who had been involved in Youth Training of any sort were much more likely to be in a job than those who spent the initial period unemployed (Main and Shelly, 1990). For the individual, therefore, lifelong learning brings a return for themselves as well as for the economy and society.

During the 1980s, it was the restructuring of schools and schooling that were deemed by policy makers to provide the key to remedying these problems (for example, Ball, 1990). More latterly, the focus has widened to encompass a broader notion of lifelong learning, which continues to embrace the compulsory phases of education, but also includes activities in further and higher education, as well as continuing education and training throughout adult life (Coffield, 1999). As the current British Prime Minister put it during the 1997 General Election campaign: "Education is the best economic policy we have" (TES, 1998c, p 27).

This is not to suggest, of course, that the shift in policy emphasis during the 1990s produced a coherent strategy with respect to education and training through the life course. Nevertheless, the change is unmistakable. For example, the creation of a Minister for Lifelong Learning within the Department for Education and Employment (DfEE, now the DfES), along with equivalent positions in the devolved Scottish and Welsh administrations, signalled a formal acknowledgement of its significance[1]. Similarly, a plethora of official reports and other policy statements on lifelong learning have flowed from government departments. There have been three substantial reports (Dearing, 1997; Fryer, 1997; Kennedy, 1997), a major Green Paper (DfEE, 1998), and a White Paper on the reorganisation of post-16 education and training (DfEE, 1999). These have culminated in the wholesale reorganisation of the delivery of post–16 education and training through the 2001 Learning and Skills Act. Certainly, lifelong learning has come to occupy a position that – symbolically at least – is at the centre of government strategy (Ainley, 1998; Tight, 1998a; Coffield, 2000).

What is involved here is more than a narrowly technical adjustment to the organisation of educational provision. It is instructive, for example, that the key Green Paper was given the portentous title, *The Learning Age: A renaissance for a new Britain* (DfEE, 1998). What is suggested, then, is a transformation in learning opportunities, which is crucial to effecting a profound restructuring of wider social and economic relations. The intellectual basis for this reformulation of state policy is provided, in turn, by what has become a widespread consensus about the emergent requirements of the economy. Building on earlier analyses, it is now widely argued that the production and distribution of knowledge are increasingly significant processes in the determination of economic competitiveness and development, which are reflected, in turn, in economic growth, employment change and levels of welfare. The capacity of both organisations and individuals to engage successfully in learning processes of a variety of kinds has come to be regarded as a crucial determinant of economic performance (Lundvall and Johnson, 1994). For some commentators, this implies nothing less than a fundamental transition from an industrial to a knowledge-based society (OECD, 1996; Leadbeater, 1999). Clearly, alternative accounts of the nature of the learning society are possible and some of these are presented later in the book. However, the ideological impact of this particular version derives precisely from the fact that it is rooted in a coherent analysis of contemporary patterns of economic change.

Moreover, it is an analysis that has been widely adopted internationally, as well as within Britain. Governments in advanced industrial countries in other parts of Europe, North America and Australasia have based policy programmes on this view of an emergent knowledge-based, globalised economy. Most strikingly, perhaps, it has been advanced by supra-national organisations, including the European Commission, the OECD and the World Bank, as the basis for their highly influential policy recommendations. In important respects, therefore, the influence of this analysis within Britain reflects its wider global significance (Crouch et al, 1999).

The proponents of this sort of analysis recognise, of course, that the development of the learning society (even defined in these terms) involves complex economic and social processes. On the one hand, it holds the promise of increased productivity and an improved standard of living. On the other, it simultaneously implies that individuals and organisations face major challenges in adjusting to new circumstances. The emergent forms of economic activity affect the characteristic nature of work and the types and levels of skills required in the economy. As a result, the security and general quality of jobs are supposedly being radically altered, with profound implications for the welfare of individuals. Accordingly, it is recognised that the nature of access to learning opportunities has implications not only for general economic competitiveness, but also for the employability of individuals and the consequent impacts on their standards of living.

The policy implications of this analytical consensus could be profound. If an economy like Britain's – where factor costs are fairly high – is to be competitive, employers need to pursue innovative and technologically-intensive strategies for the production of goods and services that have high added value. Employees require not only high levels of general education, but also the capacity to adapt flexibly to changing skills requirements throughout their careers. Moreover, educational institutions should be organised in ways that ensure these standards of general education are attained, and also that the renewal of skills through continuing education and training is facilitated (Ashton and Green, 1996). As Coffield (1999) has argued, however, one of the striking features of British policies is that they have concentrated very much on the implications of this analysis for educational institutions and for individuals, more than for the state and employers. For example, the long-term preoccupation with raising 'standards' in schools and colleges is a clear reflection of the former. Equally, the emphasis in initiatives such as the UfI and the National Grid for Learning is on the need for individual workers and students to acquire the necessary skills and competencies (Gorard and Selwyn, 1999).

Social exclusion

The second major strand of arguments for the learning society is based on ideas about social justice. Here, it is claimed that access to education and training is unfairly distributed in Britain; and that it is the same groups of people who are denied learning opportunities throughout their lives. Indeed, these inequalities may also persist across generations (Sargant et al, 1997). In the standard form of this argument, the education and training system is seen as a good one, providing a product appropriate for all. It is the problem of inequitable access that needs to be solved to ensure greater and wider participation (Titmuss, 1994).

That there are serious inequalities in opportunities for, and participation in, formal adult education and training is indisputable. Employment, mode of employment, size of company, industry sector, occupation, and social class all show systematic variations in access to training (Deloitte Haskins and Sells, 1989; McGivney, 1993). In addition, there are key differences in opportunities for formal learning by gender, age and ethnicity (Tremlett et al, 1995). The groups under-represented in education and training are, therefore, unskilled manual workers, unqualified, part-time and temporary workers, the unemployed, lone parents, women of lower social class, refugees, ex-offenders, the relatively illiterate and innumerate, and those with special needs or disabilities (NIACE, 1994). Hence, these characteristics represent the most effective predictors of whether or not individuals participate in adult learning in Britain today. Not only do current or recent experiences of learning vary by occupational class, but there is also a class pattern in whether people intend learning new things in the future (Tuckett and Sargant, 1999).

Those who are already better educated or qualified, and presumably more likely to be employed at a higher grade, are also more likely to receive training later in their lives (McGivney, 1990; DfEE, 1995), perhaps because their previous educational record is seen as providing evidence of their being trainable (Pettigrew et al, 1989). In one study, for example, only 3% of those who left school at the minimum age undertook training during the three years prior to the survey, compared to 65% of those with immediate post-initial education (Park, 1994). The best-qualified applicants also get the best employer-based training in government schemes such as the (then) Youth Training Scheme (Banks et al, 1992).

It has been argued quite widely that recent changes in the organisation and delivery of adult education and training have exacerbated these inequities. For example, the 1992 Further and Higher Education Act divided vocational and non-vocational courses, with the former attracting Funding Council support only if they lead to national qualifications. The concept of education for leisure has all but disappeared (Burstall, 1996). However, previously non-vocational courses were precisely those that could be used by women in particular to gain confidence before progressing to assessed courses. Men are more likely to be employed full-time, and to receive training, while women more often look after a family, and are less likely to be learners in general, with unpaid work at home not yet being widely accredited (Butler, 1993). Younger, male employees who are already well qualified are the most likely to receive further training (Green, 1994). Those caring for children are the least likely. Most people undertaking vocational training are young (McGivney, 1993); only 9% of those involved in post-initial education and training are aged over 65 (Harrison, 1993). In fact, vocational training seems almost to cease at the age of 50 (NIACE, 1994).

Vocational and other forms of provision show different patterns of participation, and therefore lead to different excluded groups, with women only under-represented in the former. Some of the likely determinants of these differences concern the structure of opportunities to access learning, such as the sector of employment, for example; while others concern the individual's social background, such as family occupational class. Both of these types of determinants may affect the take-up of learning opportunities, but the latter has primacy as an explanation, because background predates opportunities and because it is very difficult to change. People can often move house and jobs, for example, but they cannot, so readily, alter their ethnic or class background.

The DfEE (1998) produced a whole range of practical proposals to deal with many of these issues of inequitable participation. These included: the launch of the UfI; the expansion of further and higher education by 500,000 places by 2002; the provision of Individual Learning Accounts; doubling the help available for literacy and numeracy among adults; raising standards of post-compulsory teaching by means of a Training Standards Council and inspection system; the publication of national qualification targets; and the development of skills at work. It should be noted, however, that all recent policies, even the most innovative, remain largely directed at individuals, rather than addressing the wider social context. As the Skills Task Force (2000) recently put it, for example:

> The promotion and encouragement of lifelong learning should be greatly increased, building on programmes like the Campaign for Learning, UfI and the Union Learning Fund, particularly targeted at individuals who could most benefit from learning but are reluctant to become involved. (p 7)

This focus on the individual, in turn, underpins a tension between this inclusive strand in the learning society and the economic imperative. As the examples already discussed make clear, for example, it is often the nature of jobs and the training they involve that lies at the heart of unequal access to learning opportunities today. Despite policies and pledges, there has been static national participation in all forms of lifelong learning in recent years (NIACE, 2000). In fact, the gap in terms of access between those who are already poorly educated and those who are well educated appears to be widening; while class, occupation, previous education, and employment remain the most significant indicators of adult participation in education and training. Over half of the population now report themselves as being unlikely to be involved in any lifelong learning in the future. At least part of the reason for this depressing state of affairs is that there are tensions between the economic and social justice strands of learning society policy.

While the two strands are usually presented as being in tandem, it is actually clear that the economic imperative concentrates on the young and the employable, while the social agenda focuses on the older, the unskilled, and the economically inactive. A recent Budget, for example, phased out tax relief, and with it public support, for non-vocational adult education classes. Thus, there is no help available from the Treasury unless a course appears to be of immediate economic benefit (Tuckett, 1999). This policy makes sense for the first strand, but not for the second. This underlying tension forms one basis for much of the rest of this book.

The learning society: alternative visions

We now present some alternative visions of what a learning society is and could be. We drew attention earlier to the marked commonalities in state policies – both at the level of national governments and supra-national organisations – with respect to the building of a learning society. The latter is conceived primarily in terms of objectives of economic growth and wellbeing. More particularly, a crucial role is accorded to the individual actor in this official discourse. Economic competitiveness, it is argued, is dependent on a highly skilled labour force; and, hence, economic growth primarily reflects the capacities of individual workers to acquire these necessary skills and competencies. Some official accounts (for example, European Commission, 1996) extend this analysis to consider the distributional consequences of the achievement of such economic growth. What would be the effects on employment levels? Who would have access to jobs? What would be the impacts on wider patterns of social integration and exclusion? Others are notably silent on these issues.

While it remains axiomatic for many politicians that getting education and training right will have very great economic benefits, the suggestion that poor educational performance is a cause of poor economic performance requires a lot to establish it. Establishing a causal link from a curriculum change, for example, to economic improvement is very difficult (Yeomans, 1996; Gorard, 2001a). An equally plausible explanation of the relationship between the two is that it is easier for countries with a healthy economy to afford quality, innovative education.

The assumption that advanced economies need highly educated and trained populations and a skilled and flexible workforce for economic reasons can anyway be exaggerated. Most people will probably not get secure, highly-skilled employment whatever happens (Edwards et al, 1993). Most new businesses and associated jobs are in fact 'low tech', in areas such as retailing and traditional services (Keep, 2000). While there is a demand for high tech and high skills, there are still plenty of unskilled and low-skilled jobs, especially in some of the service industries. There is little evidence that increased expenditure on education and training leads to any improvement in the quality of employment. In fact, several of the highest spending nations have traditionally had the worst outcomes in economic terms (Smithers and Robinson, 1991).

It is also argued by many commentators that there is a gap between what is supposed to be happening in terms of the transition to a globalised, knowledge-based economy and the reality. Hence, for example, the degree of change in length of job tenure is disputable; training in transferable skills is not generally available to employees, perhaps especially in Britain; while many industries, such as those in the services sector, remain firmly local and these are often the current growth areas (Keep, 1997).

In fact, if the problems posed to the British economy by globalisation are so great, it becomes perverse for the government or organisations such as the CBI (with its notion of transferable core skills, personal profiles, action plans, independent careers guidance, and training credits) to concentrate on individuals and their lack of skills or training, or to bemoan the fact that few are willing to pay for their own training (Coffield, 1999). Increased marketisation of training may be attractive financially, but suffers two main defects. First, Britain may be suffering more from a lack of skilled jobs than a lack of skilled workers, and leaving things to the market will inevitably tend to a 'low-skill equilibrium', polarising accessibility to training (Istance and Rees, 1995). A market in training cannot overcome the wariness of employers with regard to the link between training and staff turnover (and 'poaching'), and it cannot therefore maintain a balance between general (transferable) and specific skills, under-financing the former (Greenhalgh and Mavrotas, 1994). Second, freedom of choice for the individual will lead to situations where people opt for forms of training that are not best suited to the needs of the economy. In fact, it has been reported that in the Modern Apprenticeship Scheme, ten times as many people want to study hairdressing as Information Technology (IT); whereas skills audits regularly reveal a need for IT competence. Markets may be a poor basis for social policy, since employers are too concerned with the short term (Gleeson et al, 1996). This may be why, despite universal endorsement of the policy of expanding lifelong learning, there is little evidence of powerful innovative policies being implemented in practice, either in the UK or overseas (Field, 2000).

One justification given by advocates for the advancement of a learning society is a pseudo-progression. In this version, lifelong learning is essential since the rate of industrial, technological and societal change is exponential (Cropley, 1977). The world is changing too quickly for one person's life to be considered to take place against a stable background (Employment Department Group, 1994), and the rate of change is increasing over time, so that lifelong learning is becoming more and more essential to allow people to adapt. The position was summed up by one observer thus:

> In the past the time span of important change was considerably longer than that of a single human life. Thus mankind was trained to adapt itself to fixed conditions. Today the time span is considerably shorter than that of human life, and accordingly our training must prepare individuals to face a novelty of conditions.

However, as this was A.N. Whitehead, the eminent philosopher, speaking in the 1930s (Dave, 1976, p 15), it is possible that the apparent change over generations has always been large, since by the very nature of memory and public records, more is known of now and of the recent past than more distant times.

When a learning society is seen as a future ideal state towards which Britain should be striving, any failures such as injustice and inefficiency in the current educational system may be part of the interim cost to be borne in the struggle. "Sometimes glimpses of that vision seem to take shape, shimmering like a distant oasis" (Cassels, in Keep, 1997). However, advocates of greater educational equality and industrial competitiveness are not new (Cropley, 1977), while demands for lifelong learning may be as old as recorded history itself (Dave, 1976). In 1973, a South Wales newspaper claimed that greater productivity in the depressed coalfield valleys would come not from longer working hours or greater effort, but better organisation and more efficient machinery: "Physical exertion is yielding to technical 'know how': we are truly in the age of the Technocrat".

The standard learning society analysis is too simple, suffering from what Yeomans (1996) calls 'historical amnesia'. We have been here before: as early as blaming the loss of industrial pre-eminence on a failure of the education system in the late 19th century (Rees, 1997). In Britain, many of the policy components of a learning society were described and advocated by the 1919 Smith Report. This concluded that education was not simply for personal benefit alone, but for the common good, and that it was advanced not only by educational measures but also radical social reform (Lowe, 1970).

There are some indications, therefore, that far from being a future state, elements of a learning society may actually have been stronger in the past, for some sections of society and in some geographical areas, than they are today (see Chapter Three). By this, it is not simply meant that training today might be inferior to the craft-based systems of the past, or that the skills of bricklayers in the 1990s do not match those of the 1920s, for example; or that a learning society has always existed for the most prosperous segment of the population if they wanted it (Coffield, 1999). In the first part of this century, education for all was not underpinned so much by arguments of economic competitiveness or even increased social mobility (Lewis, 1993). The main purpose of workers' education, for instance, was not to encourage talented individuals to leave their working community, but to meet the rising aspirations of labour and to lead perhaps to greater political awareness or fuller participatory citizenship. Education was part of politics, and workers' education was as much a part of the rise of labour, and the post-war settlement, as compulsory initial education (Lewis, 1993). Although there were tensions within the movement between radical and liberal intentions, and although individual class-mobility came to be accepted as an added bonus, as a whole this tentative alliance of university intellectuals and the inheritors of an older autodidact tradition was successful in its own terms.

Nowadays, the expansion of state education has institutionalised social mobility and while all mainstream political parties argue about an education-led economy or greater equality of opportunity, the more radical collective agenda of cultural and intellectual equality is ignored. Even the non-conformist inspired versions of education for cultural accomplishment have been lost for the most part (Rees, 1997).

It is suggested here that, to the extent that it is correct to describe a learning society in the past, this was partially underpinned by group loyalties to a variety of communities based in occupations and localities. If these loyalties have been undermined – by structural changes that have had far-reaching effects on occupations and localities – it might be expected that the heirs of those communities will no longer exhibit the orientations appropriate to a learning society (Fevre et al, 1999). The newer approach to education and training is inspired by individualism, and may be unable to produce the more virtuous outcomes that are popularly supposed to arise in a learning society. The individualist approach tends to produce an instrumentalist view of learning, which leads to outcomes that are a poor substitute for education and training inspired by group loyalties, or the more radical forms of education leading to political awareness. It also enhances what have been described as the "insidious effects of learning as a positional good" (Keep, 1997, p 14).

If it is argued that knowledge and skills become obsolete quickly and that competitive economies need to be more innovative, then further training for all can quite reasonably be justified by policy makers and backed up by the enhancement of workers' status that the retraining and multi-skilling provides. However, the same process can also be seen as justification for exploitation of the workforce, leading to greater productivity for the chief benefit of those at the top (Furter, 1977).

A push towards *institutionalising* adult education prolongs the dependency of individuals on institutions, possibly hindering what for many is the true outcome of education, which is to enable all to take control of their own learning, and to teach them to be independent of teachers. Lifelong learning, far from breaking the schools monopoly, can therefore be seen as an annexation of out-of-school territory by 'schoolers', using similar approaches to those that have already failed in schools, such as certificating individuals. More recently, this form of learning society has been presented by academics (Tight, 1998a) and practitioners (Mansell, 2000) as 'moral authoritarianism', and these commentators remain unconvinced of the link between educational achievement and workplace performance. In fact, formal adult education has traditionally interested only a few in Britain, where public spending, for example, has been much less than in other countries (Lowe, 1970). Why, if there is huge unfulfilled demand for learning, are taxpayers not clamouring for greater funding and why is any new funding voted for by adults almost inevitably spent on children?

In an alternative account of the learning society, learning is something that everyone does and wants to do, but informally. The 'society' element could be an attempt at coercion, and control of one of its most powerful forces for change. In the past this control may have been through the extended family, passing on false knowledge such as religious observance and denying life opportunities to children in order to preserve them as an economic asset (Coleman, 1990). This control then gradually passed to schools, which according to Cobbett taught children to be content to be 'slaves' under the pretext of teaching them to read and write (Johnson, 1993). Schools can be seen as preparing children for the world of work as defined by the employer – to do as they are told, turn up on time and move with the bell. Schooling may be marginal to real life for many people, but its compulsion has been formative in society, perhaps leading to loss of autonomy for families with deeper regulation by the state, with a clearer distinction between adults and children and between the place of work and home (Johnson, 1993). On this analysis, it is not surprising that the lengthening of adolescence in society today has led to a demand by the state and employers for a lengthening of the 'learning' (that is, instructional) process.

Current solutions to the problems of working life are often reduced to the single idea of 'qualifying' the individual to adapt and to agree to a 'useful' training, where this is defined as one suited chiefly to the requirements and structures of the existing productive system (Furter, 1977). This trick is a clever one, since it is generally cheaper to train people to do the jobs that exist than it is to provide suitable jobs for the people who exist.

An even more extreme version would be that learning is something that everyone does instinctively and therefore not something that needs to be taught, especially by the appointees of the state (Frow and Frow, 1990). Therefore, any attempt at formal education cannot affect the amount of learning taking place. It can only affect *what* is learnt, and even here the results can be unpredictable. The assumption that teachers can transmit what is useful has been generally untested. The quality control of education is usually of the teaching, not of the learning itself (Deamer, 1996).

Conclusion

At least three strands of a learning society have arisen in this brief discussion: the push for greater inclusiveness and the economic imperative, both currently in favour, and the older liberal view of a learning society as a cultured arena for civilised life. To a large extent, these differing objectives require different approaches, and would benefit different sections of society. The economic argument tends to see people as human capital, allying with the inclusive argument when there is a shortage of appropriate labour. Independent workers' education can also be seen as economic in purpose, both the liberal-based supposedly 'impartial' education represented by the Workers' Educational Association and university extramural classes, and the less formal anti-capitalist episodes (see Chapter Three). The inclusive argument for recurrent education is based on movement towards greater equality rather than towards greater quality per se. It is the liberal vision that explains the demand for learning for leisure and pleasure, for oneself and for one's peers (Hanson, 1968).

It would be elegant to conclude that a true learning society will exist when all three components are in harmony. However, it is not clear a priori that this is likely or even possible. The tensions may be just too great: between education as stimulus to action, changing one's own life as a step towards changing the world (Frow and Frow, 1990); and education as a process of social control (Simon, 1990). The twin aims of education are fitting people for their social roles and promoting their ability to think independently. The challenge for educators is to overcome the inherent contradictions between the two (Fryer, 1990). In this book we chart the extent to which this has been achieved over the past century, and highlight the policy implications for the coming century.

Note

[1] There are already clear indications that the devolved governments in Scotland, Wales and Northern Ireland are developing distinctive approaches to the organisation and delivery of lifelong learning from that which is being pursued in England (Croxford and Raffe, 2000). However, we do not pursue these divergences here. Moreover, the underlying rationales for policies, which is our principal focus here, remain remarkably consistent.

TWO

Lifelong learning trajectories

As we have emphasised, our primary concern in this book is to present the results of our research in an accessible form. Rather than beginning with normative questions about what a 'learning society' ought to constitute, the principal concerns in this book are with what the patterns of participation through the life course actually are and how best to understand their determinants. This is important not only to strengthen the social science of this field, but also to provide a proper basis for the formulation of policy.

To evaluate the various policies for fostering lifelong learning and the intellectual rationales that underpin them, which we sketched out in Chapter One, we need to have a firm knowledge of people's actual patterns of participation in lifelong learning. We also require an understanding of the factors that shape these patterns of participation. In short, therefore, we concur with Coffield (1997) that the development of an adequate social theory of lifelong learning – however complex – is a necessary precondition of understanding and creating a learning society.

In this chapter we present an overview of our preliminary theoretical model of the determinants of lifelong learning. It is this model that shaped the way in which we approached our empirical research. We then present an explicit account of the methodological strategy that informed the principal of the research studies on which we draw.

History, place and biography

Previous analysis of why people undertake education and training during their adult lives has tended to isolate individuals from the social and economic contexts in which participation in learning takes place. The dominant mode of theorising in this field has been human capital theory (HCT), where individuals participate in lifelong learning according to their calculation of the net economic benefits to be derived from education and training (Becker, 1975). Given the dominant policy consensus about the general direction of economic change towards more knowledge-based forms of production (as outlined in Chapter One), it follows that a worker will seek to participate in lifelong learning in order to capitalise on the benefits that will flow from skills renewal and development.

Hence, on this view, the principal issue that government policy needs to address is to ensure the removal of the 'barriers' that prevent people from participating in education and training. These include 'situational' factors, such as finance and lack of time because of other commitments, as well as the features of educational institutions, which make them unresponsive to potential learners (McGivney, 1990). Although some of this work provides a valuable picture of participation patterns, it remains under-theorised; and ignores the insights provided by the sociology of education more generally, which has also emphasised the constraints on access to educational opportunities experienced by different social groups. More importantly, questions of individual motivation – which predominate in human capital theory – are under-explored here; and have been generally confined to research involving those who *do* take part in education and training of some kind (Maguire et al, 1993), rather than considering those who do not. Major initiatives such as the UfI, Individual Learning Accounts, and the National Targets for Lifelong Learning reflect these priorities quite clearly. Achieving a learning society thus comes to be defined in these rather simple terms.

According to HCT, people participate in education and training in order to increase their future earnings; and these earnings may increase because they will thereby make themselves more productive workers, but this is not an essential part of the theory (Gambetta, 1987, p 132). They weigh the costs of current investment in education/training against future benefits from higher incomes. Now, this is not an obvious and incontrovertible fact of human behaviour (Schultz, 1961). While economic calculation may sometimes influence behaviour once thought immune to it, the relative merits of economic and competing explanations are a matter for empirical investigation in each case.

In reality, individual behaviour in economic markets of any kind is embedded in social relations that are shaped by social norms, interpersonal relationships, family and community structures and so forth. Hence, rather than adopting a universalistic form of explanation (such as HCT), we explore the ways in which the determinants of participation in lifelong learning vary systematically over time and from locality to locality (Rees et al, 1997). Viewed from a perspective that emphasises place, history and individual biography, then, creating a learning society – even one defined in terms of essentially economic considerations – becomes a much more complex process.

The temporal and spatial variations in empirical patterns of participation have been widely acknowledged. However, their analytical implications have been less fully explored. Understanding why these patterns take the form that they do requires an analysis of the shifts that have taken place in the structure of learning opportunities available in given areas (through, for example, changes in educational provision or labour market conditions), as well as how access to these opportunities is constrained by the social and cultural resources that different social groups command.

Moreover, the relationships between these kinds of structural conditions and actual participation are further mediated not only by the knowledge about learning opportunities that is socially available, but also by the beliefs and attitudes that are held in respect of them (Fevre et al, 1999). Our previous research suggests that the latter 'learner identities' also vary systematically over time and spatially, reflecting complex patterns of individual, family, community and wider determinations. We therefore agree with Bloomer

(2001) that it is too crude to try and divide the determinants of participation into simple categories of structure and agency, and ignore the potential interplay between them.

Accordingly, understanding the determinants of participation in lifelong learning involves tracing out the interactions between the social relations that are specific to particular places; patterns of historical change; and the experiences that constitute individual biographies. In this book, we explore these issues by reference to the results of an empirical study of patterns of participation in lifelong learning over the past one hundred years.

In particular, we draw on the results of a large-scale questionnaire survey; in-depth semi-structured interviews with a sub-sample; secondary data; and extensive archival analysis. These sources, and their analysis, are described in the second half of this chapter. As shown in Chapter Three, focusing on a single region has allowed us to make a detailed reconstruction of the changes that have taken place in patterns of lifelong learning and how these are related to shifts in the economic structure, as well as transformations in social relations more widely.

Our study explores the empirical patterns of participation in lifelong learning through the concept of 'trajectories'. At one level, what is involved here is the attempt to describe characteristic sequences of learning episodes through the life course by aggregating individual experiences into a set of typologies (Banks et al, 1992). However, there is a clear analytical element too. Hence, the resources largely determine the 'trajectory' that people join that they derive from their social background. An individual's capacity to take up whatever learning opportunities are available is constrained by his or her previous history in this respect. However, 'trajectories' do not simply reflect the constraining effects of structured access to learning opportunities. The individual educational experiences of which they are comprised are simultaneously the products of personal choices, which themselves reflect 'learner identities', the characteristic attitudes and values that individuals hold with respect to their participation in learning. What is central to an adequate analysis, therefore, is to produce an account of the interaction of 'learner identities' and the individual choices to which they give rise, with wider structural parameters (Rees et al, 1997).

The principal aim of the study forming the major basis for this book, therefore, is to develop a better understanding of the determinants of participation and non-participation in lifelong learning. For the theoretical reasons already sketched, this involves a close analysis of changes in the trajectories of participation over time; as well as the detailed consideration of the impacts of regionally and locally specific patterns of social and economic development. Time and place have come to be recognised as crucial elements in social analysis more widely, but have not previously been systematically integrated into studies of post-school participation in education and training. It is intended, moreover, that this analysis should contribute to the development of policies that will enhance participation in education and training, especially among those social groups that are currently under-represented.

Human capital theory and participation in adult learning: a critique

Human capital theory is based on the assumptions that individuals will seek to maximise their material wellbeing (or utility) in economic transactions; that they possess full knowledge of market conditions; and that they will act rationally to achieve their preferences in the light of this knowledge (see, for example, Martinelli and Smelser, 1990, p 29). Accordingly, individuals will choose to undertake education and training to the extent that they are aware of the opportunities available and that they are able to maximise material returns through doing so.

Recent developments in the sociology of economic life have renewed the critique of such neo-classical economic theory (for example, Zukin and DiMaggio, 1990; Granovetter and Swedberg, 1992; Smelser and Swedberg, 1994). Most generally, the absolute differentiation between economic and social life that it implies, and the consequent tendency for individuals to be governed by exclusively material motivations, are rejected. As Lazar (1996) has recently put it:

> ... for sociological analysis, economic action is a form of social action, not merely a matter of individuals acting in pursuit of individual interests, and must not be analysed as if it exists in a rarefied realm with its peculiar, autonomous form of motivation. (p 600)

What are emphasised, then, are the *continuities* between economic action and institutions, on the one hand, and wider social networks and organisations, on the other. Hence, for example, behaviour in economic markets is, in Polanyi's (1957) term, 'embedded' in systems of social relations, particularly networks of interpersonal relations. Moreover, economic markets have characteristic *normative* bases (in the same way as the more obvious cases of exchange based on 'reciprocity' or 'redistribution') (Polanyi, 1957). And to these might be added the pervasive influence of differential power between social groups[1].

This dissolution of the boundary between economic action and social relations more widely has specific consequences for the ways in which the determinants of individual behaviours are conceptualised. The neo-classical formulation ignores the possibility that individuals may pursue ends (or have preferences) that are different from the maximisation of material well being. This potential for a diversity of preferences may be conceived as reflecting different value positions (although the latter, in turn, may be shaped within normative structures). For example, an employee may undertake a programme of training because he or she prizes the intrinsic pleasure obtained from the programme or from the enhanced capacity to do a job, even where the material benefits to be derived are negligible. This action would be 'rational', even though the ends that are sought deviate from those assumed in the conventional economic model of preferences.

The critique of neo-classical theory also raises the question of the extent to which behaviour in markets may be conceived as the product of individual choice and decision-making *at all*. In this context, the exercise of choice by the individual is constrained by a structure of taken-for-granted presuppositions with respect to what is available and appropriately sought after. What this suggests is that there are definable relationships between individual preferences and the choices based on them, normative systems and the locations in the social structure within which socialisation occurs.

Nevertheless, it is important not to overstate the effects of socialisation: to avoid an *over*-socialised conception of the individual, where his or her action is viewed as a passive reflection of wider social forces. Even where the range of possible courses of action is perceived to be highly restricted, individuals remain able to compare options and to choose 'rationally' between them. Individuals are able to reject the preference structures into which they are socialised, as, for instance, any analysis of participation in adult education programmes demonstrates. Actors remain autonomous through exercising choice over the courses of action that they pursue, even though their choices are made within parameters that are set externally. Analytically, therefore, the task is to produce an account of the *interaction* of individual choice with its parameters.

These external parameters are not, however, confined to the effects of socialisation. Individual choices are not simply constrained by socially constituted preferences, but also reflect the social structure of actually available opportunities. Preferences themselves may be shaped − whether through socialisation or more directly − by the reality of feasible alternative actions. Moreover, the scope of autonomy and choice is not neutral in the face of processes of social exclusion and integration, but is structured by these wider social relations. Individuals do not enjoy a level playing field in access to opportunities for education and training (as for other goods and services); and this is true, in principle, irrespective of how people understand these opportunities. For example, changes in state provision of educational opportunities (consequent, say, on the 1944 Education Act) or in the organisation of economic production (leading to the expansion of women's employment) have resulted in structural changes in learning opportunities, whose implications have, arguably, only partially been absorbed into people's social understanding and normative structures.

Towards a social theory of lifelong learning

A major part of the sociological analysis of participation in education and training presents almost a mirror image of human capital theory and neo-classical economic analysis more widely. Here, the emphasis has been overwhelmingly on the constraints within which individual actors operate. For example, patterns of attainment within compulsory schooling or of participation in post-compulsory areas of education have characteristically been analysed in terms of the changing structure of opportunities that are available (for example, through state policies) and the differentiation of individuals' access to these opportunities according to their location within the social structure, particularly their class, gender and ethnic backgrounds. Clearly, much of the mainstream research on the effects of selective and comprehensive systems of secondary schooling illustrate this mode of analysis (for example, Halsey et al, 1980). Similarly, many accounts of the shift from an elite to a mass system of higher education or of participation in adult education programmes fall into the same general mould (for example, Marsh and Blackburn, 1992; McGivney, 1993). And much the same can be said of a great deal of the research on the take up of opportunities for vocational training, whether supplied by the state or (although the analysis is far less developed) by employers (for example, Banks et al, 1992; Rees, Fielder and Rees, 1992).

Frequently, this conceptualisation in terms of the restriction of individual choice over courses of action has been used to permit the reduction of the complexities of individual behaviour to characteristic educational 'pathways' or 'trajectories' (the term that we shall use here). Precisely because autonomy is bounded by external conditions, it is possible to identify regularities in individuals' educational experiences as they proceed through the life course. Hence, for example, Halsey, Heath and Ridge (1980) identified different routes through compulsory schooling, based on performance at key junctures such as the '11 plus' or 'common entrance' examinations, and were concerned to elaborate on the nature and effects of the flows of individuals from different social backgrounds through them. Similarly, Banks et al (1992) develop the notion of 'career trajectories' to encapsulate the contrasting experiences of young people during the years after they have passed the minimum school-leaving age; and again, these are related to key features of social background and previous education.

At one level, what is involved here is no more than the attempt to *describe* characteristic patterns of educational attainment, participation and so on. Individual educational experiences are simply aggregated into typologies, which may then be related to the opportunities provided and the social resources available from different backgrounds. However, the concept of the 'trajectory' embodies a clear analytical element too. Our argument here has recently been elaborated by Hodkinson, Sparkes and Hodkinson (1996) through their invocation of Strauss' (1962) well known discussion; they say:

> Strauss (1962) suggests that we often describe this predictability [of individual 'trajectories'] according to one of two metaphors. The first is the career ladder. From this point of view, early decisions around the transition to work are the lower rungs of the ladder. As our lives develop we gradually climb, in a direction that is clear and predictable to a knowledgeable outsider.... The other metaphor for career development ... is that of cooking an egg. Whether we poach it, fry it, boil it or scramble it, it will always be an egg.... Working-class males, let us say, can develop in a variety of ways, but their central 'working-class maleness'

will always allow the expert outsider to predict the range of opportunities
and type of trajectory that they will follow. (p 141)

What this highlights, therefore, is that there are two elements involved. First,
the 'trajectory' that people join is very largely determined by the resources
that they derive from their social backgrounds. Hence, to extend Strauss'
(1962) example, working-class males' experience of initial schooling and
subsequent education and training differs systematically from that of middle-
class females; their access to learning opportunities is systematically
differentiated by the social resources or capital available to them. Second, an
individual's capacity to take up whatever learning opportunities are available
is constrained by his or her previous history in this respect. Accordingly, once
an individual has started out on a given 'trajectory', then the probability of
proceeding through its subsequent stages is relatively high; the sequence of
educational experiences is to a considerable extent cumulative. For example,
if someone leaves school at 16 with no qualifications, this itself restricts
subsequent access to further or higher education and to anything other than
very limited vocational training.

We wish to argue that this concept of 'trajectory' is integral to the
development of an adequate social theory of lifelong learning. By extension
from previous research, it is possible – although empirically complex – to
identify a range of characteristic sequences of learning experiences through
the life course ('trajectories'), which constitute the core of what such a theory
should set out to explain. However, while these 'trajectories' do certainly
reflect an externally constituted structure of learning opportunities and socially
differentiated access to them – as our earlier discussion suggests – it is necessary
to elaborate a more nuanced account of their determinants. More specifically,
we need to explore more fully the ways in which 'trajectories' are 'embedded'
in social relations more widely; and to take proper account of the interaction
of individual choices and constraining parameters in the determination of
courses of educational action.

In locating 'trajectories' at the core of our theoretical concerns, attention is
necessarily focused on processes of social change. Most immediately, of course,
this relates to the sequences of educational experiences that occur through
individual life courses. However, in addition, characteristic 'trajectories' are
themselves transformed over time; the kinds of 'trajectories' that are typical
currently are significantly different from those of earlier (and, indeed, by
implication, future) epochs. In other words, there is also a process of historical
or inter-generational change, within which individual experience may be
located. Accordingly, it is possible to mark out historical periods in terms of
their pattern of typical 'trajectories' (as, for example, Antikainen et al, 1996, p
14, do for Finland). Clearly, transformations in the structure of available
opportunities for education and training are key influences here. Changes in
state education policies, in employers' strategies with respect to training
provision or in community-based programmes of informal learning are all
examples of ways in which characteristic 'trajectories' may be restructured

over time, through expanding or contracting the learning opportunities that are available. Moreover, such changes also impact on the role played by individuals' social backgrounds in differentiating access to such opportunities. For example, the post-war expansion of secondary and higher education in Britain, along with marked changes in employment structures, have contributed significantly to changing women's educational profile relative to that of men; what it means to be a woman in this context is different now from what it used to be.

It is important to note, moreover, that these historical or inter-generational changes in characteristic 'trajectories' underpin most strategies for building a learning society. What the latter involve is generating a set of typical 'trajectories' (however defined) in the future that is significantly different from the present one. For instance, official strategies at the moment are predominantly concerned with shifting the mix of 'trajectories' towards a situation where a much higher proportion of the population engage in the renewal of skills and competencies throughout their working lives, irrespective of their location within the employment structure.

In putting things in these terms, however, the partial nature of conceptualising the learning society *simply* as a desirable future objective is exposed. Viewed in this way, building a learning society becomes abstracted from what are in reality long-term processes of historical change through which patterns of learning ('trajectories') have been transformed. By focusing exclusively on the ends that remain to be achieved, a proper analysis of these processes of change may be avoided; indeed, this is precisely our claim with respect to current strategies derived from HCT.

Moreover, this future orientation also permits the presentation of a kind of 'Whig history' of the development of lifelong learning, in which the weaknesses and shortcomings of the present are conceived as the necessary preconditions of the achievement of a desired state of learning in the future. The possibility that elements of past practice were superior to the present or, to put it another way, that the development of participation in education and training may be distinctly non-linear, especially for particular population groups, is discounted, through a failure to engage with the complexities of the social processes involved. For example, in a region like South Wales, it may be that the collapse of employment in nationalised industries, such as coal, steel and railways, where initial and continuing training were provided for all employees and were integral to the internal labour markets leading to supervisory and managerial jobs, has brought about a significant deterioration in learning opportunities, at least for men. And equivalent arguments can be made with respect to the demise of community-based learning through the Miners' Institutes. There is a real sense, then, in which substantial sections of the population now have learning opportunities which are significantly worse than their parents (or, more correctly, their fathers) enjoyed (Rees, 1997).

This emphasis on the necessity of locating the concept of the learning society within an analysis of the complexities of change in social patterns of participation in learning necessarily draws attention to the specificities of *place* too. Quite simply, characteristic 'trajectories' vary from one locality to another. It is, of course, widely recognised that there are substantial variations in patterns of, for instance, educational attainment and participation more widely, between different regions of Britain and even between more local areas (Garner et al, 1988). However, the theorisation of such differentiation is much less developed. As we have noted, analytical concerns have characteristically focused on what are presented as national patterns and the location of individuals within a spatially undifferentiated social structure of class, gender and ethnic backgrounds (but see, for example, Coffield et al, 1986; and Ashton et al, 1990). Certainly, there have been very few (if any) attempts to relate historical or inter-generational changes in patterns of educational participation ('trajectories') to regionally and locally specific processes of social and economic development.

However, precisely because characteristic 'trajectories' are 'embedded' in wider social relations, they reflect the spatial and temporal differentiation of the latter. Most obviously, the structure of learning opportunities and the impacts of its transformation are sharply differentiated between places. Hence, for example, although changes in state provision have been instigated largely at the national level, their effects have frequently been experienced most acutely in local contexts. Not only have many policy changes been implemented primarily at the local level, but also the interaction of national policies with local conditions has produced highly variable local impacts. For instance, the national policy of expanding learning opportunities for younger adults through, say, Youth Training, in reality had very different effects according to the local context of secondary and further education provision, employer participation and so forth; and this is reflected in wide differences in take-up, completion, and eventual outcomes for young people (for example, Rees et al, 1996). Moreover, the effects of changes in industrial structure and associated employment opportunities, while deriving from wider national and international economic developments, are experienced in local labour markets and the educational and training opportunities associated with them (Ashton et al, 1990). For instance, colliery closures in South Wales were the result of shifts in international energy markets and national state policies, but their impact was to remove from particular local areas jobs and the training that went with them (Rees and Thomas, 1991). Likewise, decisions of multinational companies to locate advanced manufacturing plants in regions like South Wales have introduced wholly new opportunities with respect to education and training, whose effects have been quite localised (Rees and Thomas, 1994).

Equally, while the processes of social differentiation of access to learning opportunities are pervasive, the form that these processes take may be affected by the local context (a point that has not been adequately recognised in conventional studies of educational participation and attainment). For example, the significance of someone's gender to their education and training is partly determined by the structure of local employment opportunities, as the collapse of a male-dominated employment structure in South Wales has illustrated (Istance and Rees, 1994); although this is clearly mediated by class background and the consequent extent of dependence on local opportunities (Lovering, 1990). Accordingly, there are complex interactions between people's locations within the social structure, their spatial locations, and their access to learning opportunities. In short, then, the structure of learning opportunities to which individuals have access is not uniform from place to place; teasing out the precise empirical significance of this spatial differentiation is a major, albeit complex, part of the required analysis of characteristic patterns of 'trajectories'. And this, in turn, raises the possibility that strategies for building a learning society will have to take account of what may be significant variations between localities in learning resources.

Characteristic 'trajectories' do not, however, simply reflect the constraining effects of structures of learning opportunities, even where the latter are properly conceived as 'embedded' in historically and spatially differentiated social relations. The individual educational experiences of which they are comprised are simultaneously the products of personal choices between alternative actions. This is seen most clearly where an individual opts to pursue a course of action that deviates from an established 'trajectory'; what Ahleit (1994) refers to as the 'biographical discontinuities' that result when, say, a redundant miner or a mother whose children have left home chooses to enter a university access programme. However, even where individuals' behaviour is consistent with typical patterns of learning ('trajectories'), it is always possible for them to do something else; their actions thus remain the product of choices and need to be understood as such.

To reiterate a point made earlier, therefore, the analytical puzzle is to unravel the interaction of individual choices and constraining social parameters. This is, of course, a familiar and perennial problem in social analysis; and, in what follows, we do not claim any definitive contribution to resolving it. Rather, our concern is to make an essentially pragmatic contribution to exploring the salience of these issues to an understanding of patterns of learning through the life course (Hodkinson et al, 1996).

At the most basic level, then, the choices that individuals exercise over their participation in education and training reflect the kinds of knowledge that they possess of the learning opportunities available. More interestingly, however, their actions are chosen in respect of preferences that are defined within what we refer to as 'socially constituted rationalities'; that is to say, individual choices are made over courses of action to be followed, but not in random ways.

In the particular context of educational experience through the life course, we suggest that a key concept in understanding the latter is that of 'learner identity'. As Weil (1986) puts it, 'learner identities' refer to:

> ... the ways in which adults come to understand the conditions under which they experience learning as 'facilitating' or 'inhibiting', 'constructive' or 'destructive'. Learner identity suggests the emergence or affirmation of values and beliefs about 'learning', 'schooling' and 'knowledge'. The construct incorporates personal, social, sociological,

experiential and intellectual dimensions of learning, as integrated over time. (p 223)

'Learner identity' thus encapsulates how individuals come to view the process of learning and, accordingly, provides the framework through which alternative courses of educational action are evaluated. Moreover, as Weil (1986) indicates, an individual's 'learner identity' is essentially personal, with emotional as well as intellectual dimensions (Sennett and Cobb, 1972). And yet, however personal 'learner identities' may be, they remain the products of individuals' social experience. And here too, we wish to emphasise the ways in which the latter is pervaded by history and place.

Most obviously, then, compulsory schooling is a powerful source of 'learner identity'. Quite simply, those who have had a successful experience of learning at school are more likely to have developed a positive 'learner identity' and therefore be more ready to engage with learning opportunities in later life. But 'learning identity' is not simply a matter of success or failure at school; it is also the product of more complex processes. For example, the forms of curriculum, pedagogy and assessment associated with, say, the 1960s grammar schools, served to construct the learner in quite different ways from those made available within the secondary moderns of the same period or the progressive comprehensive of the 1970s. The 'learner identities' that educational institutions aspire to engender in their students therefore vary both between different types of institution and historically as well.

These factors thus underlie the ways in which the structure of learning opportunities (which, as we have seen, has itself been changing) has been evaluated differently by successive generations. To use a specific example from our current research, it may well be that the training opportunities that became available after coal nationalisation in 1947 were regarded very differently by the first generations of miners to experience them, whose schooling was overwhelmingly confined to elementary levels, compared with those who entered the industry subsequently, following what by then was universal secondary education. Indeed, as we have argued elsewhere, for the earlier generations, the workplace training which they received, far from being understood in narrowly vocational terms, may well have constituted the most significant element of their educational experience as a whole (a point that complicates currently fashionable arguments about the vocational 'relevance' of school-based education) (Rees, 1997).

It is also clear, however, that 'learner identities' are not simply the product of formal education; they also emerge in relation to more informal learning opportunities, with rather different implications for the evaluation of alternative courses of action. Traditionally, the fields of sport and music have provided a minority of young people with the opportunity to develop a different conception of their own abilities from that gained through formal education (Furlong, 1991). For older learners, experience within political and community organisations can have a similar effect (Weil, 1986).

Indeed, again as we have argued elsewhere, in particular places and epochs, this latter kind of activity has been much more significant in shaping 'learner identities' than the formal education system. For example, historically in industrial South Wales, there is evidence of conflict between rather well articulated ideological systems, within which individual 'learner identities' were developed, whose origins were very much in community-based activity. Hence, it is suggested that non-conformism gave rise to a conception of education as individual cultural accomplishment, which contrasted sharply with the collectivism associated with what Lewis (1993) terms 'workers' education' through the Workers' Educational Association, the National Labour College and so on.

What these brief examples begin to illustrate, moreover, is the complexity of the social experience within which 'learner identities' are rooted. Certainly, such experience extends beyond the formal institutions of education and, indeed, community-based learning too. Hence, for instance, the workplace is one key arena within which the 'learner identities' forged through the formal education system may be renegotiated (or, alternatively, reinforced). As the experience of the coal industry suggests, what is involved here can extend beyond the specifically vocational; as we have suggested, nationalisation may have contributed as significantly to shifting characteristic *educational* experiences in places like South Wales as did the changes in education policy which comprised part of the same post-war settlement. Similarly, the development in recent years of a significant advanced manufacturing sector in the region, based to a great extent on foreign direct investment, may in due course contribute towards an equivalent redefinition of educational experience and associated 'learner identities'. Moreover, these changes may have particular impacts on specific social groups: most obviously, women.

These latter arguments also pose in an acute way the issue of changes in 'learner identities' over time. Hence, for example, 'educational and training cultures', embodying distinctive dispositions among peers towards education and training, may develop to reflect not only current socio-economic circumstances in a given area, but also the residue of the past (Rees and Rees, 1980). For instance, willingness to undertake job-related training may reflect both the traditions of such provision in a locality, as well as the requirements of current employment patterns. Moreover, family life is a key vehicle through which such inter-generational transmission occurs. Some young people have grown up in families where continuing education and training is part of the routine cycle of employment life for family members; it is a naturalised form of experience. For others – currently the majority – the opposite is true. In these circumstances, then, participating in learning after compulsory schooling, when it does take place, demands a reworking of personal history.

Participation in adult learning: operationalising a theoretical model

The theoretical model that we have outlined provided the basis for our empirical research into the determinants of patterns of participation in adult learning. In operational terms, therefore, it was necessary to draw on a variety of sources and corresponding analytical techniques. The major elements of our approach to our empirical research are described briefly here (Gorard et al, 1997a; Gorard et al, 1999a).

Our methodological strategy involved an in-depth analysis of a *single* region, industrial South Wales (see Chapter Three). This made practicable the use of a variety of data sources, both contemporary and historical. Using South Wales as a 'social laboratory' to chart long-term historical patterns, moreover, permitted the uncovering of fundamental relationships and processes in the determination of participation in lifelong learning which at least provide the starting point for studies elsewhere. In short, therefore, the implications of this study are not confined to the specific regional context in which the empirical research was carried out.

We used three principal methods of data collection. These were: (i) a questionnaire survey; (ii) semi-structured interviews; and (iii) archival analysis. In addition, the regional context, as well as conditions in the three local study areas, were investigated through documentary analysis and semi-structured interviews with key respondents (Gorard, 1997a; Chambers et al, 1998). The three principal sources are discussed in turn (see also Gorard et al, 1997a).

Questionnaire survey

The sample for the major questionnaire survey was drawn from three localities (Blaenau Gwent, Bridgend and Neath-Port Talbot), chosen to reflect the diversity of social and economic conditions in industrial South Wales (see the Appendix). In somewhat simplified terms, the region can be seen as comprising three distinct local types. The valleys, particularly those to the east and centre of the region, have a history of coal mining, with allied engineering industries, from the 19th century onwards. They are heavily urbanised and densely populated in pockets, although farming continues on the hills between them. These sites are typified by local areas such as Aberdare, Rhondda, Merthyr, Rhymney and Blaenau Gwent. These areas are now characterised by major industrial decline and consequent social and economic disadvantage.

Heavy manufacturing industries developed strongly after 1945 in some sites along the coast of the region. These are urban areas, primarily producing metals such as steel, steel-based manufactured products and petrochemicals. These industries, like the coalmines, are also declining, but the decline has not yet been as dramatic as the large-scale closure of the pits. Such sites appear in Llanelli, Swansea, Port Talbot, Neath, and Newport, although Newport like Cardiff has some new development giving it a hybrid character (Welsh Office, 1996).

New manufacturing industry tends to be closer to the M4, but slightly further from the coast. Relatively new factories, many built by overseas companies, have caused some urban areas to expand, and the communities that have sprung up as a result suggest one possible industrial future for South Wales – that of providing a relatively skilled but relatively cheap labour force for foreign investors. These towns are typified by Bridgend, Pontyclun, Llantrisant, and Cwmbran (Welsh Office, 1996). Thus, our three sites can reasonably be used to typify the region as a whole: one in the heart of the depressed coalfield; one in a large urban centre historically linked with heavy industry; and a third in a rapidly expanding town south of the coalfield.

Within each site, sampling was focused on three electoral divisions, again selected to represent local conditions. Household lists were identified from electoral registers and an initial sample of some 800 respondents (one from each household) was derived by means of repeated systematic sampling. This sample was stratified so that respondents were divided equally between men and women; and spanned the age-range 35-64 years old evenly. A booster sample of around 200 respondents was drawn from the children of members of the initial sample, to allow detailed exploration of family relationships. This sample was also divided equally between men and women and covered the age-range 15-34 years old evenly. The primary response rate was 74% and this was supplemented by substitution. A total of 1,104 usable questionnaires were completed.

The questionnaire was designed to collect data of four principal kinds: the social/demographic characteristics of individual respondents; detailed histories of respondents' post-compulsory educational and training careers; simplified histories of respondents' employment careers; and simplified histories of the educational and training careers of respondents' children. Information on individual histories was collected on a modified "sequential start-to-finish date-of-event basis" (Gallie, 1994, p 340). We collected information on participation in all forms of education and training, including less formal activities such as evening classes and leisure activities, as well as further and higher education, and workplace training of all kinds.

While careful pre-piloting and a pilot study provided the basis for question design, there remain problems with this approach arising from the fallibility of respondents' recall. However, the alternatives of longitudinal panel designs and cross-sectional designs also face major problems (Gorard et al, 1997a).

Semi-structured interviews

A 10% sub-sample, representing the characteristics of the main sample, provided the basis for 105 extended, semi-structured interviews. These interviews again focused on the respondent's recollections of how his or her education and training career unfolded. However, here it was the ways in which this is understood by respondents that provided the focus. Respondents were encouraged to speak freely on these issues, or even to conduct demonstrations (of a skill, for example) or to show us around their homes (to see a personal library, computer or admire their DIY, for instance).

Archival analysis

The full historical range of the study was made possible by the analysis of materials held in the South Wales Coalfield Archive. This was carried out by colleagues in the Department of Adult Continuing Education at the University of Wales, Swansea, where the Archive is located. The tape transcripts of oral history interviews held in the Archive, although carried out originally with different objectives in mind, provide a primary source of data on the nature and determinants of participation in education and training during the first half of the 20th century.

Other sources of data

In order to understand the position of traditional providers, we conducted 30 interviews with educational and training organisations and companies in South Wales, who could comment authoritatively on changes since 1945 (Chambers et al, 1998). We also supplemented our household survey with the learning histories of a further 483 households in Wales, obtained as part of our work with NIACE Dysgu Cymru (see Gorard, 2000a). We tracked changes in participation in work-based training and qualifications via the Labour Force Survey, and in further education (FE) and higher education (HE) via the Individualised Student Record System (Gorard and Taylor, 2001). We supplemented our household interviews by contacting 32 informal learners, using ICT as a platform for their learning experiences either at home or at drop-in centres.

Methods of analysis

Following extensive preliminary analysis, there were two major elements in analysing the data derived from the questionnaire survey. First, the complexity of the 1,104 individual education and training histories was reduced by converting each one into a sequence of episodes (for example, an educational programme, new job) in which participation in education and training did, or did not, occur. These sequences, in turn, were classified into 11 'lifetime learning trajectories', which describe almost all of the variations in individual histories. For most analyses, these can be further grouped into only five types of 'lifetime learning trajectories'.

Second, logistic regression analysis permitted the identification of those characteristics of individuals (independent variables) that provide good predictions of which 'lifetime learning trajectories' they follow (dependent variable). This method of analysis is especially fruitful, as independent variables may be added into the regression function in the order in which they occur in real life: that is, the statistical procedure models exactly the social phenomenon it is analysing ('trajectories') (Gorard et al, 1998a). Hence, at birth, these independent variables include the respondent's gender, the year and place of birth, and parental occupational and educational background.

By the end of initial schooling, we can include details of siblings, the type of schools attended, school examination entry and performance, and so on. Eventually, we can use everything we know about each individual to predict his or her learning trajectory. We believe that this innovative method of analysis constitutes a significant advance over previous approaches in this field (Gorard et al, 1999a).

Conclusion

At one level, our discussion suggests no more than the need to transcend conceptions of the learning society that are rooted in economistic models of market behaviour. Although, as we have argued, such conceptions currently dominate official discourse, this conclusion may, nevertheless, be regarded as unexceptional.

However, what is significant is that it is rooted in an analysis of the social relations of lifelong learning, rather than simply expressing an alternative set of normative preferences. Hence, choices with respect to participation in learning opportunities may be rational, without conforming to the preferences presumed in human capital theory. It is recognition of this simple point that, at least in part, explains well documented reluctance to take up opportunities (as, for instance, in the case of Youth Training). More generally, there is no reason to expect a simple consensus over the implications of education and training programmes: opportunities provided by the state or by employers may well not be construed as such by potential trainees or employees, for example.

It is also important to note that our stress on the complexity of the social relations of lifelong learning is more than some post-modern celebration of diversity for its own sake. In particular, locating these social relations within a framework that embraces both change over time and differentiation between places (see Chapter Three), has important implications for strategies for building a learning society. Most obviously, the inadequacies of conceiving the learning society simply as something to be achieved in the future are exposed. To be effective, strategies need to take account of the actual processes of change in learning opportunities that different social groups have experienced. Moreover, in doing so, the differentiation in this experience between both social groups and localities cannot be ignored. Indeed, rather than a uniform learning society, the aim of development is better conceived as the creation of a diversity of learning societies, which build on the real-world complexity of the social relations within which lifelong learning takes place.

Note

[1] Some economists and, perhaps more interestingly, transnational policy bodies, such as the Centre for Educational Research and Innovation at the OECD and the World Bank, have begun to acknowledge the limitations of conventional human capital approaches.

THREE

History, place and the learning society: the case of South Wales

As we argued in Chapter Two, an adequate theory of lifelong learning must take into account social and economic changes over both time and place. In the study that provides the principal empirical basis for the remainder of this book, we focus on one geographical region, which permits the in-depth analysis of changes over time and of the complex interplay of social, cultural and economic factors. This chapter briefly describes the region in question – industrial South Wales – and the long-term restructuring that it has undergone through the 20th century, which is the time period covered by our study[1].

One of the consequences of this long-term restructuring is the marked differentiation of social and economic conditions between localities within the region. Accordingly, we also describe the three sites in industrial South Wales that provided the focus for the primary data collection for our study. Information from secondary sources, from literature review, and from our key informants provides the basis for these accounts.

It is important to emphasise that in providing these sociographic accounts of the places in which our research has been focused, we are doing more than providing 'background information'. It is integral to the analytical approach that we have developed (and that we have set out in Chapter Two) that people's decisions as to whether they participate or not in adult education and training are crucially shaped by the opportunities that are available to them; the ways in which they understand those opportunities and their relationships to them; and the resources (individual, familial and community) on which they can draw in accessing these learning opportunities. All of these factors are specific to particular historical epochs and to the places in which people live and work. Therefore, a clear analysis of how the social and economic relations characteristic of localities have changed over time is essential to a proper understanding of the learning trajectories that individuals follow and how their patterns have shifted over the decades too[2].

It could be argued, of course, that industrial South Wales provides an especially rich geographical context for a study of this kind, given the extent and rapidity of social and economic change that it has experienced over the past century. While this is true, it partly misses the analytical point too. In effect, once our conceptual framework is accepted, then any locality can be seen to provide a fruitful site for empirical research, as every place has specific characteristics that shape participation in adult learning. Correspondingly, on this view, the implications of any regional study are not confined to the particular location, but have wider resonances.

Industrial South Wales: an economic region

Industrial South Wales covers an area measuring 80 miles from East to West, and 30 miles from North to South. It is bounded to the south by the coast and to the north by the Brecon Beacons, beyond which lie the sparsely populated areas of mid-Wales. The region is deeply scored by steep-sided valleys that run north-west from the coastal plain. Accordingly, east-west transportation links are confined to the motorway and major arterial roads, and the InterCity rail-link, running along the coastal plain to the south and the heads of the Valleys to the north (Humphrys, 1972).

The region comprises some 20% of the total area of Wales, but housed some 70% of the population in 1970. South Wales developed a strong economic coherence, based on its marked dependence on a very narrow range of industries. By the latter part of the 19th century, employment in the region was heavily concentrated into coalmining, iron and steel production, and the transportation, manufacturing and services associated with these two staple industries. This concentration of economic activity into a very narrow range of industries was more marked in South Wales than other, comparable parts of Britain.

It is important not to overestimate, however, the length of time that South Wales has been industrialised; the iconic coalmines of the Rhondda valleys, for example, functioned for only a hundred years or so. Many workers were in-migrants from rural areas and the area remained very much influenced by an agricultural ethos well into its industrial period. Population growth was very rapid during the period up until the First World War, with immigration rates matching those of the US at the same time. For example, the population in the Rhondda valleys was 4,000 in 1861, but thirty years later had grown to 163,000 due to the expansion of the mines. In-migrants, initially from other parts of Wales, moved into the region. Then came the Irish and English, leading to a net gain in population of 129,000 from 1901-11 and the consequent destruction of some Welsh-speaking areas, especially those to the east (Howell, 1988).

Booming economic conditions, therefore, produced almost instant new communities, concentrated into ribbon-like developments along the valleys (Nash et al, 1995). The dominant of the staple industries was coal, with around a quarter of a million miners employed in, 1913. In good times, the wages in mining were relatively good (especially compared with agriculture) and there was a high demand for men. The influx of new workers deluged many traditional aspects of the region, and the mining communities developed their own distinctively 'modern' lifestyles, in which education and cultural activities more widely played a characteristic role.

The interwar period witnessed the collapse of this Imperial economy in South Wales. Coal and metal manufacture, both heavily dependent on export markets, were very severely affected by the Great Depression. For example, whereas there were 234,000 miners in 1913, there were only 136,000 by 1939. By the 1930s, unemployment in Tredegar was 27.4%, in Newport

34.7%, and by 1935 over 50% in Merthyr Vale. Consequently, between 1921–39 400,000 people left South Wales, causing the age profile of those remaining to rise, as the leavers were mostly young people (Humphrys, 1972). Unemployment disappeared temporarily during the Second World War, but the underlying industrial decline continued.

Between 1945–70, the pattern of industrial life in South Wales was transformed. By 1970, nearly everyone was in a job that did not exist in the same place in 1945. The coalmines were nationalised in 1947, but the numbers employed in mining dropped again from 112,000 in 1944, to 106,000 in 1960 and only 60,000 by 1970. The major decline of the coalfield took place between 1959–70, when 86 collieries closed (Rees and Rees, 1983). Mining had so far declined that only 30,000 were employed by 1979 (Howell, 1988); and this rump of the industry disappeared almost entirely in the aftermath of the 1984–85 miners' strike.

This loss of employment was partially compensated, however, by the growth of new types of manufacturing industry and, more particularly, by the growth of jobs in the services (most markedly in the public sector). Hence, for example, by 1971, 60,000 people in South Wales worked for US manufacturing companies (an inward investment trend that had begun during the 1920s). During the 1970s, major new inward investment streams got underway, with significant manufacturing plants being established by Japanese, South Korean and, increasingly, European companies ('Wales 2000', 1996). These used South Wales as a springboard from which to supply the rest of the European continent.

There was, of course, considerable movement of younger men who lost their jobs in coal mining into some of these new manufacturing activities. Many urban centres in the (former) coalfield thus became little more than dormitory centres. Equally, however, many of the jobs in new manufacturing plants were taken by women. More significantly, the growth of jobs in services – both private and public sector – offered new employment opportunities that were taken up by women. The transformation in gender roles (albeit very partial), which these changes have implied, have been paralleled by equally significant shifts in wider patterns of social and cultural relations.

Nevertheless, South Wales – and the former coalfield, in particular – remains a region characterised by extensive social and economic disadvantage. Unemployment is relatively high and earnings are among the lowest in Britain. Moreover, economic activity, especially among men, is exceptionally low. For example, of the 459 local authority districts in Britain, 9 of the 10 with the lowest economic activity rates for men, and 7 of the 10 for women, are in Wales (Istance and Rees, 1995). The extent of these problems has been recognised recently by the designation of South Wales as one of the most deprived parts of the European Union (and consequently eligible for Objective One funding).

It is in the latter context, in particular, that lifelong learning has come to be seen as having a critical role to play in the envisaged economic regeneration of the region. One vision of the future for the region – and, indeed, Wales as a whole – is as a second 'Celtic Tiger', following the model of the Irish Republic. Education and skills development have been widely identified as providing the cornerstone for such a development. However, it is important to understand that the promotion of new initiatives with respect to adult education and training needs to be located in the context of a past in which adult learning has also played a critical role.

Education and training in Wales

Schools and schooling

Education in Wales provides something of a paradox: a history and reputation of respect for learning, combined with relatively poor measures of educational attainment in the present day in almost every assessment. Education has often been treated as a 'given' by writers in Wales and desire and respect for it as almost 'primordial' (Roberts, 1983). There has been a tendency to characterise the Welsh as being a nation of education-lovers, as though there was some endemic trait in the make-up of its inhabitants (Lowe, 1970). More sophisticated analyses, however, have emphasised more complex determinants, while continuing to emphasise the high regard in which education is held in Wales. For example, the Gittins Report (Central Advisory Council for Education [Wales], 1967) on primary education in Wales argued:

> The Welsh have traditionally regarded themselves as having an unusually high respect for education.... The wide interest in education, which undoubtedly exists in Wales, can be seen not only as an outgrowth of its cultural tradition but as a consequence of its economic poverty. (quoted in Istance and Rees, 1994, p 11)

By the 1970s, however, some observers were suggesting that these attitudes to learning were changing. After the 1944 Education Act, it was suggested that the grammar school tradition, which dominated Welsh secondary education, produced a polarised distribution of attainment, with a substantial 'elite' of high attainers, but equally a very large proportion of school-leavers with no formal qualifications at all, leading to a waste of talent and social division (Istance and Rees, 1995). Following the advent of comprehensivisation in the 1970s, Wales' relative advantage in terms of high attainers disappeared, leading some commentators to suggest that children in Wales are 'schooled for failure' (Reynolds, 1990, 1995). However, recent re-analyses of the relevant figures in context suggest that schools and students in Wales are in reality doing as well as their equivalents in England (Gorard, 1998a, 2000c). Indeed, average levels of attainment at GCSE in Wales, for example, now exceed those in England.

Nevertheless, concerns continue to be expressed over the extent to which the Welsh education system is successful in preparing 'ordinary' young people for the kind of labour market that either exists currently or is envisaged for the future. Despite the well-publicised attempts to improve the vocational preparation of young people within the educational system, commentators have continued to voice doubts over their efficacy in the Welsh context. Accordingly, the British two-track distribution of educational experience is perhaps at its most exaggerated in Wales (Gorard et al, 1997b; Gorard, 2000b). A crucial question, therefore, is the extent to which this continues into post-compulsory education and training.

Adult education and training

Although there is always a danger of romanticising the past, there are accounts of a long-standing tradition in Wales of support for adult learning (Istance and Rees, 1994). Before the era of compulsory universal education, there was a history of Sunday schools, voluntary societies and schools based on ironworks, collieries, and tinplate works, paid for by benevolent employers, philanthropists and the workers themselves (Evans, 1971; Nash et al, 1995). The first organised form of adult education may have been the Sunday schools and Church Literacy Societies, and this tradition of teaching adults in Sunday schools may have been a distinctively Welsh phenomenon (Ellis, 1935). Added to these were the *Eisteddfodau*, the workers' society lectures, the Drama movement, the YMCA, and traditional societies that were especially prevalent in Wales; as well as the less formal learning that took place in the pit, workshop, public house and barbers' shops (Lewis, 1993).

This has led some observers to detect a deeply-rooted desire for continuous learning in Wales, so that "public participation in various forms of education is very much greater and the habit of community cooperation is very much stronger than in England" (Lowe, 1970, p 315). "Together they have helped to produce that interest in religion, philosophy, letters and music that is characteristic of the Welsh people" (Welsh Department, 1937, p 7).

The two roots of adult learning in South Wales were, therefore, religion and the workplace. The first led by the late 19th century to Sunday schools, concerts and penny readings organised by the local chapel, and YMCA classes, whose traditions of discussion and close textual analysis became one model for what followed (Jones, 1991). The second led to the Workers' Educational Association (WEA), Trade Union activities, workers' societies and Institutes, the Plebs' League, and the Labour College Movement; as well as the educational activities of the left political parties and the Communist Party, in particular.

What was especially significant about these developments was that they were largely organised at the local level, with a very close relationship between the providers, backers, and users. There is, therefore, a tradition in Wales of education for cultural reasons, as well as for personal and social mobility, which is in marked contrast to the current emphasis on learning for economic reasons (Rees, 1997). Hence, for example, the WEA was formed in Wales in 1903 as a federation of working class societies and educational groups with links to the Trade Unions, perhaps as an attempt to curtail the independence of workers' education movements (Welsh Department, 1937). Certainly, the

WEA shared control of education in liberal subjects with university tutorial classes, the YMCA and the National Council of Music. By 1918, the success of the university extramural classes was so great that, according to one observer, they could have been extended 'without limit' (Ellis, 1935).

Equally, however, 'workers' education' also flourished in South Wales. There was a relatively large number of postal students ('distance-learners') at Ruskin College before 1914, as well as a smaller number of residential students. The Great War led to a surge of demand for new classes, partly to explore what was happening, and partly as a symptom of local unrest and resistance to the War. The ensuing coal strike coincided with the growth of the Plebs' League and the Central Labour College, which was largely dependent on the support of the miners of South Wales (Lewis, 1993). The demand for classes continued to grow after 1918, particularly in and around Swansea, pushed perhaps by the events in the Soviet Union and pulled by the onset of the Great Depression.

A residential adult education college was founded at Harlech in 1927, taking over students after the closure of the Central Labour College. The college had an inherited tradition of collectivist education, with ex-students returning as influential figures in their local community. For some, this influence meant a cascading of radical socialism; for others it meant socialisation into a liberal democracy. Coleg Harlech was also over-subscribed, and despite the fact that some men left their jobs after the courses in order to study for further courses of training, it was those who returned to their previous environments from the residential college after a "glimpse of the vision splendid" (Ellis, 1935, p 201) who were most influential in sustaining a demand for more learning. Hence, for example, by 1920, WEA classes and local debating societies in Neath were well-attended and there was said to be a "deep hunger for learning among the people" there (Eaton, 1987, p 153). There were also weekly classes for the miners, paid for by the education authority and well-attended lectures in the library.

This period also encompasses a spate of growth in the number of Workers' Institutes in South Wales, such as the Victoria Institute and library started in Port Talbot in 1887 (Jones, 1991). These were often paid for by a penny in the pound taken from miners' wages and matched by the coal owners, or by philanthropists. After 1919, the Miners' Welfare Fund paid a penny for every ton of coal raised in Britain, and this money was used to help improve or increase the number of local 'Stutes (Nash et al, 1995). For example, the Oakdale Workmen's Institute and Library was founded in 1917, financed by a loan from the Tredegar Iron and Coal Company and repaid by the miners over decades. This included a library, reading room, committee room and concert hall. It was used for concerts, *Eisteddfodau*, political meetings, lectures, and clubs and societies, as well as entertainment. Evening classes at the Institutes and halls included reading (Evans, 1971). By 1926, over 2,000 students, mostly miners, were attending 65 Independent Working Class Education classes in South Wales; while a further 500 or more students were in 31 WEA classes, growing to over 1,000 by 1929, of whom over 80% were manual workers (Lewis, 1993).

Unemployment during the Great Depression of 1929-35 was at its worst in South Wales, and although a quarter of a million people left to go to England in search of work, there were entire villages of men on the dole. Nevertheless, South Wales had at least 135 Workers' Institutes that were well-attended, despite or perhaps because of the Depression. The peak use of the libraries came in 1926, with a record of 49,161 annual loans in one small community and new branch libraries, such as that at Aberafan opening in 1936. The issue of non-fiction books, in particular, grew during the depression (Eaton, 1987). It may be that a strong desire for learning in society appears more often in or immediately after periods of widespread excitement (Lewis, 1993). Education may only be able to assist with major social change, as long as people have the free time to pursue it. This may be why in Wales, if not in Austria (Jahoda et al, 1972), self-teaching, voluntary organisations and political activity all *increased* during the unemployment of the Great Depression and why the trend continued post-1945 and the creation of the welfare state (Hanson, 1968).

By 1935/36, there were 517 separate adult courses in Wales of at least one year's duration and these were in addition to those in what were termed recognised places of learning. They might be considered the equivalent of uncertificated courses today, being partly invisible and the forgotten sector of education. They catered for 10,246 students and the majority were in South Wales and run by the WEA (224 classes). Even so, the supply of classes was not equal to the demand. Most were training lectures, attracting students over 25 years of age, most frequently from mining and quarrying occupations (Welsh Department, 1937). The growth in demand for day and weekend courses, in addition to the more normal evening fare, also led to the establishment of 20 Labour Colleges in South Wales by 1937, catering for 2,243 students. By 1938, there were 31 such adult day schools, taking 5,716 students for classes on current political issues, such as the rise of fascism, so that many local men and women were both well-read and well-informed during the interwar years (Lewis, 1993). It is important to note that these developments were all in addition to more traditional formal state-funded and private education.

Post-1945 developments

This tradition of voluntary provision of opportunities for adult learning in South Wales did not disappear after the Second World War and the profound restructuring of educational and other economic and social provision that ensued under successive post-war governments. For example, by 1950, the Miners' Institute in Tredegar had a library of over 23,000 books, and an elaborate programme of evening classes and the position was similar across all of the coalfield valleys (Francis, 1976). However, by this time, Institute members worked mainly in *nationalised* industries such as coal, steel and railways; and within these industries both initial and continuing training came to be provided for all. These organisations had an internal labour market leading to supervisory and managerial posts and it may well be that these forms of adult learning, directly related to employment prospects, came to play a more significant part in the learning activities of the region than those undertaken within the voluntary sector (Istance and Rees, 1995). Certainly, although the WEA continued after 1944 as a supplier of liberal non-vocational courses, it had a declining wider role.

Moreover, the post-1945 settlement involved the wholesale restructuring of formal educational opportunities, most obviously through the provisions of the 1944 Education Act. However, there was also a rapid increase in higher education. Indeed, this period, in which the University of Wales had an intake of which some 40% were from working-class backgrounds (Jones, 1982), represents a time when many adults had greater opportunities in Wales than may have been available to their peers in England. Equally, the growth of provision within the further education sector, much of it closely associated with the developments in the staple industries of the region, also brought about a significant widening of opportunities to undertake education and training after leaving school.

These post-war educational opportunities became available in a period that has been described in retrospect as economically 'affluent' (Kelly, 1992). It should be noted by planners of any future learning society, however, that it is much more likely that these affluent conditions created a fertile environment for the development of adult learning than the other way round. There was near full employment, relatively high job security, and a rise in real income for many people (McIlroy, 1990). There was moderately redistributive taxation in favour of lower income groups; and underpinning all of this was the welfare state, an edifice completed by the great series of legislative changes during the post-war years.

For the first time, then, manual workers drove to work in their own cars, while professionals decorated their own houses. A tendency for people to marry earlier, and have fewer and earlier children, brought more leisure in middle-age; a leisure assisted by a host of new labour-saving devices in the home. The population was ageing and an increasing proportion of workers had clerical and administrative jobs with shorter hours. The growth in both public and private transport created mobility. More people lived in their own homes as 'nuclear' families and started homely interests such as gardening and there was an upsurge of interest in music and other arts. Publishers such as Penguin popularised the paperback book from 1935, so books became cheaper, libraries became better stocked and reading as a pastime increased dramatically, despite the concurrent growth in television output. Television and radio were also a powerful educational force, realised most formally by the creation of the University of the Air (later the Open University) during the 1960s (Kelly, 1992).

In South Wales, therefore, some of the characteristics of a learning society may already have been in place earlier in the 20th century. For example, from the brief account we have given, it is clear that during the early decades of the century there was at least limited access to adult learning, not only for economic objectives or to gain occupational mobility, but also for cultural and developmental reasons. Moreover, given the nature of the society, this access was as strong among the working class as it was among other social groupings, as a result of the voluntary activities of working people themselves and their representative organisations, as much as the sponsorship of the state (Burge et al, 1999).

By the middle decades of the 20th century, although the influence of these voluntary forms of learning was waning, access to educational opportunities (broadly defined) was boosted by the activities of the state. The latter were not confined to the radical improvements that were made in the provision of formal education and training. It was also important that the dominant industries within the region, in part at least because they were nationalised, offered extensive opportunities for both initial and continuing training; and these provided important supplements to – and may, indeed, have been more significant than – what was on offer within the formal education system and what remained of the voluntary forms of learning provision (Rees, 1997).

The limitations on learning

It is, of course, important not to overstate this case for the earlier existence of a learning society in South Wales (Gorard et al, 1997b). Hence, it has been suggested that the very strength of the adult educational system has been a weakening factor in Welsh society, raising false hopes of better employment, leading eventually to a sort of 'brain-drain' emigration from Wales. For example, the chief limitation on the expansion of adult extramural classes in 1918 was the lack of qualified tutors, most of whom worked on a voluntary basis. According to one report, the best teachers went to England after their training to get a better job (Ellis, 1935). Those remaining tended to be both uncertificated and parochial in their viewpoint, with no knowledge of areas beyond their own district. Similarly, during the chronic unemployment of the Great Depression, the migration of tutors to England led to the collapse of many adult classes, despite the concurrent rise in local demand (Lewis, 1993). When times are hard it tends to be the better-educated who leave Wales, and neither now nor in the past has there been a clear policy to replace them or tempt them back.

Also, the apparent 'golden age' of voluntary adult learning was heavily gendered. Formal educational development for young women in South Wales was constrained by contemporary perceptions of 'proper' family life, the law, medical opposition, prejudice and inherent conservatism. Similarly, the provision of adult education for women was an area of 'gross neglect' in South Wales, with only three women of the 200 or so students in WEA classes of 1911-12 (Lewis, 1993). Women's groups did use the facilities of the Workers' Institutes, but were never allowed to be part of the organisation, while the attendance of children was heavily discouraged (Nash et al, 1995). On the other hand, much adult learning was (and remains) informal, and therefore unrecorded. In some cases, the relevant statistics for Wales are not available for a variety of administrative reasons (Gorard, 1997a). In others, the participation of women has simply been rendered invisible in accounts written by men. Moreover, according to some observers, women have always predominated in elements of formal postwar adult education (Kelly, 1992). This is true not just of the LEA-provided evening institutes, whose intakes were over 70% women (from 1946-66), but also the classes of the WEA and university extramural provision (a rise from 55% women students in 1946 to nearly 70% by 1966). There was in addition a huge rise in the postwar popularity of Women's Institutes and Townswomen's Guilds, whose members numbered three quarters of a million in the 1960s.

What is clearer, however, is that women's access to workplace learning was severely restricted. In part, this simply reflects the dominance of the region's employment by industries – coal mining, metal manufacture and the railways – from which women were to a very large extent excluded. Inevitably, therefore, they were denied access to the training opportunities that became available in these industries, especially during the post-1945 period. Moreover, some of the employment sectors where women were heavily represented – domestic service, for example – offered only limited opportunities of formal training. In others – such as teaching and the civil service – training was available, but the numbers involved were small and mostly limited to women who were unmarried (Williams, 1983).

Whether or not we conclude that there was a learning society in industrial South Wales during the earlier decades of the 20th century, there can be little doubt that it does not exist currently. Within the voluntary sector, the great tradition of 'workers' education' has dwindled away to almost nothing. The WEA and YMCA continue to provide classes for adults, but the numbers of students are still diminishing. The last Workers' Institute in Wales was completed in 1961; and they have all gradually switched to being primarily places of entertainment, rather than (at least formal) learning. Symbolically, the Oakdale Institute was closed in 1987 and has been relocated to the Welsh Folk Museum, a poignant memorial to the passing of at least one form of a learning society (Nash et al, 1995). The trades unions focus on practical issues of health and safety and negotiation, rather than the great topics of political economy.

Adult education provided by LEAs has decreased enormously during the 1990s. It is unlikely that this is simply due to lack of demand, but is also a result of the lack of centres and courses on offer. Reducing the number of centres may make sense financially, but it increases the average travel time for students in an area of limited public transport. Moreover, the tradition of 'liberal adult education' has also been hit by externally imposed financial constraints. Adult education provided by university continuing education departments, for example, continues to attract greater numbers of students, but this reflects strong trends towards greater vocationalisation of provision. More generally too, the number of books issued by libraries in South Wales, as in the rest of the UK, is in decline despite a growing population. In Neath, for example, the number of books issued each year dropped by 11% from 1974-86 (Eaton, 1987). It may be, however, that this is compensated by the growth in the purchase of books and magazines, perhaps reflecting the emergence of more individualised and home-based forms of learning (Field, 2000).

Most strikingly, however, the learning that was associated with the traditional industries of the region has disappeared as those industries have themselves been eradicated or massively reduced in scale and their working practices reorganised wholesale (Chambers et al, 1998). It is, of course, the case that the new forms of employment that have emerged in South Wales over recent decades have created their own patterns of workplace learning. Indeed, there are clearly examples of first-class training practices, especially among some of the large, frequently foreign-owned establishments (Rees and Thomas, 1994). Nevertheless, there must remain major concerns over the extent to which employees in South Wales are being offered levels of training opportunities that are comparable to those enjoyed by earlier generations, let alone what would be necessary for South Wales to become the motor of a new 'Celtic Tiger' economy. Certainly, it is instructive that, for Wales as a whole, of 940,000 employees, only 14,000 had taken part in any training in the four weeks prior to one major survey, of which 8,000 had had training off-the-job, 4,000 on-the-job and 2,000 both (Welsh Office, 1995b).

Conclusion

Industrial South Wales has undergone an economic, social and cultural transformation during the 20th century. Before the First World War, a characteristically 'modern' society emerged, based on the staple industries of metal manufacture and, above all, coal mining. The protracted demise of that distinctive economic and social system comprises the region's history for much of the remainder of the century. The collapse of employment in coal and steel – despite nationalisation and extended state support – has only partially been offset during recent decades by the growth of jobs in new forms of manufacturing and, more particularly, the service industries.

Despite the vicissitudes of economic life, through much of the 20th century, the regional society has sustained relatively vibrant forms of adult education and training. Through the activities of voluntary organisations within civil society, as well as those of employers (especially after nationalisation) and, of course, the state, many sections of the South Wales population have enjoyed access to a diversity of types of learning for much of the century. While by no means perfect, many men and rather fewer women have been able to participate in significant learning activity during their adult lives. More recently, however, many of the conditions on which this learning activity was based have been eroded; and it is by no means clear that adults currently enjoy even the level of opportunities that previous generations had.

At a minimum, therefore, we believe that our brief account of developments in South Wales is sufficient to remind readers that, in some respects and for some groups, South Wales was more like a learning society in the past than it is now. This is an important corrective to those accounts that describe a steady improvement in learning opportunities over time, leading almost inevitably to the achievement of a true learning society at some, unspecified point in the future: a Whig history. Progress towards a learning society is not a simple, linear process; and it is certainly not inevitable either.

Notes

[1] Industrial South Wales was defined in this study to exclude Cardiff and its immediate environs (the administrative capital of Wales and so protected from changes in economic climate), the Vale of Glamorgan (seaside towns benefiting from tourism, small-scale farming, and commuter areas), and small areas in Powys and Dyfed (sparsely populated, no heavy industry).

[2] One of the paradoxes of this approach is that sampling strategy becomes very complex, as it is unlikely that any such strategy will be effective over the whole of the time period under consideration (one hundred years in this case).

FOUR

Patterns of individual participation in adult learning

In this chapter, we begin to present the empirical findings that our research has generated. In a sense, the cornerstone of these findings is the analysis of the patterns of individuals' participation in adult learning; and this is where we begin here. It is ironic given the prominence attached to lifelong learning in policy debates that relatively little has been known hitherto about what patterns of participation are actually like. Moreover, even less systematic, empirical investigation has been directed at exploring what are the factors that shape these patterns of participation over individuals' lifetimes. And we begin to address these determinants of participation patterns in the latter parts of this chapter.

It is necessary at the outset, however, to be clear about some of the limitations of the research we have carried out. Perhaps most fundamentally, it should be noted that in describing people's patterns of participation, we encompass a wide diversity of forms of learning activity. There are the well-recognised differences between formal learning activities, such as taking courses in further or higher education, and informal practices, such as learning through leisure-time hobbies or participating in voluntary organisations. Equally, there are important distinctions between learning activities that people are *required* to undertake, at the behest of an employer or to qualify to undertake a pastime such as running a club, and those in which individuals take part voluntarily.

In much of what follows, these important distinctions are not a central part of our discussion. However, the general theoretical points argued in Chapter Two apply across all these different categories of adult education and training. Moreover, of course, given that we do include such a wide variety of learning activities in our analysis, it is perhaps even more striking that the extent of participation is so limited for a large proportion of people.

Learning trajectories

As we saw in Chapter Two, what is involved in an exploration of empirical patterns of participation in lifelong learning using the concept of trajectories is an attempt to describe characteristic sequences of learning episodes through the life course by aggregating individual experiences into a set of typologies (Gorard et al, 2001a). There is also a clear analytical element. Hence, the trajectory that people follow is largely determined by the resources that they derive from their social background. An individual's capacity to take up whatever learning opportunities are available is constrained by his or her previous history in this respect. However, trajectories do not simply reflect the constraining effects of structured access to learning opportunities. The individual educational experiences of which they are comprised are simultaneously the products of personal choices, which may themselves reflect 'learner identities'. What is central to an adequate analysis, therefore, is to produce an account of the interaction of such learner identities, and the individual choices to which they give rise, with wider structural parameters. The policy implications of such an analysis, as presented over the next three chapters, are profound.

The questionnaire survey produced 1,104 education and training histories for our primary respondents, and 2,484 histories for their families. These can be aggregated into a typology of eleven lifelong learning trajectories that encompasses almost all of the individual variations. This may be further aggregated into a five-fold typology; and it is the latter simplification that is used in this book (see Gorard et al, 1998a, 1998c, for further details). Table 4.1 summarises the frequencies of the basic five trajectories.

The 'immature trajectory' describes the small number of respondents who have yet to leave continuous full-time education, whether still at school or not. These are largely ignored in the analyses below.

Non-participants

The non-participants are those who reported no extension of their education immediately after ending compulsory schooling, no continuing education in adult life, no participation in government training schemes and no substantive work-based training. This group has no analogue in previous models based on research in this area, since they are the group most frequently ignored as they are unapproachable through lists of participants (and only available due to the door-to-door method of access used here). For around a third of respondents in total, their experience of lifelong learning ended with initial schooling or even earlier. Although this needs to be qualified in light of the evidence of informal learning from the semi-structured interviews (see Chapter Seven), it nevertheless confirms previous accounts of the size of the task confronting policy makers seeking to promote lifelong learning (Beinart and Smith, 1998).

The non-participant group is older than average for the sample, and therefore at least part of the explanation for the differences between this group and the

Table 4.1: Frequencies of each lifelong learning trajectory

Trajectory	Frequency	%
Non-participant	339	31
Transitional	222	20
Delayed	144	13
Lifelong	353	32
Immature	42	4

other three are age (or period) related. These differences could be based on changes in the local opportunity structure, due to economic and educational reforms. However, the delayed learners (to be discussed shortly) have a very similar age profile to the non-participants, which suggests that age alone is an insufficient explanation. Non-participant learners have older children on average, but they also tended to have them at a younger age. They more often attended secondary modern, but not grammar or technical, schools at school-leaving age. Non-participants are more frequently white, female, and living in Blaenau Gwent, and more likely to be economically inactive, with less prestigious class backgrounds. Fewer than in the other four groups attended school regularly, or took any qualifications at 15 or 16 years of age. They are the least qualified group at age 16, and throughout their lives. To a large extent their family members have similar educational and vocational profiles. On average, their mother, father, sibling, current partner, and first child left full-time continuous education earlier, and had lower level qualifications throughout their lives. Markedly fewer report a leisure interest requiring sustained study or practice.

Delayed learners

Those on the 'delayed' trajectory are like the non-participants in having a gap in participation between leaving school at the first opportunity until at least 21 years of age. But they followed this with a minimum of one substantive episode of education or training as an adult. This is after they have made the transition from school to work (compare the deferred beginners described by McNair, 1996, and the discontinuous learners of Hand et al, 1994). A few of these are 'third-age' learners, for whom the first substantive learning episode is after becoming permanently economically inactive through retirement or long-term illness. These may be more activity or learner orientated than goal orientated (Harrison, 1993).

The delayed learners differ in many respects from the non-participants and from the lifelong learners (to be discussed), being, for example, somewhat less likely to have attended a secondary modern or a grammar school (that is, displaying more diversity). They are more likely to have attended a minority school type at age 15, including elementary, fee-paying, denominational, and technical. They are more likely to live in Neath-Port Talbot, but to have been born elsewhere in South Wales. Our findings in this regard have recently been confirmed by an analysis based on the National Child Development Study. Those who left education when faced with a choice to stay on, but then returned later, could be distinguished by their social, economic and educational backgrounds (Thomas, 2001).

Transitional learners

The transitional learners reported the continuation of full-time education or a period of initial work-based training immediately after completing compulsory schooling, but no subsequent education or training. Theirs may be thought of as 'false start' trajectories, similar to the 'by default' learners described by Hand et al (1994). Transitional learners differ from the other groups in several respects, being, for example, more often male and slightly younger than the non-participants, but more often female than the lifelong learners. They are less likely to live in Neath-Port Talbot, and more likely still to live in the same area as their parents. They tend to have undertaken longer episodes of post-compulsory education outside work, perhaps continuing their education part-time immediately after leaving school at 16 years of age.

Lifelong learners

The remaining respondents have been optimistically classified as 'lifelong learners', since they have reported both transitional and subsequent learning episodes. These are more like the categories of learners usually discussed in the literature (by Tremlett et al, 1995, for example) and very similar to the continual learners sketched out by Hand et al (1994). However, it should be emphasised that ours is a very generous interpretation. It is possible in this typology for a lifelong learner merely to have stayed on at school for one extra term on reaching the leaving age of 14, and to have later undertaken a one-week induction training course at the age of 45.

Lifelong learners are more frequently male, born outside their current area of residence, less often from Blaenau Gwent, with both parents living outside their current area of residence (frequently outside South Wales), and with a Chapel/non-conformist religious background. They attended school regularly, more often at grammar schools among the older age groups, took examinations at 16, gaining higher qualifications at age 16 and throughout their lives. As with the non-participants, their family members have similar educational histories.

Why do some people participate and others not?

To begin to explain how these patterns of participation in lifelong learning arose, our regression analysis is used to identify those characteristics of respondents that enable good predictions of the 'trajectory' they follow. The full model includes over 40 independent variables that have a (statistically) significant relationship with trajectory patterns, but the sense of these can be summarised in terms of several broad factors such as time, place, gender, family background, and initial schooling, all of which appear to contribute to relatively stable lifelong learning trajectories.

It is important to note that all of these factors reflect characteristics of respondents that are determined relatively early during the life course. This can be expressed more formally, as the variables were entered into the logistic regression function in the order in which they occur in real life. Hence, those characteristics that are set very early in an individual's life, such as age, gender and family background, predict later 'lifelong learning trajectories' with 75%

accuracy. Adding the variables representing initial schooling increases the accuracy of prediction to 86%. And this rises to 89% and 90% respectively, as the variables associated with adult life and with respondents' present circumstances are included. This accuracy is itself a major research finding, showing how important these early factors are in determining patterns of later participation, and therefore highlighting the difficulties for policy makers in producing any changes in these patterns in the short term.

Time as a determinant

The age of respondents, and therefore the periods at which they left school or moved jobs, is a major determinant of lifelong participation. There is already evidence that however clearly established trajectories may be, their pattern and frequency changes over time with economic, social and policy changes (Banks et al, 1992). Generally, the frequency of participation in formal education or training has increased over the 50-year period of our study. More respondents in successive generations report staying-on in school or college after school-leaving age (even though this age has itself increased twice during the same period). In addition, formal participation decreases with the age of each individual (as in Greenhalgh and Stewart, 1987).

However, age is not a simple linearly increasing determinant of participation in the region of study that has witnessed a dramatic boom, bust and retrenchment in the past 50 years (Gorard, 1997a). For example, it may be that adverse economics have more impact on the employment prospects of younger cohorts at any period. The training and socialisation available in the three local nationalised or state-dependent industries – coal, steel and rail – have disappeared to a large extent, along with the job opportunities that they provided. Therefore, our study is in agreement with Gershuny and Marsh (1994) that the effect of time is an important one for the dependent variable, in this case training, in their case unemployment; but that the effect of time varies for each birth cohort. Even where the working lives of two individuals overlap, they may have an age-related differential proneness to participation in training, for example.

The proportion of respondents displaying each trajectory varies significantly by age. Some of these differences are structural/methodological and to be expected. For example, those still in full-time continuous education are much younger. If these, and the 15-24 age group that they mostly comprise, are ignored, there has been a clear trend towards increasing participation in some form of adult education since 1945/46, when the oldest respondents (in the 55-64 age cohort) left school (see Table 4.2).

However this increase is not chiefly to do with a greater return to education as an adult. The proportion of delayed learners has held relatively constant, or even decreased (but here the difference could be age rather than period related). The proportion of lifelong learners has increased a little, but the greatest growth has been in the proportion of those only using education as a transitional state. Over time, as it were, people who do not participate in any

Table 4.2: Learning trajectories by age cohorts (%)

Trajectory	15-24	25-34	35-44	45-54	55-64
Non-participants	13	26	28	37	43
Delayed	4	8	20	17	22
Immature	38	1	–	–	–
Transitional	22	33	17	16	12
Lifelong	24	31	35	31	22

adult learning are being replaced by people who continue their initial education for longer, but who then do not participate in any lifelong learning thereafter (see Chapter Six for a more detailed analysis).

When respondents were born presumably determines their relationship to changing opportunities for learning, and to social expectations. It is significant that respondents with similar social backgrounds from different birth cohorts exhibit different tendencies to participate in education and training. Time, therefore, may be a composite here for a variety of factors such as changes in local learning opportunities, economic development, the increasing formalisation of training, the antagonism between learning and work (see Chapter Eight), and the changing social expectations of the role of women (to be discussed).

Older respondents often reported quite radical changes of job or responsibility with no training provided at all. Examples included coalminer to catalogue shop manager, steelworker to electrician, librarian to upholsterer, and plasterer to market-gardener, and all with no training at all. Such people thought that learning was simply common sense, and that formal training was largely unnecessary. "No, nobody worried about things like that then. It's quite a new thing isn't it?"

To some extent these feelings are still common, but in reaction to the apparently more formal systems of training today. One woman said of her government training scheme:

> "It was a complete waste of time. They didn't teach you anything. You had to learn it for yourself.... It was a case of here's the stuff, have a go ... but all they were there for was drinking coffee and having a fag ... my mates all thought the same."

What has increased, perhaps, is the amount of unnecessary learning taking place (see Chapter Seven).

Similarly, the salience of educational qualifications was widely perceived to have increased as a consequence of shifts in the nature of employment. One father, for example, contrasted his own experiences with those of his son.

> "... so they [his parents] kept me back from my 11 plus ... I didn't go to school that day.... As soon as I was old enough to work, they wanted me to work.... [But] he's not coming out of school until he's 18, you know.

It's as simple as that, because we know how important it is, especially today."

Time is such an important analytical variable, allowing a consideration both of changes within the lifetimes of individuals and of changes across age cohorts, that it underlies much of the rest of this chapter, and forms the basis for an extended consideration in Chapter Six.

Place as a determinant

The importance of place in understanding the determinants of adult participation has been argued in Chapter Three. Most respondents in this study are local, having been born and educated in South Wales; and place has so far been found to play three roles in this study. First, Wales is different in many ways to other parts of the UK: against the British trend, it has a decreasing proportion of the workforce who are self-employed; and a lower incidence of job-related training than every region of England outside the east Midlands, for example (DfEE, 1997a, 1997b). Similarly, the chances of people participating in government employment and training programmes, and hence the chances of taking NVQs, have regional variations (Shackleton and Walsh, 1997). This has to be taken into account when examining the frequency of training episodes.

Second, in much the same way as Daines et al (1982) found differences between their six research sites, there are clear differences between patterns of participation in our three research sites (the sites are described in the Appendix). Third, participation, especially later in life, is more common for individuals and their families who have moved into the research sites from elsewhere. There may be two processes at work here. Trained and educated individuals are more likely to be part of a nationwide occupational labour market and have to move with their jobs. Those who are prepared to countenance moving to get a job are perhaps also more likely to enrol in courses. Similarly, those who had been away from Wales were more likely to participate in later learning. This is partly a function of occupational class and educational attainment for those in national labour markets, or who had been to university in England.

Apart from a small number who live outside South Wales and tend to be more highly educated, the picture for each research site is fairly simple. Those living in Blaenau Gwent, the most deprived area in the study, are more likely to be non-participant or perhaps transitional learners. Those in Bridgend, the most rapidly expanding area in the study, are more likely to be either transitional or lifelong learners. And those in Neath-Port Talbot, with a more recent history of established industry, are more likely to be delayed learners and most likely to be lifelong learners (Table 4.3).

Whichever site respondents live in now, their pattern of mobility in the past is as significant in defining their participation as the available local opportunities. For example, Table 4.4 shows that the further they were born

Table 4.3: Learning trajectories by area of residence (%)

Trajectory	Bridgend	Blaenau Gwent	Neath-Port Talbot
Non-participant	28	41	30
Delayed learner	30	32	37
Transitional	38	36	26
Lifelong learner	37	22	41

from their current area, the higher their chances of some form of learning experience after initial schooling.

The pattern of mobility and participation is quite clear. The lifelong learners are slightly younger, on average, than the non-participants, yet they have moved twice as often. Being prepared to, or being in a family prepared to, move between these four areas is related to participation in later education or training, whereas it appears to have little impact on school-based or transitional learning behaviour. It has been observed that whereas geographic mobility increases social mobility, it reduces the chances of meaningful vocational choice at initial education (Husen, 1986). Mobility can be both a factor in the determination of participation and the result of it. More formal schooling can lead to a greater chance of migrating to an area away from one's immediate family, especially from rural to urban areas. However, the process is not a simple one – such as a brain drain – as other factors also play a part such as social class and the motivation that comes from ambition.

Nearly three quarters of the respondents (72%) currently live in the same site in which they were born. Similarly, both of their parents, where the address is known, mostly still live in the same area (80%), and even where one of the families lives elsewhere it is most likely to be in South Wales. The sample is therefore a very stable one in terms of residence (as expected), making it ideal for the examination of local area effects on participation in adult education and training. It means that our detailed history of local structures of opportunity is particularly relevant to an understanding of the patterns emerging from the data.

However, these figures, as expected, show marked differences between the research sites. The recently expanding industrial area of Bridgend has a less settled population than either the established manufacturing region of Neath-Port Talbot or especially the depressed steel and mining valleys of Blaenau Gwent. Those living in Blaenau Gwent have on average moved only half as many times as the rest of the sample, having lived in the area on average for

Table 4.4: Learning trajectories by place of birth (%)

Trajectory/Born	Same site	South Wales	UK	Abroad
Non-participant	35	31	22	18
Delayed learner	17	14	22	18
Transitional	18	14	17	23
Lifelong learner	26	40	35	41

seven or eight years longer. In general, the further away from each research site the respondent and their family were born, the more moves they have made in their lives.

Those who have moved between regions are even more likely to participate in lifelong learning than those who have always lived in the more advantaged localities. It may not be an exaggeration to say that those who are geographically mobile tend to be participants in adult education or training; while those who remain in one area, sometimes over several generations, tend to be non-participants. Some people appear to be trapped in an area by the relative cost of living, and lack of transport. Since most respondents had not left South Wales, the biggest influence of place was a direct one, based on the availability of local opportunities for education and job-related training (mainly in steel and coal for men at the start of the period under study). These opportunities have clearly changed over time. The restructuring of local employment opportunities – the trends towards services, manufacturing assembly, female employment, and flexible working patterns – is one example. In general, employees no longer have the training (or the danger) associated with the nationalised industries. The new jobs are more frequently temporary, or part-time, and have in the main been taken up by women. One man, now in his 40s and unemployed after temporary work in a factory, left school at 15:

"I went into the coalmines [like all his school friends], but that was closed then in 1969. I had an accident just before it shut ... and it was while I was out that Llanhilleth shut, and everybody was transferred to other pits."

Asked why he had never taken part in any voluntary courses or leisure interests, he replied:

"I'm not brainy enough I suppose.... Well, I never looked to be honest."

He was clear that most of the jobs he was likely to encounter required no special skills or training, and equally clear that there was little point in learning except for a job.

To some extent, this local view of the value of training was clarified by a Training for Work manager in one of the research sites:

"People can't move out of the area, to Newport for example because of the house prices, and there is no public transport at night or early morning for shift workers, so unless they have a good car people can't commute.... Bosch, Sony, and Panasonic are always advertising for jobs, as their workers leave through boredom with the conveyor belt production. But they go on to another similar job hoping it will be less boring, or to Benefit, and not to training [except for the limited induction training accompanying the new job]."

"Some jobs have two hundred plus applicants if they are reasonable, and so applicants are thrown out if they are overqualified, or underqualified, even if they have been doing the job elsewhere for twenty years. Bosch recently selected for a job like this but still had two hundred plus applicants left in the pile, and used things like height as criteria for selection.... There *is* a trend away from reliance on qualifications to ability and experience, but often it comes down to who you know, not what. People are taken as temps for trial before the job is advertised."

"I was a returner at the age of 26, did not want to work in a factory. In the valley others often just drift along and think why bother. You need a good car to work elsewhere, and you stay because the nuclear [sic] family is still important here, with grandparents helping with childcare. Abergavenny is 14 miles and it takes two hours by bus, so you need a good car. I live in Ebbw Vale and I hate people from Tredegar, while Newport is a foreign land. The brighter ones from here go to university and simply don't come back. People say 'I left school at 16, picked up money shovelling, you did As [A levels] and you're unemployed, and he went to university and now works in a cracker factory'."

All of our interviews with trainers and teachers, from both industry and education, stressed this 'parochialism' of local people. This was particularly so in Blaenau Gwent. As working conditions in the mines deteriorated, miners, if they wished to continue in mining were forced to travel to other valleys to work, and this was not a popular option. While there were some other industries operating in the area, these tended to be small firms paying low wages. The introduction of redundancies at British Steel (Ebbw Vale Plant) in the 1970s coupled with the decline in the pits was exacerbated by this reluctance of paid-off workers to look for work out of the area, which has, in this account, contributed to second and third generation unemployment.

The trainers and educators emphasised the difficulties that this creates. The reluctance of people from Tredegar or Blaina to travel to Ebbw Vale and vice versa has forced educators to adopt strategies of taking education to the people. In this respect, the more fluid structures of community education or virtual colleges (see Chapter Nine) may prove more successful than the activities of Ebbw Vale College, for example.

"Somebody in the South East of the borough would find it very difficult to get to the North West with the sort of public transport we've got. If you've got a car that's alright but this part of Gwent is one of the lowest areas of car ownership in Wales.... Of course community education centres [like the Scientific and Technical Institute built in Ebbw Vale that has been in continuous operation since 1849] are much more evenly distributed throughout the borough. They're very accessible to people."

A Blaenau Gwent careers adviser agrees that:

> "We've had to retrain the people in this area, before anything else, to move from one area to another.... When I started I couldn't get the kids to come from Brynmawr or Ebbw Vale for training. I'd bring kids over here and they'd say 'is this Tredegar?' They'd never been to Tredegar!"

This reluctance to move may be based on past patterns of employment:

> "If your father was in the works, there was a job for you when you left school. That was the pattern. It was the same in the other valleys, they had mines they did, not the steelworks, but they had the pits and the mines. There was always that type of work [for men, by implication]."

A manager in an engineering firm concludes:

> "There's not many people who will travel from Tredegar to Ebbw Vale, which is the next valley over. They won't travel. It's just that they won't. If they can't get the employment they want in their locality that's it."

There is some recent evidence that young people (particularly those with qualifications) are showing more willingness to travel. However, LG (the Korean company then new to the adjacent area of Newport) has had extreme difficulty recruiting workers from Blaenau Gwent, despite laying on free buses to work. All trainers commented on the deep-rooted third generation culture of unemployment in the area. Many of the families known to them appear disinterested in both education or working. One trainer cynically and, as we shall see, very unfairly commented that the only level of education many aspired to was knowing how to sign their name at the dole office.

New industry has moved into the area slowly. In the 1970s there was an influx of what a Tredegar careers advisor described as 'fly-by-night' companies, which were primarily there to receive the Welsh Development Agency subsidies. This era is over, and there are now a number of relatively established employers committed to the long-term development of their workers through training. Manufacturing is still largely male-dominated, with the female workforce tending to be concentrated in the retail and care sectors. There is reportedly an acute skills shortage, and this has been exacerbated by the presence of large foreign owned companies such as LG, Sony and Bosch. Trainers felt that Ebbw Vale was turning the corner (at that time), with the success of the rugby club and the Garden Festival boosting confidence in the town, but that this would be a slow process. A local careers adviser reports that:

> "Japanese [and other] companies moving into the area are surprised at the skills shortage. They look at the high unemployment figures but when it comes to recruiting staff they have great difficulties.... They think there's hundreds looking for those jobs, but there are not. If the

kids have anything about them in terms of ability they are going back
to school aren't they?"

The suggestion here is that employers see extended initial education as a
cause of a low skill workforce, rather than a solution to it – a very common
theme in our interviews.

In Neath–Port Talbot, educators and employers also emphasised what they
saw as the very low levels of ambition among people, and their consequent
reluctance to travel any distance to work. The Principal of a local college
characterised his students as both parochial in their attitudes and as having
very low personal expectations. He saw this as being translated into minimal
performance in school, which created problems when they moved on to the
college. A local careers advisor commented that families see very little value
in the type of education on offer, since "they don't see education as leading
anywhere". Both of these trainers noted that high rates of unemployment
lead to a lack of motivation and a culture of short-termism. Local employers
commented both on the marked lack of basic literacy and numeracy skills
among their workers and on their reluctance to train in order to improve
their promotion prospects.

The Principal of the local college disputes the claim made in his presence
that the standard of local education is poor since Port Talbot has a very low
proportion of residents with higher qualifications according to the 1991 Census.
Thus, a local employer claimed that he could not recruit the right type of
people to 'drive Port Talbot forward'. Whereas:

> "The really interesting question is how many of those people [graduates
> from the college] have come back into this community with a job that
> is commensurate with their educational attainment? The sad answer is
> its much closer to nought.... You can't blame the local people. You can't
> blame the schools. You can't blame the colleges. Yes, you can look at
> elements of blame but unless you've actually got something there for
> them, it's [Port Talbot] always going to be a net exporter. You look at
> the Afan Valley wards. Look at the population there and it's the classic
> skewed age profile, an increasingly ageing population. No industry and
> those communities are starting to die on that."

This view, from a regional perspective, attacks the simplistic basis of recent
human capital approaches to economic development (see Chapters One and
Two). Even in the best-planned economies, such as Singapore, graduates are
now working long-term as maids and waiters. In Port Talbot they simply
leave, since having a trained workforce cannot, of itself, produce work.

Gender as a determinant

Although the significance of gender changes over the period of this study, it
remains one of the clearest determinants of participation throughout, affecting

not merely the frequency and length of learning episodes but also their type and outcomes. In general, women were more likely to be non-participants from the 1940s to the 1970s, and have been more likely to be transitional learners since. Women have traditionally been under-represented at every level of learning above initial education (Hopper and Osborn, 1975), although they were traditionally over-represented in extramural classes. Men consistently report more formal learning than women. Although the situation is changing (see Chapter Six), these changes are different for each gender. Women are still less likely to participate in lifelong learning, but are now more likely to be 'transitional learners'. Extended initial education (including apprenticeships) is now relatively gender neutral (Gorard et al, 1999b, 2001b), while later education or training is increasingly the preserve of males (see Gorard et al, 1998d, 1999a).

When trajectories are considered for men and women separately (Tables 4.5 and 4.6), it is clear that the increase in participation for males took place chiefly for those finishing initial education in the 1960s (the 45-54 age cohort), while for women it took place a decade later in the 1980s (among those in the 35-44 age cohort). One implication of this is that whereas the reduction in non-participation for men was replaced by an equivalent increase in lifelong learning (until the 1980s), for women the increase in lifelong learners was matched by an increase in the proportion of those participating only in extended initial education and training (the transitional learners).

Part of this difference is related to differences in the pattern of work and the training opportunities that ensue. Men are still twice as likely as women to work full-time, in part because of childcare responsibilities, but also as a result of some women's preference for part-time work (DfEE, 1997a). In general, women without children are more likely to have jobs, while for women with children their employment cycle is job, family, workforce re-

Table 4.5: Men's learning trajectories by age cohort (%)

Trajectory	15-24	25-34	35-44	45-54	55-64
Non-participant	19	25	23	20	34
Delayed	8	11	19	20	22
Transitional	34	31	15	17	16
Lifelong	39	33	42	43	29

Table 4.6: Women's learning trajectories by age cohort (%)

Trajectory	15-24	25-34	35-44	45-54	55-64
Non-participant	22	28	32	49	54
Delayed	3	6	20	15	23
Transitional	38	35	18	15	8
Lifelong	38	30	29	21	15

entry (Gershuny and Marsh, 1994). There is some evidence to suggest that the association between work and identity is weaker among women than men. Most training is full-time for those working full-time, and so is more common for men, and single women (Greenhalgh and Stewart, 1987). In fact, married women who receive full-time training show a net movement out of the workforce, so that the proportion without any training actually increased from 1965-75. More women are now working (economic activity up from 57% of those aged 16-59 in 1971 to 71% in 1995), while fewer men are (a drop from 91% to 85% over the same period). However, the rise in employment for women has been chiefly in part-time posts (DfEE, 1996), which are less likely to lead to training and qualifications (Shackleton and Walsh, 1997).

Some of the same factors determining employment prospects for women also apply to off-the-job learning. Women may face more of a hindrance to participation than men due to having children and other relatives to care for (Frazer and Ward, 1988) and are, in consequence, unable to travel as far to institutions. Women are more likely to cite domestic reasons for non-participation or drop-out, while men more frequently cite work reasons. Men and women have been observed to participate in courses in different subject areas (NIACE, 1994). On the other hand, women are more likely to gain an NVQ via government programmes (Shackleton and Walsh, 1997), and a recent report suggests that, in fact, women and men train equally often, but that women's episodes are simply briefer (DfEE, 1997a).

By the 1990s, young women were taking academic qualifications below degree level more frequently than men, while young men were more likely to receive formal vocational training (DfEE, 1995). This is partly because women more frequently stay in immediate post-school education, at least for the first two years. After this point the number of men prevails, since a large proportion of the women move on to something else (Dolton et al, 1994). There are regional differences between this gender gap in participation, larger in Scotland but smaller in Northern Ireland, for example. Similarly, the gap varies with age cohorts, reducing over time, but is generally larger for those living with a partner (Felstead, 1996). Several of the barriers to training may affect women more than men, including lack of awareness of opportunities and the likelihood of domestic responsibilities (Maguire et al, 1993), especially for a lone parent. Socially, women may be at a disadvantage in gaining acceptance for their own interests, as evidenced by the finding that emancipation is a common theme in the motivation for women to return to formal education (Schratz, 1996).

A regular story that most dramatically displays this difference between men and women is a kind of enforced altruism (an example perhaps of what we describe in Chapter Two as socially constructed rationalities). For example:

"[I left my first job as an analytical chemist because] the thing was my husband was in the Air Force you see so as soon as we got married we went to live in Germany and were just travelling around.... [I had no further jobs while married because] well we had the children, you see, and in those days people didn't. It was almost a – in some spheres – a slight on the husband implying that ... he couldn't support you."

This woman, in her sixties, has since separated from her husband, taken a new career as a teacher with regular training, become an inspector of schools, and since retirement has taken classes in Welsh, Spanish, antiques appreciation, and contract bridge. She is therefore an 'ideal type' lifelong learner, thwarted earlier in her trajectory only by social custom. It is clear from this story that gender is significant in a relationship, as well as a factor in its own right. Like many other lifelong learners, this woman has had a period away from South Wales.

This altruistic phenomenon is still prevalent (although perhaps less widespread). A similar story was told by a woman in her twenties, who obtained a diploma in business studies (the first formal qualification in her family):

"Well, I found work then. We moved away to Birmingham up there [as a management trainee], but Steve didn't like it up there. And he was promised a job back here, so we came back but it fell through and then the kids came along."

They are now living in the depressed area of Blaenau Gwent, and her husband is still unemployed. The respondent works part-time as a packer in a local factory, and helps voluntarily with a local playgroup, where she is learning Welsh and taking qualifications in childcare.

Gender is a relevant aspect of social structure, and it is one that creates a clear 'climate of expectations'. It is within the limitations and constraints imposed by these expectations that individuals may seek to make rational choices, and it is only within the patterns of behaviour that these constraints produce that the exceptions of people 'breaking out' can be properly understood. In what follows, we draw on our re-analysis of the coalfield archive material to illustrate these general arguments.

As we have seen (in Chapter Three), at the turn of the century South Wales was one of the largest and most important centres of learning in Britain. It was in the midst of absorbing agricultural populations from mid-Wales, the West Country and further afield, and transforming them into a new society. The colliery workforce almost trebled through in-migration over 30 years by 1920. Perhaps those who came seeking a better life were self-selected pioneers, or perhaps the challenge that their old skills were largely redundant, and they had to learn about the alien environment of the pit, led to a community of learners (a male community of course). According to our archive oral histories, much of the learning was of the techniques and terminology of mining, especially safety since "if you don't learn it properly you'll most likely get a stone on top of you", but the teaching that went on in the pit was far more than was necessary for the job. At the South Wales Miners' Federation meetings, or the 'double-parting' where they took breaks underground, men such as Will Jon Edwards learnt of Spencer and Darwin, and above all of politics.

A culture of learning existed within this coalfield society. Underpinned by a non-conformist ethic was an ethos that encouraged self-improvement and a general assumption that young men should study for self-advancement. Will Lake used the remainder from his first wage as enrolment fees for mining classes, one of many 'boys' wanting to climb the ladder to colliery management. In 1906, over 3,000 students were engaged in mining study in Glamorgan, where courses were run in 66 villages. Men like J.L. Williams came to the valleys aged 18 in 1906 looking for freedom from the conditions of the farm, higher wages from the 'black gold' and 'more self-education'. He attended evening classes run by the county council, but later went to study at the Central Labour College, becoming an adult education organiser and eventually an MP.

The effort to study after a full day's work was considerable. Walter Haydn Davies recalled that "to study mine surveying [we] used to walk over the mountain from Bedlinog to Bargoed where the classes were held". Albert Davies had to wear his coat to do his homework in the bedroom, since only the family room had a fire. Miners subscribed to journals and took correspondence courses, paying as much as four guineas subscription (a very large sum). However, this was not encouraged as what Walter Haydn Davies termed 'self-centred individualism', but as long as it did not detract from the collective good. By 1913 more students were attending further education in Merthyr Tydfil than in any period since, until the growth in learning opportunities was curtailed by the Great War.

After the war, Harold Watkins found that the mood of students in Glamorgan had changed. Interest in commercial subjects and mine management waned, seen perhaps as being too self-interested or more to the benefit of the bosses than the learner. Many now wanted "to find out about things", especially economics. Will Coldrick had combined pit work with a study of commerce, but during the war he attended independent working class lectures (WEA), and later went to the Labour College. The Labour College Movement held that general and technical education were not enough: a different kind of education was also needed. Anti-capitalist feeling increased, and qualified miners such as Jim Vale declined offers to become managers, since 'going over' to the bosses had become another form of self-centred individualism. Learning for these men became more clearly a transformational, rather than a promotional, process, ideally leading to advancement of one's class or community as well as one's family. As social and economic difficulties affected the coalfield, with the depression and the coal disputes leading to entire villages 'on the dole', this learning ethos was apparently undiminished (in direct contrast to findings of Jahoda et al, 1972, in Austria). In fact, during the depression attendance at Workmen's Institutes increased, and, as noted in Chapter Three, the peak use of libraries came in 1926. By 1935 there were 517 separate adult courses in addition to 'recognised' places of learning, catering for 10,246 students and the supply was still not equal to the demand (Welsh Department, 1937).

On the other hand, the role of women in the functioning of the coalfield has been described as 'essential' but, because coal was the basis of all local paid employment and women were prohibited from the pit, their work was unpaid. Of perhaps 150,000 people in the Rhondda valleys in 1911, only 7,000 were women in paid employment, mainly young and unmarried. This also kept women outside many of the opportunities for formal learning available to the men at the time. The Board of Education later stated that the "majority of the women's classes are not intended to be a preparation for posts in industry ... but are because women wish to acquire greater skill and aptitude as homemakers". It was expected that women would give up paid employment on marrying, and a typical occupational lifespan of the women interviewed for the archive was only 5 to 10 years. If a woman aspired to a profession and a career, her best option was to lie about her marriage, as Mrs D.J. Davies did. A societal prohibition on paid work was extended quite easily to educational aspirations, and the Director of Education in Merthyr during the Great War even objected to married women, 'past the prime of life', attending classes in domestic studies: "The Committee's Evening School Regulations should be amended to exclude them".

When economic difficulties faced families in the coalfield, the impact on women may have been greater than on men, and increasing numbers of girls were required to leave home to work as domestic servants in English cities. Mrs Fine left when she was 16 to become a 'between maid' in a TB clinic in Hertfordshire, with a half day off and a break of two hours in a day lasting to 10pm. She married aged 20, "otherwise I would have been in service I expect".

Women had limited access to many social institutions in the valleys such as the Institutes and pubs, so the chapel became a focal point for the formation of women's clubs. Until the 1930s funding was a problem; as women could not be employed, they were not unemployed, but they could be the 'womenfolk of the unemployed'. Starting as occasional meetings offering limited learning opportunities, often in space reluctantly provided in the men's Institutes, by 1939 there were more women's than men's clubs in South Wales. This provision of clubs by and for women is an important feature of interwar coalfield society that has not previously been emphasised.

Today's respondents tell stories that resonate with the earlier tales of these coalfield wives, and our interviews have highlighted examples of female non-participants whose educational and vocational aspirations have been restricted and undervalued by brothers, husbands and fathers. Some have given up jobs and related training on marrying. Others have had their choices restricted, as in the case of three sisters, all in their mid-twenties, whose father demanded they leave their jobs to run the family shop. Another woman left her job to look after her new husband's children. Female working and learning futures are shaped from a very early age as one woman, then 42-years-old, describes:

"My mother's one of those old-fashioned types that a boy has got to do it [education] but a girl is not important.... 'Oh don't worry, it's only our Anne. Anne stays at home and does the work'."

Consequently, Anne's desire to be an electrician was thwarted by its stereotype as 'being no job for a woman', and instead of fulfilling her own desire for college, she ended up subsidising her brother's university education.

When progress towards a learning society in Britain is accounted separately by gender, women respondents today still tell stories that would have been recognisable to Mrs Davies in 1911, and that have been referred to as 'enforced altruism'. And yet it is women's participation that has driven most of the apparent increase in formal education and training over the past 50 years. For men, there is such an emphasis on the 'barriers' to participation, such as cost and travel, that it is difficult to imagine Walter Haydn Davies and his friends walking over that mountain in winter. Perhaps what these accounts reveal is that the barriers are not the chief problem? If not, then the 'blame' for non-participation may lie in the motivation of individuals, but it may also lie partly in the perceived nature of the opportunities on offer.

Other social determinants of lifelong learning

The next chapter considers the crucial role of family and initial schooling in forming learner identities for individuals that then impact on their participation in later life. This chapter concludes by considering patterns in several other background characteristics which, like place, age and gender, show interesting variations between trajectories, yet unlike them are omitted from our more general statistical model. These variables are omitted because the variation applies to too few cases in our sample (for more on these see Gorard et al, 1997c; Gorard, 1998a).

Ethnicity

The first of these is minority ethnic background. The term 'ethnicity' is used tentatively here, since most standard classifications used to measure this notion are in fact a confusing mixture of religious, 'racial', national, and cultural characteristics (Gorard, 2001b). This study uses self-reporting to define the categories. As expected from the 1991 census data, the proportion of respondents of recent ethnic minority origin was small, smaller in fact than the 1.5% figure for the whole of Wales (OPCS, 1993), but close to a representative figure for the three research sites in industrial South Wales chosen for this study. For the purposes of this analysis, all categories other than 'white' are grouped together. Although representing only eight cases in total (0.7% of the total) the non-white respondents provide an interesting alternative entry point to the complex data patterns emerging from the survey.

This variation in South Wales in terms of recent minority ethnic background is too limited to be of general use as an explanation. However, the data available supports that of Tan and Peterson (1992). Once other factors are taken into account, non-whites are at least as likely to participate in training as whites. In areas other than employer-provided training, non-whites may be more likely to participate (see also Shackleton and Walsh, 1997). The study therefore disagrees with the findings of Greenhalgh and Stewart (1987) in this respect. The evidence also disagrees with that of Gambetta (1987) who found that migrants from Southern Italy to the study area were less likely to continue education after school. In this study, in-migration and mobility are key indicators of prolonged educational participation.

The non-whites are better qualified than average at the end of full-time education and throughout their lives, and this has previously been found to hold in the whole of Wales (Welsh Office, 1995a) and for the work-based training of black women in England (DfEE, 1995). It is reflected in the higher qualifications of their siblings, and predicted to some extent by the qualifications and occupations of their parents, which are considerably elevated compared to South Wales as a whole.

Language

Similarly, very few respondents speak a language other than English at home – 1.7% in total (with 1.4% speaking mainly Welsh or Welsh and English). This low figure for Welsh-speaking in industrial South Wales is one result of the rapid expansion of the coalfield (see Chapter Three). It is also clear that the analysis that follows is specific to the situation of Welsh-speakers in this minority environment.

Those speaking a language other than English are generally older (mostly aged over 55), having moved between regions of the UK or even abroad less often and lived in South Wales longer than average. All were born in Wales, even the three who speak a language other than English or Welsh. Welsh-speakers are predominantly male, from a Chapel/non-conformist family background, and living in Neath-Port Talbot or Bridgend. All of the respondents in Blaenau Gwent speak English only.

In terms of participation, the Welsh-speakers leave full-time continuous education later, while speakers of other languages leave at the end of compulsory schooling and have few chances to return to any formal learning. Table 4.7 shows the differences in numbers of episodes of education and training undertaken, the length of time involved in study, and the proportion of respondents' lives spent in study. Although some of these differences may be age-related, it is important to recall that the Welsh-speakers tend to be older, attending school before ROSLA, and that the overall percentage of their life in education or training since leaving school is almost double that of average.

Their levels of qualification are as expected from the participation figures, with Welsh-speakers generally coming out best and other language speakers worst at the end of full-time continuous education, and these differences are currently being preserved over their lifetime. The picture for respondents'

Table 4.7: Participation in adult education and training by family language

Mean\language	English	Welsh	Other
Age at end of full-time education	16.3	17.7	15.0
Number of episodes of education and training	1.5	2.1	1.3
Years in education and training	2.3	5.0	1.9
% of life spent in education and training	13.4	20.5	4.9

qualifications and participation in education also appears in their lifelong social class, with Welsh-speakers having more prestigious occupations, and this pattern continues into the next generation.

Religion

Respondents were asked about the religion dominant in their family background. As expected, Anglican (52%) and Chapel (26%) backgrounds are common, while non-Christian religions are very rare. Over the 50 years concerning this study, those respondents describing themselves as from a Chapel/non-conformist background have declined (see Pope, 1997) and been replaced in the main by those with no religion. This may have significance if the tradition of chapel and Sunday school was indeed part of the foundation for those components of the learning society previously described in South Wales (see Chapter Three).

Indeed, there is evidence that the families of chapel-goers generally participate more in all forms of education and are more highly qualified. They more commonly report having a leisure interest requiring sustained practice or study, and attending school regularly. One reason for this could be the increased and enthusiastic participation in education as a child reported by several such respondents at interview. For example:

> "My father was secretary of the chapel, then he was deacon of the chapel.... I think he had visions that I would become a minister. He was never disappointed that I didn't mind but he always teased me – 'y parch' ... that's why he gave me the name."

> "I think the pressure is there. In a little village like where I come from.... I mean passing the 11 plus was a big thing ... if you failed the 11 plus you were finished. It wasn't just [pressure from] parents with us, because when I was in Brynamman the difficulty I had was finding time to do homework, believe it or not. There were so many things going on there it was unbelievable."

"When I was in school we won the Urdd Eisteddfod play ten years on the trot.... Mind you look at the people we had there.... We had debating societies every Monday and we had to prepare a speech.... It was a lovely place to grow up in. You were influenced by your peers as well, not just your parents.... The only time I was ever locked in was to have piano lessons. I had recitation lessons ... my father decided I was going to have singing lessons."

"And I think it held you in good stead later on ... you were never afraid to stand in front of an audience. I mean you did so much of it in chapel and in young people's and the Urdd."

"Amman Valley Grammar school ... in those days produced teachers and preachers."

This respondent was a male educator and examiner in his fifties, who had been away to university and retained that early enthusiasm for learning and teaching throughout his life and tried to pass it on to his children. His story also illustrates the importance of initial schooling for the later trajectory, and since it is related to a selective system that has now disappeared, there is a period effect here as well. However, part of the explanation may also be the relatively elevated class profile of the non-conformist families.

Conclusion

The general determinants of lifelong learning, as proposed by this study, include gender, family background, initial schooling, occupation and motivation. However, the most significant factors may be summarised as time and place. Their significance lies as much in their interactions with the other variables as in themselves. When and where an individual is determines their structure of opportunities such as access to courses, but it also determines the relevance of gender, family background, initial schooling, occupation and motivation in mediating those objective opportunities. Place and time affect the opportunities available to people, and these opportunities are key to an understanding of participation and non-participation. One cannot, for example, ask why someone did not take an option that was non-existent at the time (Gambetta, 1987). Similarly, one cannot really ask why someone did not take an option that was non-existent in the place that they lived or were able to travel to.

"Patterns of participation in adult learning are strongly related to educational advantage and to age, but also vary significantly across regions of Great Britain" (Sargant, 1996, p 197). In reality, place is not as fixed as time, since the individual can move, but the population in this study is relatively fixed and few people have moved considerable distances in their lives. In fact, the concept of mobility, for those families able and prepared to move, is crucial to patterns of participation.

It is also important to note that all of the factors we uncovered reflect characteristics of respondents that are determined relatively early during the life course. The analytical implications of this are profound. It provides strong empirical support for the utility of the concept of 'trajectory' in analysing participation in lifelong learning. Not only is there a clear pattern of typical 'trajectories' that effectively encapsulates the complexity of individual education and training biographies, but also which 'trajectory' an individual takes can be accurately predicted on the basis of characteristics that are known by the time an individual reaches school-leaving age. This does not imply, of course, that people do not have choices, or that life crises have little impact, but rather that, to a large extent, these choices and crises occur within a framework of opportunities, influences and social expectations that are determined independently. At this level of analysis, it is the latter that appear most influential.

What appears to have happened in the 50 or so years since the 1944 Education Act is that initial education has been extended, so that the majority of students continue to participate in education or training after the age of 16, and a substantial proportion would now expect to continue to higher education at 18 years of age. The changes have been particularly remarkable in the relative participation rates of women. However, this has so far made little discernible difference to many people's lifelong patterns of participation. If it was lack of involvement in paid work that was at least partly responsible for the non-participation of women in work-based (and workers') education earlier this century, it may be the subsequent changes in the nature and forms of work that are partly responsible for the fact that women's participation in formal learning episodes has not increased in proportion to their involvement in the workforce. To some extent, extended initial education has replaced formal job-related training, and to a larger extent, extended education now involves those who in previous generations would never have experienced any formal adult education or training. Unfortunately, this experience of extended education is not sufficient by itself to encourage later participation. Of the 1,104 participants in the study aged 16-65, over 31% had experienced no education or training outside compulsory education: no further education, no job-related training, no evening classes, no health and safety training, no hobby requiring study or sustained practice. Over the 50 years covered by the survey, these non-participants have decreased in proportion as they are constrained to stay in formal education after the age of 14, then 15, then 16, but they are replaced, in the main, by those who report no further participation once they do leave. We examine these changes over time in more detail in Chapters Five and Six.

FIVE

Families and the formation of learner identities

In this chapter, we consider the early-life experiences of each individual that help form a lifelong 'learner identity' that itself appears to become a determinant of their future patterns of participation. The first of these is family background, and the second is initial schooling.

Family as a determinant

Family background, assessed in terms of income, parents' education, or parents' occupation, is a key predictor of lifelong participation in education or training, as it is of success at school (Gorard et al, 1999c). In some periods and regions, it may be the characteristics of the father that are dominant (Cervero and Kirkpatrick, 1990), and in others those of the mother (Bynner and Parsons, 1997). In this study, the father's occupation, the mother's education and place of birth predominate, and there is no agreement with the finding of Gambetta (1987) that the significance of parental education varies by occupational class. There is little evidence from this study that the UK is moving towards a 'classless' society in terms of learning, or that cycles of advantage and disadvantage are reducing. Social reproduction is still a key factor, and the link between household of origin and later occupational status may have actually strengthened since 1945 (Gershuny and Marsh, 1994).

Several previous studies have examined educational attainment and occupation (for example, Halsey et al, 1980), while there is a smaller body of literature that considers participation in education or training as its primary variable, and an even smaller body that relates the participation of generations within the same families. In compulsory education, traditions of similar educational routes (or initial educational trajectories) within families are quite common. Models of reproduction involving post-compulsory education and training, on the other hand, have generally found much weaker links between the involvement of parent and child (for example, Cervero and Kirkpatrick, 1990). The correlations between parental education and the child's later participation in the longitudinal model created by Yang (1998) are so low that, even when combined with many other predictor variables, such as school attainment and attitudinal data, only 23% to 30% of the variance in participation is explained (and this model had only considered a restricted range of adults aged from 16-32).

Theoretical models of post-compulsory participation are generally complex, involving structural, socio-economic and psychological factors (see, for example, Cross, 1981), but nearly all are variants of an accumulation form. In the accumulation-of-prior-learning theory, it is claimed that the best single predictor of later participation is earlier participation. Nevertheless, the correlations are very low, and therefore "the lifelong education cycle cannot be comprehended without the inclusion and analysis of other factors influencing the accumulation of educational experiences" (Tuijnman, 1991, p 283). These other factors include area of residence (a proxy for local economic conditions), gender, and parental occupation and education (Gerber and Hout, 1995; Zhou et al, 1998). This last factor is the focus of the following sections, where it is suggested that parental patterns of participation in education and training are at least as important in determining the patterns of participation for a child, as are the child's own experiences of learning.

Educational patterns within families

The analysis here uses three indicators of participation in lifelong learning: the highest lifelong qualification so far, the age of leaving full-time continuous education, and the individual's learning trajectory. The first of these indicators is the highest qualification of parent (origin) and child (destination) as shown in Table 5.1, where 'A level' refers to A level equivalent qualification or above, using the DfEE standard classification for National Training Targets (see Marshall et al, 1997). 'Elementary' refers to qualifications below A level, including employer-based certificates. The frequency of each level of qualification is higher among children than their parents, but despite this growth in qualifications, more children have the same, or lower, level of qualification as their parents than do not. There is clearly some form of family relationship here. A similar, though somewhat weaker, pattern is observed when qualifications of the smaller number of grandparents and their grandchildren are considered (therefore, the parents and children of the respondents). Thus, whatever the mechanisms of this relationship are, they continue over at least three generations. All of these patterns are observable for both male and female respondents, and although men are generally more highly qualified in all three generations, the biggest change has been the increase in the qualifications of women over time. The table of reproduction is even more similar between each generation when it contains only cases of one gender.

Table 5.1: Qualifications of parents and children (numbers) (% in brackets)

Parent\child	None	Elementary	A level	Total
None	798 (44)	538 (27)	490 (28)	1826
Elementary	52 (18)	99 (32)	103 (50)	254
A level	72 (20)	135 (31)	195 (49)	402
Total	922	772	788	2482

The age at which children leave full-time continuous education (FTCE) has also increased over time. Although the age of children leaving FTCE is predictable from the age at which their parents left, the relationship is a relatively weak one. For example, the correlation between the ages of fathers and their children on leaving FTCE is +0.33, which means that the relationship explains only 10% of the variance in the figures. This relationship is getting weaker over time. It may be that the picture is confused by the changing forms of participation over time, as training moves from employer-funded work-based provision to state-funded and college-based forms. FTCE measures only encapsulate one part of an individual's education and training history, and it is partly for this reason that the project uses the concept of lifelong learning trajectories hereafter.

Our sample included 200 respondents whose parents were also part of the sample, and it is possible to compare the relationship of trajectories within these families, although some of these cannot be used since the child is still in FTCE (see Table 5.2).

Several patterns are evident in the table. The proportion of lifelong learners remains constant over one generation. All other trajectories show large changes in frequency. In general, non-participation and delayed learning have declined, while transitional participation has doubled in one generation. Some of this apparent increase may be due to the children's trajectories encompassing fewer opportunities for later learning than their parents so far, simply because they are at an earlier stage in their lives (that is, they are right-censored). However, this overall trend is the same as that from other analyses using all respondents (mentioned earlier).

Intriguingly, transitional participation is now the modal trajectory for the children of parents in the non-participant and delayed trajectories, while the children of transitional learners themselves are more likely to be lifelong learners. The numbers involved are small, but a tentative suggestion can be made here that may soften the rather pessimistic analysis of changes over time presented elsewhere in this book. Increases in participation in post-compulsory education since 1945 have not, so far, produced a proportionate increase in lifelong participation. Nevertheless, there is a slight indication here that such an effect may take at least one generation to be noticeable. That is, the massification of further and higher education has not produced a generation

Table 5.2: Learning trajectories of parents and children (numbers) (% in brackets)

Parent\child	Non-participant	Delayed	Transi-tional	Lifelong	Total
Non-participant	20 (31)	5 (8)	25 (38)	15 (23)	65
Delayed	5 (25)	–	10 (50)	5 (25)	20
Transitional	3 (16)	4 (21)	4 (21)	8 (42)	19
Lifelong	5 (10)	3 (6)	19 (37)	24 (47)	51
Total	33	12	58	52	155

Table 5.3: Participation in adult education and training of parents and children

Parent\child	Participant	Non-participant
Participant	77	13
Non-participant	45	20

of lifelong learners, but it *may* help to do so for their children, since there are more transitional learners over time and the majority of children of transitional learners are actually lifelong learners.

One would expect there to be more lifelong learners in the younger generation than the older one. There are, but it is noteworthy that half of the children who are lifelong learners have parents who are lifelong learners themselves. Similarly, more than half of the children who are non-participants have parents who are non-participants. It is clear that, for whatever reason, patterns of participation 'run in families' to a great extent.

Tables 5.3 and 5.4 examine the same data on trajectories in a more collapsed form. In the first example, all trajectories involving *any* participation after initial schooling are grouped together (participants), and contrasted with those cases reporting no formal learning episodes (non-participants). In the second example, all trajectories other than lifelong learner have been grouped.

From this table it can be calculated that the odds of participation if one's parent also participated in adult education and training are (77:13)/(45:20) or 2.63. At this level of analysis, reproduction of patterns of participation within families is stronger, but it should still be noted that due to the increase in transitional, front-loaded participation, the majority of children of non-participants are participants. When the same analysis is applied to lifelong learning, supposedly the target of much post-war government policy, the lack of overall progress is more apparent (Table 5.4). The odds of being classed as a lifelong learner if one's parents were, as well, is (24:27)/(28:76) or 2.41. A clear majority of people are not lifelong learners, even more so if their parents are not lifelong learners.

Those who become lifelong learners without a parent of similar trajectory are generally younger than the others in the table (so the differences cannot be explained by right-censoring, or incompleteness, of the life histories), with no children of their own, and living in the coalfields north of Cardiff. They are mostly males, from atheist and non-conformist religious backgrounds. All took some qualifications at age 16, and most gained the equivalent of five or more GCSEs at grade C and above. Those with lifelong learner parents who have not become so themselves are somewhat older, often with several

Table 5.4: Lifelong learning of parents and children

Parent\child	Lifelong learner	Not lifelong learner
Lifelong learner	24	27
Not lifelong learner	28	76

children, with the first child coming when the mother was aged 18 or less, and living in the former steel region of Neath-Port Talbot. They are more commonly female, and from Anglican families. None has five or more GCSEs at C and above. Thus, as well as being trajectory determinants for individuals (see Chapter Four), age, gender, area of residence, initial education, and having children are all also correlates of those who are 'mobile' in terms of trajectories within families. An accumulation theorist might claim that the latter differences between the upwardly and downwardly mobile groups are due to their differing qualifications from initial education, but it has already been shown that the qualifications themselves are predictable from the other background characteristics (Gorard, 1997c). That is, the qualifications and early adult participation are acting simply as proxies for events and processes in even earlier life.

A difficulty that emerges in attempting to explain the patterns shown above, by analysing the narratives from the prolonged interviews, is that there are very few references to older family members in the context of later formal learning (although partners, friends and children are frequently referred to as both barriers and stimuli for later participation). This is likely to be a natural phenomenon in that respondents referred to their parents when discussing the transition from initial schooling, while they more often referred to their dependants when discussing decisions about participation in later life. For this reason, the majority of the discussion that follows relates to only one component of lifelong learning, soon after initial education. In most of the interviews, when the respondents talked about their parents and children, they were talking about another participant in the study. In these examples, the study has therefore collected two perspectives on four generations in each family, and these families are used to introduce the themes presented here. One of the early conclusions that can be drawn from these accounts is the confirmation that although respondents may be occasionally inaccurate about themselves, they are generally even less accurate in their accounts of each other.

The interviews show how significant parents can be in setting an individual on course for a life of learning or its avoidance. Parents in the 1940s and 1950s are often reported to have been concerned more with the outward appearance of school, to want their children to be as neat and tidy as possible, and to try and avoid 'the Board Man' coming to see them. Schooling itself and learning were not seen as important, and one reason may have been the ease with which jobs were available locally.

Parents sometimes also reinforced the effect of other social determinants, such as gender. One woman had missed a lot of school through illness:

> "It was really because you didn't grasp it like the others grasped it and I think I tend to do a lot of work backwards anyway so I see then backwards and I think 'I can't do this'. I don't know it and I get fed up of people telling me how bright my brother was and I couldn't do nothing. So, I thought why bother?"

Interviewer: "What about your mum and dad, what did they think about your education, did they push you?"

"No. My mother's one of these old-fashioned types that a boy has got to do it but a girl is not important."

Even today, economic imperatives, such as the need to earn money, may lie behind the stories of parents unwilling to see the value of further education. One man is the son of another respondent in the study. Neither have any qualifications from school, nor any later education. Both later learnt a craft or 'trade', and both ended up in jobs not primarily involving that trade.

Interviewer: "Did you enjoy it? [that is, school]"

"Well ... not really. I don't think any kid enjoys school really.... I didn't want to try the exams or anything. I just wanted to get out of school really."

Interviewer: "What was your parents' reaction? [to wanting to leave]"

"I told my father I could stay on and play rugby for another year, and he said 'no'."

It is noteworthy that this man, like many others but unlike their own parents, now wants his children to gain some qualifications and perhaps stay on in education a little longer, even though he knows little about the opportunities available. This is apparently because the easy-to-get jobs have disappeared in the region – a very common theme.

Reproduction

There is clearly a gendered pattern in family attitudes to lifelong learning. 'Reproduction' here is used to refer to the influences producing identical learning trajectories for both parent and child in the same family. Such reproduction is nearly always gendered. In one family, the 62-year-old father had a succession of varied jobs after leaving the Parachute Regiment, including several such as draughtsman for which he had no qualifications, before returning to higher education much later. He says of his transition to the workforce at age 15:

"The headmaster told us on our last day there that if we could add up our wages, check our wages, he thought our education had been sufficient in so many words.... Well at that time in that area there was loads of work around.... I didn't see anything except working in one of the local factories or on the buildings like my father."

His wife had stayed on in full-time education much longer, eventually leaving to become a housewife and mother. Perhaps partly due to her influence, and what are described as her 'thwarted' ambitions, he later took a degree intending to be a science teacher. His sons now have low-skill manual jobs and no qualifications, while his daughter has taken an Open University degree during her pregnancy. In the previous generation, the father's father had left school to get a job, while his mother had tried to continue her education with a place at a 'posh' school. So for three generations of this family, the women have a more extended education than the men, but in the first two generations, so far, the men have had greater opportunity for work-related training.

A similar picture emerges from the family of a 53-year-old woman. Her mother and father had no qualifications, her mother never had a job, while her father was a fitter. She has had many low wage jobs with no training, although she had gained A levels before leaving full-time education. In her own account she and her husband were not very supportive of their daughter. She would have liked her daughter to continue in education, but:

"My husband says 'well if they don't want to learn just leave them alone. They'll learn the long way'."

The daughter, who is still only 17, has dropped out of her A level and says of her parents:

"Well, once I had a job they were all right."

A 21-year-old man acknowledges the influence his parents, among others, have had on his educational choices, and explains how he ended up in the same career as his father. On taking A levels:

"Yeah, that's the natural progression – I didn't really want to go into employment at that age.... That's always been instilled into me to get an education first ... by my parents ... very few of my friends went into employment at that age."

As a result he started a teaching degree:

"Well, my mother was a teacher, that was a big factor like, but saying that I've always.... My mother used to come home and tell me stories about the satisfaction when a pupil got something right ... and I was listening one night and thought it sounds a worthwhile job."

But he dropped out of that to become a policeman like his father:

"I think I've been a little naive. I've never really thought and planned. Like my choices, I've never really ventured outside my parents.... My father used to talk to me about his job and that seemed fun as well."

Another man of similar age was asked what options he would have had if he had left school at 16.

> "Leave school? Get beaten up by my dad for starters.... No, I wasn't brought up to know about any other options. I just expected to do A levels...."

Explaining why he has chosen medicine as a career:

> "It's just that I've lived with this all my life. My dad's a doctor and I've been to his surgery.... I just always enjoyed seeing what my dad did and the work he was doing."

'Reproduction' also takes the form of non-participation in education. A 44-year-old woman had left school as soon as possible in order to leave home:

> "There were 13 of us and we all left home at 16. Our dad was ... we never got on with our father."

Her daughter also left education at 16. Both mother and daughter now work in the same factory. Her son is currently unemployed, and although he originally moved to FE college, he dropped out to work as an untrained mechanic.

> "My old man's a bus driver and I've always been involved with cars and buses and stuff like that."

A 47-year-old man, whose father was also an early school-leaver and a coalminer, had left school at 15 because:

> "It's just the normal thing I think around here unless I went to a grammar school or whatever."

In some cases, both generations of the family are illiterate. In one example, both son and father attended the same literacy class, to no apparent effect. Not only are many jobs not open to this pair, all other learning opportunities they have sought have rejected them. The son in particular is ambitious to be a care assistant.

Three overall patterns of parental reproduction of trajectories have emerged from the interviews. First, there are the parents who would not countenance an education of the sort they never had, whatever the intervening societal changes. For example, a man of 56 recalls how his father made all the major decisions about transition from school at 15:

> "School trips, I could never go on.... He organised the job for me and took me out of school before I could try ... I wanted to stay in school ...

to try my O levels ... but you couldn't get an apprenticeship over 17 so ... he said I've got a job for you in W.H. Watts.... I was there about three months and I went home one day and he said I've got you a job at Ivan Waters ... it'll save you the bus-fare from Bridgend. He wants you to start next Monday."

Second, there are the parents who cannot imagine an education other than the one they had. A woman of 30 recalls how her parents had met at university and the influence that had on her choices:

"I think they thought it would be a better school ... it was a religious school as well, a convent school. My mother went to a convent school herself and she felt quite strongly that she wanted us to have the same experience.... I think they really expected us to go to university. They expected it and we were really forced into it, and it was always held out as a really enticing prospect. You know, if you do well you will be able to go to university and going to university is great."

Third, there are families where everything can be provided for a formal education that the parents never had but now want for their offspring, except the necessary finance. The ensuing reproduction is clearly unintentional. A woman of 40 followed the route of informal learning, when the economic situation meant that her early educational promise was not fulfilled:

"My family, especially my grandfather, very big ... no he was more than a socialist, he was actually a communist. He was an activist for the Communist Party in the Rhondda. He did quite a lot for education in the, you know ... very, very staunch union.... I spent most of my very young years with my grandfather. I mean I could read when I was three.... Yeah my mother had to stop buying the News of the World because I could read it.... I was not allowed to read comics. If I wanted to read it had to be a book.... If I'd worked harder I think that I could have got ... you know I've got four O levels, I could have got a lot more but it was just at the time really, uh, all living at home with mum. Mum was a single parent. She was widowed at 27.... My dad died when I was eight, and there's my sister and brother ... quite a difficult time then."

Near reproduction

The last example shows that the difference between repeating the formal educational route of a parent, or finding a new one is often very slight. 'Near reproduction' is used here to describe the situation where the trajectories of both parent and child in the same family are related without being identical. These examples can help to illustrate the point made by the survey results that families are important as determinants of participation, but that there are many other influences and boundaries affecting an individual's decision.

A 51-year-old woman had wanted to be a nursery nurse, but was frustrated by the economic position of her family. Having attended a secondary modern school and obtained no qualifications, she has been a full-time mother with many and various informal learning activities, such as becoming an organist and running the local mothers' union. Her sister exemplifies the relevance of initial schooling since although a twin she went to the local grammar school, gaining O levels and continuing to train as a pharmacist. However, that difference in participation did not last, as she dropped out of training and joined the police force. The respondent's daughter is now intending to become a nursery nurse one generation later. Her son is considering university, but is not supported by his unqualified father who would rather he got a job. His parents "left it up to me" to go on and take A levels at a local college, and it was "sort of my decision" but:

> "Everyone I knew was going on to do A levels or things like that at Neath Tech. My mother says they never set up anything to pay for me to go to college because they really thought I'd be thick like them. And my sister's going now as well, so they're getting a bit worried about money you know."

A woman of 40 had a very determined father, who ensured that she stayed in school, eventually gaining a higher education qualification. Her father had little formal education, but according to her account she is now trying to repeat her father's role with her son:

> "I personally didn't really want to stay on in school but my father was one of these people who said you must go on and you must stay at education, and he pushed us all three of his children on to further education ... he was a self-made person. He came very much from a working class background but you know by the time he had retired, he was director of his own company. So I suppose he knew the values of education and wanted it for us.... No, no he was not educated.... Somebody came along with an opportunity to go nursery nurse training in Cardiff which I could do at the age of 16. So I decided that was it. I was gonna do that.... He wouldn't let me go, he wouldn't let me go...."

However, her son of 17 claims that he has always planned to go on to higher education, and is thinking of training as a teacher, but that his mother does not seem to take any particular interest in his work and does not mind what he studies:

> "When I get my reports they sit me down and talk to me but that's about it."

Another male respondent said:

> "I basically wanted to leave school and start earning money."

He moved to an apprenticeship with Port Talbot Steelworks, which he heard of as his father works there. Although both parents left school at 16 as well, his mother later took an A level and his father returned to take a degree. Although the respondent took no qualifications at school, he later took OND and HNC at work, thus becoming a 'delayed learner' like both of his parents.

As with gendered reproduction, there are several stories of parental pressure *not* to continue with any education, thus conforming to the existing family pattern. For older respondents, their fears of extended education surfaced as early as the age of 11. Another interesting thing to note is that many older respondents talk of getting a job because they were plentiful but the family was poor, while they encourage their own children to study since jobs are now harder to come by, but presumably the family can countenance supporting an extended initial education. Again we meet the theme that learning is an alternative to work, rather than a preparation for or accompaniment to it. For example a man of 57 says of his parents:

> "Thinking back it did do a lot of damage really education-wise like you know and when it came to my 11 plus.... I was in a very poor family. My mother and father was afraid in their hearts that I would pass for County School because it meant then that they would have to get me a uniform where I could go with the holes in the back of my trousers to an ordinary school.... But then you had to have books and your satchels and you know so they kept me back from my 11 plus.... I didn't go to school that day.... As soon as I was old enough to work they wanted me to work...."

And of his son:

> "Like at the moment now I wouldn't say we were, we're just getting by. He's not coming out of school until he's 18 you know. It's as simple as that, because we know how important it is especially today."

A woman of 44 tells of a similar reaction to the 11 plus, and to sixth form entry.

> "My father was a miner, and I think my parents, if anything, were a little bit intimidated by it like when I passed my 11 plus. Plus all the other kids had new bikes, my mother said 'Oh my God, how can we afford the uniform?'... My mother's, my parents' reaction again was 'How can we afford to keep you at school with four brothers?'"

Other families were almost the opposite in their reactions, perhaps because some could afford to be. However, the story of one 53-year-old woman illustrates the determination of some mining families to learn whatever the obstacles, in a way that is reminiscent of stories from the archive material in this study dating from the first part of the century (see Chapter Four and Burge et al, 1999).

> "My parents were all for education ... at that time but also unless you had money you couldn't go on in schools.... So he actually went down the mines at 14. But what he did he went to evening classes and he walked five miles over a mountain every week to a Technical College in the next valley, no lights in the road, all through the winter and everything and got his ... whatever qualifications he needed to do mining and engineering and he got his degree at 30.... It's something similar to the likes of the Open University today."

> "He always used to say 'I wish I'd had your opportunity'.... They didn't force me. They didn't have to because I wanted to do it."

> "I do feel that my education as far as fulfilling myself has been a bit of a waste. I feel I would have liked to have done more with it, but at the time it wasn't possible because you didn't have childcare.... It's a full-time job and my husband was not keen."

A man of 39 whose father and grandfather were steelworkers and mother and grandmother were housewives, was pressurised to stay in further education:

> "I think to get out of the rut really. To get out of the situation of being a steelworker, because even though there's a certain amount of pride attached to being a steelworker if you like ... there's the thought that there's something better."

Although he defied his parents and left school at 16 to join the steelworks and earn money, he returned to education later and is now a teacher.

One young respondent left school at the earliest possible opportunity, just like his parents, and neither he nor his mother have participated in any formal learning episodes since then. However, the son has picked up interests in gardening from his grandfather and in engineering and automobile mechanics from his father, and learnt his 'trade' of carpet-fitting from his father's best friend. Significantly, although labelled a non-participant in education and training, this man has learnt skills in all three areas that are used by his friends and family, emphasising again the importance of recognising informal learning (this issue is discussed in Chapter Seven).

Non-reproduction

'Non-reproduction' is used here to refer to families in which the parent and child have markedly different patterns of participation. They illustrate two key points. First, and perhaps most obviously, there are some exceptions to the patterns described already. Second, even where children follow different paths from their parents, this is frequently described as being heavily influenced by the parent anyway. Most families with markedly different trajectories within two generations are 'upwardly mobile' (that is, towards greater lifelong participation, but mainly from non-participation to transitional). For example, a 65-year-old woman left school at 15, but remained under the influence of what she described as a typical strong Welsh mother, and a literate coalmining father with no formal education. She was still seeking the approval of her mother in order to participate in further education when her own daughter was 15. She worked to bring up her family, and returned to take her O levels only when she was aged 40, since her mother did not approve of childcare. She:

> "Would have liked to join the navy at 18.... Oh no way, my parents wouldn't let me go."

So she worked for the Coal Board, where male employees were given free coal for their families, but women were not. This was one of the incidents that she believes made her and her daughter a 'feminist'. Her daughter is now a professor of astro-physics.

Of course, families are occasionally 'downwardly mobile' in terms of their training trajectories. One 35-year-old man bemoaned the fact that he did not do what his father and grandfather had done.

> "Well his father was a stonemason [as well]. My father started his business when he came out of the war, with his father.... He did a lot of building around Bridgend ... for 30 odd years I suppose ... [If I had stayed on] I probably wouldn't have been a refuse sorter now. I'd probably be a stonemason now ... I know so. I dropped a gooly I did but there we are."

There are two very common stories that involve greater participation for the younger generation. In the first, simple form the parent wants the child to do more or better than they did, perhaps to avoid the conditions of work that they had to endure – and in the examples below these aspirations are largely fulfilled.

> "My mother and father would have been devastated if I hadn't passed, totally devastated. My father was a collier but the attitude in our house was if you don't learn you won't get on, and you'll go down the colliery."
> [woman, 54]

A 50-year-old man whose parents had left school by 14, had become a teacher:

> "I think they most probably saw it as a way to help us get a job most probably and have a better standard of life than they did."

> "I think my mother would have done far better if she had been allowed to stay in school. She was the eldest of 10 children and obviously she had to either look after the children or go away and make money to send back to her mother.... My father was quite widely read, and would have done quite well if they had been allowed to go on...."

The second, and more complex, form of the story is where the respondent describes a change of attitude over one generation. Several families had similar stories, where the respondent had left school and never trained at a time when local jobs were apparently plentiful, and were encouraged to work by their parents for short-term economic reasons. The respondents are now encouraging their children to stay in education or training, because jobs are scarcer and times are apparently easier. A 42-year-old man left school at 14, to work with his father, and now pays for his children to have extra private tuition for their examinations so that they "don't have to sweep the streets".

> "The teacher went on to my father about me taking the 11 plus and he said well if he doesn't want to do it ... I didn't do it."

> "Well I got a job as a mechanic with the same company that my father worked for so ... but I don't think that's the case today.... I think things have changed a lot since then. You need qualifications when you go for a job. You know, I've got a totally different attitude now to what I had then because my kids are coming up. Well my daughter has just tried her GCSEs."

A woman in a similar situation explained:

> "What you have to bear in mind, when I came out of school the jobs were plentiful. So, it wasn't a big deal if you didn't have great qualifications because you could get a job easy enough anyway."

Initial schooling as a determinant

The adult trajectories for each individual start at the UK compulsory school leaving age (15 before 1972, and 16 thereafter). As we have seen, this is a critical moment, as the course of each person's future career may be determined at that point (Scottish Office, 1991). Compulsory schooling ends and people have a choice (albeit within quite closely defined parameters) of staying on at school, moving to some other form of education or training, getting a job, or unemployment (Dolton et al, 1994; Employment Department Group, 1994). The system is to a large extent selective in nature if not intent, and it is generally those who have done well at school who will continue in full-time education (Smithers and Robinson, 1991; Istance and Rees, 1994). There are generally few second chances despite policy changes to improve people's chances at age 16 (Roberts and Parsell, 1990).

People's early experience of education can affect their attitude lifelong (Taylor and Spencer, 1994), and the memory of compulsory education can produce later passivity when faced with vocational education and training (Hand et al, 1994). Experience of initial school is therefore an important marker for further study. A sense of failure at school has been found to reduce the chance of further education (Gambetta, 1987), and in some cases gaining qualifications is an essential precursor to continuation. The probability of experiencing most kinds of training rises with school attainment (Tan and Peterson, 1992).

However, the clearest simple indicator of success at school is family background, and a disadvantaged social-class background not only reduces the chance of further education, it also interacts with failure at school, such that those from poorer families may be less likely to compete for educational resources throughout their lives, if they face a problem. Some writers have suggested there may therefore be a cycle of disadvantage for an underclass excluded from formal settings as a result of their inadequate schooling, resulting from their background (Bynner and Parsons, 1997). A study of the first cohort to stay in initial schooling until age 16 found that 50% had later problems with arithmetic, while 20% had problems with reading. It also suggests that few had taken any steps, even by the age of 37, to overcome these problems, and that the penalties for illiteracy were getting worse.

Experience of initial schooling may therefore be crucial in shaping long-term orientations towards learning; and in providing the qualifications necessary to access many forms of further and higher education, as well as continuing education and training later in life. There are important 'age effects' here, however, relating especially to the reorganisation of secondary schooling in the maintained sector.

For the older cohorts, the 11 plus was a clear watershed, as we have seen even, perhaps especially, when they did not sit the examination. Even in the later comprehensive system, many stories described life chances that were apparently impossible once initial schooling ended. Such accounts illustrate only one of the many relationships between family, school, work and later learning. In several cases, where initial schooling was ended solely for economic and family reasons, the frustration became a platform for the motivation to return to study as an adult. It is also the case that failure at school can act as a similar stimulus for further study (Gorard, 1997c).

The type of school attended (or not attended), the initial trajectory towards taking qualifications or getting out and getting a job, and in many cases particularly good or bad experiences of school, are also associated with later attitudes to learning. Although her parents had no higher qualifications themselves, a female teacher reported:

> "Well the thing is when I took this scholarship ... my parents were very, very supportive. Yes, they thought it was wonderful."

Even in a comprehensive system of schooling, one's life chances of participation can be effectively determined by the end of initial schooling. For example:

> "Well I didn't take no exams at all because I wasn't very good in school.... When I left school then, I did, the job I wanted was to be a care assistant. But I didn't, 'cause I didn't get the papers ... because you had to have the papers and 'cause I, as my mam said, I was backward in my reading and writing."

This gentleman in his thirties, living with his mother who helped him during the interview, could only find temporary work as a night security guard for £1.50 per hour (this was before minimum wage legislation). He was saving up to take a course in adult care, which he would probably never do since he was unable to read. He spent every holiday voluntarily caring for the residential disabled, or taking them on holiday. He fed them, dressed them and took them to the lavatory, but he could not get the job he wanted since he had no qualifications and little chance of getting them.

Schools in our sites, such as Sandfields in Port Talbot, which had been providing a mostly vocational education for difficult-to-motivate children is now bound by the National Curriculum. According to a careers adviser:

> "It is now completely academically orientated ... a totally inappropriate form of education. The relevance of education as it is provided to most of these kids ... is deeply questionable.... It is very difficult to motivate pupils [with academic routes] and this is compounded by parental influence.... They don't see education as leading anywhere."

However, a local employer reported trying to encourage the same school to arrange visits to look at their engineering plant, but with no success. Many pupils take the almost ignored Certificate of Education (CoE) examinations, at a time when local employers still do not recognise that even a GCSE grade G is an achievement. In his opinion, this is not a new phenomenon, which used to be explicable by the full employment linked to 'Treasure Island' (as the steel plant was popularly known) in Port Talbot. Qualifications were once seen as being of no value since it was so easy to walk into a fairly decent job, which did not require high levels of certificated skills or even high levels of literacy or numeracy. It is interesting that a new generation may also see qualifications as irrelevant to them but now because there are no longer many jobs locally. In their terms, a job is better than a qualification, and a piece of paper cannot create a job for you. Perhaps neither explanation is correct. Many residents simply do not value what school provides, and perhaps the experience of school colours their attitude to later participation in learning.

The Head of a comprehensive school in Blaenau Gwent explains further:

> "It's a bleak prospect for youngsters you see. They're faced with the dole. We've got families I suppose in Ebbw Vale where no adult in the household has ever worked. You know that's no sort of a model for a youngster is it? To think – 'Oh well, I can manage on whatever I get'….
> It is a working-class area but it is becoming an area without work."

One view is that this 'what is the point' attitude is prevailing over a traditional respect for education in Wales or at least a view of education as a means to occupational mobility. A community educator believes that learning used to be seen as a liberating force (albeit in a vocational context):

> "A way to avoid going down the pit or ending up behind the counter at the Co-op and parents would push their children to do well at school so they would at least have choices in what they worked at. Now, that philosophy has gone. The philosophy of education being a liberator seems to have gone."

Again, we meet the theme of moving away from a true learning society in some respects. The same educator speculates that the lack of physical horizons in the valleys affect people's mental horizons, with people seeing no further than their own valleys. A careers adviser from Tredegar believes that there has actually been a drift of people into the area because they know there are no jobs and it is therefore easier to claim the Jobseeker's Allowance, saying "it's a thing I've never seen before". They tend to 'drift up' from Newport and Cardiff (where there is much higher employment) having no real interest in getting a job or going on a training scheme.

The Head of a comprehensive school in one of the research sites had lived in the same area all of his life. His reminiscences provide another example of the view that recent increases in transitional participation and the consequent rise in qualification rates are more a consequence of the lack of suitable jobs than a desire by individuals to invest in their 'human capital':

> "I came from the Garw valley, a mining area. My father was a miner. Hard work. I and my friends and peers were encouraged to go elsewhere. 'If you don't bloody work, you will end up down the mine.' The kids at Ynysawdre School saw education as a route out of the harsh physical environment…. Now there is a southern drift in the valleys of an aspirant working class, and fewer job opportunities locally. The four mines operating in Garw have now closed. The hopes and expectations of young people have changed. Now there is a kind of 'nihilism'."

Learner identities

Normative analyses of groups tend to suggest clear and fairly rigid patterns for the determinants of post-compulsory training, perhaps because prior choices may constrain future ones (Dale and Davies, 1994). The irony is that the existence of choice for the individual can lead them to conservatism (Schratz, 1996). Even under pressure, many people retain their conservatism, so that most unemployed people look for jobs in the same occupation as their previous one, despite the fact that it has led to unemployment (Mid Glamorgan TEC, 1996). Similarly, most people look for work in the same area as the one they live in, which may also be the only one in which they have been unemployed. Individual analyses, on the other hand, allow us to consider the role of key personal events in shaping the future for each individual (Bowman et al, 2000). Studies suggest that where people 'break the mould' it may be the result of a crisis such as redundancy, illness, divorce, or a death (Taylor and Spencer, 1994). However it is also possible that an interest in learning may be apparent early in an individual's biography, but having not been satisfied initially, perhaps due to marriage or migration, is only later converted to concrete interest (as seen in some of the previous examples).

Personal motivation is an important consideration, which may itself have social determinants, influencing awareness of the 'appropriate' opportunities (Sargant, 1996). A disposition to learn (or not) may therefore be the most relevant determinant, and yet the most underestimated by survey methodology (Harrison, 1993). Since post-16 learners are overwhelmingly voluntary (Edwards et al, 1993), there are in most cases at least two possibilities facing them: to participate or not. Unfortunately, many people may feel that once school is over, education is over and that 'real life' is something else (Lowe, 1970; Squires, 1993). And while the decision to participate must be reinforced by action, a decision not to participate need not be.

When considering individuals' own accounts of their experiences of education and training after school, it is their very diversity that is initially most striking. Respondents tend to emphasise the distinctiveness of their learning histories, the particular family circumstances or labour market shifts to which they had to react and so on. Consequently, there are seldom simple patterns in these individual accounts, even among those who follow the same 'trajectory'.

This complexity is at least consistent with the theoretical framework that was sketched in Chapter Two, where the choices made by individuals concerning their participation in learning is a key element. Equally, however, for the respondents themselves, any choices that were made are perceived to have been heavily constrained by external circumstances. Perhaps most obviously, many older women describe the ways in which the learning opportunities available to them were limited by local employment, social expectations as to what was appropriate or by a 'forced altruism' with respect to family commitments. Even some of the younger women respondents provide similar accounts, confirming the points made earlier about the very partial nature of changes in women's 'trajectories' over time.

Moreover, for a number of those – women and men – who had participated actively in post-school learning (albeit mainly in the form of conventional further and higher education), this is seen as a product of what was normatively prescribed within the family or, less frequently, the wider community, rather than their own active choice. Certainly, it is clear that, to make sense of individuals' learning histories, it is necessary to understand the ways in which learning opportunities were understood when decisions over participation were being made. There is strong evidence that these 'social constructions' of opportunities, in turn, are shaped by a range of contextual influences.

One of the clearest examples of the latter relates to the impacts of the experience of compulsory schooling. 'Success' or 'failure' at school lays the foundation for what appears to be an enduring 'learner identity'. It is striking, for example, how numerous respondents who had experienced the 11 plus examination testified to its major and often long-term effects.

For respondents too young to have gone through the tripartite system, although 'success' and 'failure' are less starkly defined, it remains the case that they identify positive experiences of schooling as crucial determinants of enduring attitudes towards subsequent learning. For many individuals, then, the significance attached to 'doing well' at school within families and even the wider community has long-term consequences. In particular, while 'passing' the 11 plus is certainly not a sufficient condition for becoming a 'lifelong learner', a number of respondents do attribute their post-school education and training to the influences of their adolescent experiences of the traditional grammar school, especially in the wider context of the South Wales coalfield, where the conventional non-conformist emphasis on the intrinsic value of education continued to be influential.

In contrast, those who 'failed' at school often come to see post-school learning of all kinds as irrelevant to their needs and capacities. Indeed, they frequently refer to adult education and training as 'school', suggesting the enduring influence of their earlier experiences of learning. Hence, not only is participation in further, higher and continuing education not perceived to be a realistic possibility, but also work-based learning is viewed as unnecessary. There is thus a marked tendency to devalue formal training and to attribute effective performance in a job to 'common-sense' and experience (see Chapter Seven). While this is certainly not confined to those whose school careers were less 'successful' in conventional terms, it is a view almost universally held among this group of respondents. For example, one of our respondents had left school at 14 and gone straight into a successful career in British Steel Tinplate, despite having no formal qualifications or even training.

"You learn as you get along.... You got to train yourself and you use your hands and ears. No one came along and said 'You mustn't do this' or 'you mustn't do that'.... I mean commonsense will tell you not to do certain things.... I can pick up most things purely by watching someone else doing it...."

In reality, of course, it is difficult to interpret the implications of these findings. Reluctance to acknowledge a significant role for formal training may not impair an individual's ability to do a job, especially where the requirements are minimal. Conversely, there is considerable evidence from the semi-structured interviews that many people are able to acquire substantial knowledge and skills – both inside and outside of employment – without formal training.

"I haven't got a GCE or a BSc or whatever they're called these days ... but as I say you don't have to be academic to be able to do things.... It's the same with the French polishing, you see. I used to do it as a favour. I got a book from the library. I had a blind chappie who was a pianist, like, and he used to tune pianos and doing them up. He asked me if I knew anything about polishing and I said 'not the foggiest'. So I went to the library, got a book on it. We got the French polish and promptly went into business. It was just a sideline when I was working for the printers."

As we have seen, experience of family and early school life along with age, place and gender appear to create a relatively stable attitude to further learning opportunities – a learner identity. This can then act as a filter to decide what is 'appropriate' by each individual. If true this could help explain both the patterns of family reproduction over a period of marked change in opportunities, and the relative lack of progress towards a learning society in the UK (and our model of learner identities has already been used to explain equivalent situations in other studies, see Ball et al, 2000). It means that wider participation is unlikely to be achieved simply by considering the role of structural barriers to participation (see Chapter Six).

Conclusion

The determinants of participation in the present study are calculated rather differently in our study than is usual in the wider literature. Instead of selecting explanatory variables simply in terms of the amount of variance in participation that they can explain (the stepwise method), the independent variables are added to the model in the life order of the respondent. On this analysis, the accumulation of prior learning hypothesis appears much weaker, and the role of parental background appears much stronger. Thus, the reason why early learners are more often lifelong learners could be the same as the reason for their early participation, and based on family background, gender, and regional conditions. This would be as convincing an explanation as the accumulation model. This may explain, in part, why the results of our analysis are different from comparable studies using only 'snapshot' techniques. For example, while initial educational success may be a good indicator of later participation according to some accounts (Tuckett, 1997), the success itself can be at least partly predicted by social and family background in the model proposed here.

There is considerable reproduction of learning trajectories within families when calculated as odds ratios. This reproduction is of a specific nature: strongest among lifelong learners and non-participants, and weakest among delayed and transitional learners. The fluidity of trajectories is much greater in the latter families, and is the main area of change over time. In very simple terms, traditional sociology of education analyses of compulsory education have emphasised the role of the family in determining an individual's route, while analyses of post-compulsory participation have emphasised barriers, opportunities, and above all the accumulation of prior learning experiences and qualifications. Clearly, the role of family background decreases with age, but there is sufficient evidence here to suggest that families continue to play a key role in the transition from initial to post-compulsory education training, and beyond. It may be hypothesised that families, as well as educational experiences, are important influences in the creation of relatively stable learner identities.

These results also have important implications for policy development. Hence, non-participation is largely a product of the fact that individuals do not see education and training as appropriate for them and these views, in turn, are structured by factors that occur relatively early in life. This suggests that policies that simply make it easier for people to participate in the kinds of education and training that are already available (for example, removing 'barriers' to participation, such as costs, time and lack of childcare) will have only limited impacts.

SIX

Lifelong learning trajectories and the two dimensions of change over time

There is another, perhaps more precise, way of examining the four main lifelong learning trajectories discussed in Chapters Four and Five. They can be broken down into two components. The first refers to participation in education and training immediately after passing the compulsory school-leaving age. The second comprises those forms of participation that occur later in individuals' lives as adults (Gorard et al, 1998c).

In terms of our learning trajectories, therefore, a non-participant clearly registers neither component; a transitional learner only the first; a delayed learner only the second; while a lifelong learner has both.

In initial support for this model, it is striking that the number of episodes of participation in adult learning, the number of years spent in education and training, and the percentage of each respondent's life spent in education and training for the lifelong learners is almost the exact sum of those for the delayed and transitional learners (Table 6.1). It is as though a lifelong learner is a combination of a transitional and a delayed learner.

By dividing the respondents into two equal-sized age cohorts, it is also possible to gain some indications of changes over time in the social determinants of these two components of participation, as the two cohorts reflect patterns of participation at different historical periods (see Gorard et al, 1999a). Table 6.2 shows that the major change in terms of patterns of participation over time has been a large increase in transitional participation (immediately after passing the official school-leaving age). There has not been an equivalent change in later-life participation (participation after a break from education until individuals are at least 21 years of age). In fact, the actual frequency of later learning has fallen slightly over time. This latter pattern is not due simply to the fact that the younger cohorts have had less time to participate in education and training and thus to develop 'fully adult'

Table 6.1: Lifelong learning by trajectory (first dimension)

Score\trajectory	Delayed	Transitional	Lifelong
Number of episodes of education and training	1.9	0.9	3.2
Years in education and training	1.9	2.1	4.7
% of life spent in education and training	7.0	13.9	21.5

Table 6.2: Changes in the frequency of participation over time (second dimension) (%)

Age	Transitional	Later-life
21-45	67	45
46-65	46	47

trajectories. This can be seen from the fact that the average age at which all episodes of later-life participation occur falls within the age range of the younger cohort.

The analysis presented in this chapter is based on these two distinct 'dimensions' of change over time. It considers variation over the life of each individual, and variation between age cohorts over historical time. Looking at the data in this way transforms the kind of conclusions drawn, when judged in comparison to more traditional commentaries when these two sources of variation are conflated.

Predictive power

The data in Table 6.3 encapsulate the two time-based analyses attempted in this study. The percentages are the proportion of cases correctly allocated to each trajectory component (transitional and later-life participation), using as independent or predictor variables only individuals' background characteristics from each stage of life (at birth, by school-leaving age, and so on). The figures in brackets show how improved this prediction is compared to a model based on a 'best guess' for that stage of life.

It is possible to see how an individual's learning trajectory is shaped over their lifetime, and also to see how the determinants of these trajectories have changed over the 50 years examined in our study. The majority of the variance

Table 6.3: Accuracy of predictions of trajectory components for each stage of life (%) (and 'best guess')

All cases	Birth	Childhood	School leaving age	Adult	Present
Transitional	68 (0.25)	70 (0.32)	72 (0.36)	*76 (0.41)*	*78 (0.50)*
Later-life	62 (0.20)	65 (0.26)	68 (0.30)	72 (0.39)	*78 (0.52)*
Younger					
Transitional	70 (0.12)	72 (0.15)	79 (0.36)	*80 (0.39)*	*83 (0.48)*
Later-life	62 (0.22)	64 (0.27)	67 (0.31)	71 (0.42)	*78 (0.51)*
Older					
Transitional	68 (0.33)	70 (0.35)	71 (0.37)	*74 (0.43)*	*79 (0.57)*
Later-life	65 (0.23)	69 (0.32)	73 (0.38)	74 (0.43)	*83 (0.62)*

Note: the figures in italics could not be used in a recursive model involving only strictly prior events.

explained in the overall model (all cases) occurs with what is known about an individual at birth. This is not to suggest that their patterns of participation are fixed at birth, but that within the societal constraints and opportunities available at the time, variables like year of birth and gender predict the bulk of the variance that is explicable. As we have seen, the predictive power rises by around six points using data collected during initial schooling, and a further four points by school-leaving age. Only for later-life participation is there a significant increase in predictive power of around nine points using data about occupation and adult family life. Viewed in this way, there is ample evidence for the existence of regular patterns of participation whose determinants are largely grounded in early life.

When the sample is divided into two roughly equal cohorts (540 cases aged 21-45, and 556 aged 46-65), the patterns change in a remarkable way. For later-life participation, all three models have approximately equal power at each stage, and involve most of the same variables. The determinants of later-life participation have not changed all that much over time, which may be why patterns of lifelong learning have not improved as much as might be expected. Generally, however, the model for later-life learning is more powerful when the cases are separated by age.

Transitional participation is much less predictable from birth for the younger group, and the bulk of the explicable variance is determined at school leaving age; whereas for the older group the bulk is explained at birth. Perhaps the major reason for this change lies in the differential participation rates by gender for the two age cohorts. Participation immediately after school is now gender-neutral (in frequency if not type) and so gender is no longer a useful predictor (to be discussed later).

The changing role of determinants

In general, the relevance of age to patterns of participation is uncomplicated. The continuous increase over time in immediate post-school education and training (transitional participation) means that it is much more common for the younger respondents of both age cohorts. In fact, the probability of immediate post-school education and training decreases to 0.96 of its preceding value for every year in the age of the respondent (Table 6.4).

In general, age is much less relevant for predicting patterns of later participation in learning episodes (later-life participation), since these have not changed as much over the 50 years examined in our study; and not at all for the younger cohort. While males are more likely to participate in formal learning at any age, when the sample is analysed as a whole, this overall picture conceals an interesting change over time. Whereas in the older age cohort, gender was only relevant to the decision to participate in transitional episodes, with later-life learning being gender neutral (in quantity if not in type); in the younger cohort transitional participation is now gender balanced, and the difference lies only in later learning. It is almost as if the women who are now staying on in education and training longer and are the basis for the

Table 6.4: Personal characteristics and associated changes in probabilities of participation

Predictors	Transitional: all cases	Later-life: all cases	Transitional: younger	Later-life: younger	Transitional: older	Later-life: older
Age	0.96		0.93		0.96	0.96
Male	2.15	1.69		4.35	3.03	
English spoken		0.36				0.29
Born local		0.56	0.33			0.40
Born local*male				0.37		1.88
Other Religion/ none	0.60	0.56			0.51	0.39
Anglican	0.68	0.77			0.63	0.72

Notes: For clarity in the following tables, real-number variables such as 'Age' have been written in italics. Their coefficients are multipliers. Someone aged 27 is 0.96 times as likely to participate in transitional education and training as someone aged 26, and 0.92 times as likely as someone aged 25. The coefficients of categorical variables such as 'Male' show the change in odds compared to the base category. A man is generally 2.15 times as likely as a woman to have reported an episode of transitional learning.

* shows interaction between two variables.

increase over time in transitional participation, are doing so in replacement for later-life participation. This could be part of the explanation why it has already been observed that the decrease in non-participant trajectories over time has not created a proportionate increase in lifelong learners. 'Peter' has been robbed to pay 'Paul' (Gorard, 2000d).

The same finding also demonstrates that the link between transitional and later-life participation is not causal. Although it is true that those participating later in life have a higher level of general education, it is clearly not true that simply extending initial schooling will necessarily affect later patterns of participation.

The language spoken at home makes no difference to participation patterns for the younger age group, partly because there is so little variation (see Chapter Four). For the older respondents, speaking a language other than English at home is strongly related to later-life participation, and this may be partly due to the link between speaking Welsh and socio-economic advantage in South Wales (see Chapter Four), and partly due to the relationship between participation and geographic mobility. Those born outside South Wales are almost twice as likely to participate in later-life learning, and three times as likely to participate in transitional learning if they are in the younger age group.

The interaction between gender and place of birth is significant for later-life learning only. In the past, locally born males were more likely than females and those born elsewhere to return to at least one episode of learning after full-time initial education. Now, local males are only one third as likely as the other groups to do so. This is a dramatic change over 50 years, showing that for men at least, South Wales may indeed have had more of the characteristics of a learning society in the past than it does now.

The family religion is also not relevant for younger respondents, but for the others the importance of a Chapel/non-conformist upbringing is emphasised. This might be explained in terms of the 'learning identity' associated with non-conformism and the coalfield valleys in which it was prevalent and its link to 'workers' education' (Lewis, 1993).

The characteristics of parents are key determinants of individual learning trajectories (Table 6.5). Sometimes the mother is the better predictor of the child's participation, sometimes the father, but the pattern for both is similar. Respondents are more likely to participate at any age, the older their parents were when *they* left full-time initial education (increasing their odds by about 1.2 for every year a parent stayed in full-time education). Respondents are around twice as likely to participate at any age, if their parents have qualifications; and between one and a half and twice as likely, if their parents have a skilled or professional occupation. In this way, respondents match their parents' learning experiences very closely in relative quantity, if not in type (see Chapter Five).

For the older group, the type of school attended at school-leaving age was a key determinant of participation. Those from Grammar schools, for example, were three times as likely to stay on at school-leaving age or move to a job with training as those in other types of school (Table 6.6).

This Grammar school impact is also clear for both age cohorts in patterns of later-life learning. School type is not important as a determinant of transitional participation for the younger group, partly because they exhibit less variation with the general disappearance of the tripartite system, and partly because of the more recent increases in transitional participation of some sort (including government-sponsored schemes for those not at school and not in work). Regular attendance at school is a good predictor of both

Table 6.5: Family background and associated changes in probabilities of participation

Predictors	Transitional: all cases	Later-life: all cases	Transitional: younger	Later-life: younger	Transitional: older	Later-life: older
Age father left FTE	1.18		1.22			1.27
Age mother left FTE		1.12				
Father qualified	0.49	0.57	0.51		0.46	0.44
Mother qualified					0.33	
Father service class			1.19	1.94		
Father intermediate			1.69	1.93		
Mother service class	1.48	1.75			1.83	1.79
Mother intermediate	1.63	1.64			1.46	2.03

Table 6.6: Initial education and associated changes in probabilities of participation

Predictors	Transi-tional: all cases	Later-life: all cases	Transi-tional: younger	Later-life: younger	Transi-tional: older	Later-life: older
Comprehensive school	0.56	0.76		0.91	0.76	0.53
Grammar school	1.64	2.19		2.77	2.83	1.71
Secondary modern school	0.56	0.59		0.95	0.81	0.41
Attended regularly	1.94	1.58	2.16	1.66	1.76	1.84

periods of participation, and is perhaps also related to the formation of a learner identity (see Chapter Five).

The variables discussed so far have explained over 70% of the variance in adult patterns of participation. All those to come explain only 5% to 10% more, and many of these variables, such as the influence of siblings or the length of residence in the research site, will have been significant throughout the life of each respondent anyway, thus reinforcing the primary relevance of background characteristics. Later-life participation is between a half and a third as common in Bridgend and Blaenau Gwent as in Neath-Port Talbot, and this geographical disparity appears to be increasing since area of residence is more important for the younger cohort (Table 6.7). Transitional participation in the older cohort was more common in Bridgend, however, and less common in the other two sites. It is hypothesised that these differences in the impact of place over time are related to changes in the relative opportunity structures for work, education and training in the three research sites (Chambers et al, 1998).

In summary, when local economic conditions are good, participation in transitional learning episodes appears to decline. When jobs are scarce,

Table 6.7: Regional influences and associated changes in probabilities of participation

Predictors	Transi-tional: all cases	Later-life: all cases	Transi-tional: younger	Later-life: younger	Transi-tional: older	Later-life: older
Bridgend		0.60		0.35	1.67	
Blaenau		0.60		0.40	0.88	
Number of moves		1.09	0.85			1.15
First move local	0.57		0.39	0.46		
Father lives locally		0.54				
Years in South Wales		0.99				
Live with parents		0.33		0.39		

immediate post-school participation increases, since work and formal education are seen as alternatives rather than partners. For later-life participation almost the opposite holds. Later-life participation is higher in times of fuller employment. Moving between areas such as South Wales, the UK and elsewhere increases the likelihood of participation in later-life learning, unless the first move is within South Wales, or if a parent also lives in South Wales. Generally speaking, geographic mobility is associated with greater participation. Once all of the variables concerning adult life are added to the picture it becomes difficult to decide on the direction of their relationships. It is not clear how many of these 'predictors' could also be the outcome of participation. Perhaps the simplest to explain, in terms of strengthening an early identity as a learner or non-learner, are the educational level of the most educated sibling, and having a leisure interest requiring sustained self-study or practice. Both of these characteristics are positively linked with an increased likelihood of formal participation (Table 6.8). Occupational class shows a very strong relationship to all forms of participation, and it must be assumed that the model is non-recursive, allowing occupation to be both a determinant and a potential outcome of learning episodes. The strength of this relationship appears to be growing over time. In general, not having a partner, or having a partner in a professional or skilled occupation, and either few or late-born children increase the likelihood of participation.

Testing the two component model

If there are indeed two relatively distinct sets of determinants of participation in post-compulsory education and training as outlined above, then one would expect the determinants of lifelong learning to be similar in some respects to

Table 6.8: Adult life and associated changes in probabilities of participation

Predictors	Transi-tional: all cases	Later-life: all cases	Transi-tional: younger	Later-life: younger	Transi-tional: older	Later-life: older
Service class	3.94	1.84	6.58	3.44	3.14	2.47
Intermediate class	1.66	1.45	2.01	2.05	1.36	1.38
Leisure interest		2.01	1.75	1.68		2.53
Sibling qualified	0.63	0.53		0.54	0.60	0.52
Single			1.61			
Partner service class					2.00	
Partner intermediate class						1.35
Number of children	0.81				0.82	
Age giving birth	0.98				0.98	

both transitional and delayed learning and dissimilar in most respects to those of non-participation (perhaps the inverse of them). In the same way, one would expect the determinants of transitional and delayed learning each to be similar in some respects to non-participants, but dissimilar to each other. There are many indications above that these descriptions are valid, but a more formal method would be to attempt a binomial classification of each case into one of two possible trajectory types. If it is easier to distinguish the characteristics of a transitional learner from a delayed one, than a transitional from a non-participant, for example, this would provide substantial support for the two component model. The method chosen for this purpose was to enter the potential determinants of educational participation into logistic regression analyses in successive steps (discussed previously). Each step represented a period in the life of the respondents.

Immediate post-compulsory education and training

It is possible to create a logistic regression function that is 100% accurate in discriminating between those who stay on in education or training after school and those who do not, and with a low log-likelihood suggesting an excellent fit between the model and the data. However, it involves a very large number of predictors, which has two practical drawbacks: the number of cases dwindles making the better fit less surprising, while the number of coefficients in the resultant equation is unwieldy. The next model (and that which follows for predicting later-life learning) is therefore a compromise between goodness-of-fit, size of usable sample, correctness of prediction, and parsimony. The model is 80% accurate and an adequate fit with the data given the size and age range of the sample.

In theory, it is possible to calculate the odds of anyone in South Wales continuing after school in education or training from the coefficients for each variable in the model (such as age, gender and so on). For example, a 50-year-old woman born in Neath-Port Talbot, who attended school regularly but left school at 15 without taking any qualifications, has since worked as a domestic cleaner and raised two children, would be estimated to have around 19% chance of education or training in the two years after initial schooling. On the other hand, a 30-year-old man born in Cardiff, who attended school regularly and took seven O levels at age 16, has since worked as a salesman, and has one child, would have around 90% chance of education or training in the two years after initial schooling.

Transitional, not later-life, learning has been the growth area in the last 50 years. For example, whereas a majority of 16-year-olds joined the labour market in 1978, by 1988 fewer than 20% moved directly from school to a job and nearly half stayed in education (Banks et al, 1992). Part of this is due to the appearance of training schemes such as YTS (and its developments), but much more is due to changes in state benefits, and a lack of suitable jobs (in 1973, 60% of males aged 16 or 17 and 55% of females were employed, but by 1985 these figures had dropped to 20% and 25%, respectively). Further (including sixth-form) and higher education are still the main growth areas today, while job-related training is relatively static. Many people stay in education solely because they cannot get a job (Gleeson et al, 1996), and more because their parents, who finance them, want them to.

In broad summary, the present study suggests that those in previous generations who were non-participants, might in a present generation be transitional learners – taking a course soon after initial school but then never returning to formal education or training. One reason why this might be so was given by Hopper and Osborn (1975). They state that formal education is likely to cease after entry to the workforce for nearly everybody, and this is a function of the [then] current system. Those who are least successful in school are least able to continue, or where barriers are removed, are least likely to want to continue. Those who are able to continue are likely to have had all the education that they want or need by the time they join the workforce. This front-loading of provision means that there should be few potential adult students and therefore little provision is made for them, so that there are few adult learners in fact.

This analysis gives a clue to unravelling apparent evidence for the predictions of human capital theory (HCT). HCT predicts that most training for an individual will be early in their work career, since the returns on any 'investment' at a later date are lower (Tan and Peterson, 1992). However, until it is clear that there are opportunities for all to train throughout their lives, this assertion remains untested. The fact that most provision is currently front-loaded and that most participation is currently early in one's career cannot be used to deduce that either is the cause of the other.

To a large extent, the same factors that are generally important in participation, such as age and gender, are still important as social determinants of transitional learning, of moving quickly from initial schooling to formal participation in further education or training. To these are added three measures relating to school-leaving age: whether the individual had regular or prolonged absences from school, whether they sat for any 16+ qualifications, which for most cohorts really means the same as whether they attended a selective school, and finally the number of children they had by the age of 16. The number of children may be a determinant of further participation – it is harder to study and look after a new child – or it may be a related but non-causal link in a typical trajectory of school, family, and part-time work (Greenhalgh and Stewart, 1987).

Later post-compulsory education and training

There are a larger number of determinants of later learning, and although some of the variables are the same as for transitional learning, their relevance is not. For example, those with no qualifications are much more likely to return to study than those with qualifications below the GCSE benchmark. In addition, the majority of the determinants of later learning are unique (for example, the social class of a life partner). In fact, using earlier patterns of participation as a predictor for later learning does not improve the accuracy of the model at all. Therefore, participation per se is not a good predictor of more participation.

The regression model for later-life learning requires more information about each respondent than that already mentioned. Referring back to the example of the 50-year-old woman born in Neath-Port Talbot, who attended school regularly but left school at 15 without taking any qualifications, has since worked as a domestic cleaner and raised two children, then her school attendance and taking of examinations are now insignificant in determining her participation in later education or training. However, the example must be extended to include the type of school she attended (a measure of both age and ability as determined by the 11 plus), her qualifications at 16, whether she reported a hobby requiring study/practice, the social class of her partner and most-qualified sibling, the age at which she had her first child, length of residence in South Wales and where her mother was born. If this woman went to secondary modern school, does yoga and swimming with her friends, has a husband who is an electrician, a brother who is a teacher, and a mother born in Port Talbot, and this woman has lived in Neath-Port Talbot all of her life having her first child at age 23, then she would have around 80% chance of education or training in later life.

If the 30-year-old man born in Cardiff who attended school regularly and took seven O levels at age 16, has since worked as a salesman, and has one child, is also known to have attended a comprehensive school, passing four of the seven O levels, with no reported hobby, a partner who is a housewife, no siblings, a child born when he was 23, a mother born in South Wales, and he has lived in South Wales all of his life, then he would have around a 75% chance of education or training in later life. This is quite a remarkable turnaround, and these examples are not simply made up. They are based on two of the follow-up interviews. The working-class woman who left school early with no qualifications now has a higher probability of participating in later education or training than the intermediate class man who stayed on in education or training after 16.

There are several possible reasons for this. One, of course, is their age, with the older respondent having had more years in which to take part in something, but this ignores both the predictability of trajectories once they are embarked on, and the influence of motivation. The woman has shown herself interested in taking part in therapeutic social activities with friends and enjoyment of these is precisely the kind of experience that could lead an apparently non-participant learner to participate in more formal learning. Another possible distinction is the influence of the teacher brother, who may be both an informal tutor and a role model. The 30-year-old salesman only scores as highly as he does because he has an unwaged partner.

The influence of this unwaged category is interesting given that it is predominantly composed of women (and older men) but its effect is in addition to that caused by gender alone. Comparing the coefficients for unwaged across the two models it can be proposed that women are more likely to participate in transitional education than their gender coefficient suggests, but less likely to take part in later-life learning. However, where unwaged women have a partner, he (since they are in fact all male in our sample) is much more likely to be a learner. This could be partly due to the removal of barriers such as time (CERI, 1975) and childcare that others experience, while both characteristics could also be a symptom of relatively privileged economic position.

Barriers to creating a learning society

So what then are the barriers preventing fuller participation in lifelong learning and, therefore, seen to be hampering the establishment of a learning society? Research has suggested several barriers that potential learners face and to widen, as well as merely increase, the access to post-compulsory education and training, these barriers need to be recognised and faced. To a large extent they are presaged by the determinants of adult learning. Harrison (1993) categorises the barriers neatly into: situational, to do with the lifestyle of the prospective learner; institutional, to do with the structure of opportunities; and dispositional, relating to the learners' own attitudes.

Perhaps the most obvious obstacle that most people face when envisaging episodes of learning is the cost (McGivney, 1993). This cost could be of the direct kind, such as fees, or more commonly indirect, such as the costs of transport, childcare, foregone income, time and even the emotional cost for those with families (Hand et al, 1994). These costs are clearly more restrictive for the poor (NIACE, 1994), and to some extent for women, who are still faced with the greater burden of childcare, for which support is generally poor, and other domestic responsibilities (Park, 1994). There are anomalies in the benefits and grants systems (FEU, 1993) that confuse the financial issue. In addition to the problem of finding fees in one lump sum, several learners are surprised by the level of ancillary expenses such as examination fees and stationery costs.

The welfare system and the availability of cheap loans play a role here (Maguire et al, 1993). Benefit entitlement is incompatible with a grant from the local authority, and even when all of the costs of training are met by the individual, state benefits are often withdrawn. Unemployed people on training courses are therefore penalised by a system that says in relation to going on a training or education course or programme, "one of the conditions ... to be entitled to unemployment benefit is that you must be ... able and willing to take up any job that you are offered immediately. You might not satisfy this rule while you are on a training or education course or programme..." (Employment Service, amended 1991). During our study, 16 hours per week (21 before October 1996) was the maximum that one could study without losing benefit. In 1995, 20,000 people quit their courses because of uneven interpretation of these rules by benefits offices (Keep, 1997).

General knowledge of the incentives available to train is sketchy (Taylor and Spencer, 1994). The much-lauded increase in students continuing to higher education has been accompanied by an increase in the number in debt and the situation is worse for mature students (Gorard and Taylor, 2001). In 1995, of those over 26 in higher education many were over £7,000 in debt already (Garner and Imeson, 1996) and the situation will get worse with the ending of the older student's allowance. In general, adult education is the easiest sector for government/local government in which to economise when faced with financial stress (Kelly, 1992).

The loss of time, particularly for a social life is another cost of learning in some cases, especially in a country with a tradition of the longest average working week in Europe, for males in the manufacturing sector at least (CERI, 1975). For everyone, television has emerged as a powerful educational force, at least potentially, and a stimulant to new interests, but it can also be seen as disruptive. Adult education is now suffering not so much from lack of leisure time, but from the multiplicity of opportunities available for that time. Taking a course often involves an adjustment in lifestyle that may be possible for an individual, but is more of a problem for those with dependants or in long-term relationships. Relationships can be strained, particularly for women taking courses to progress beyond the educational level of a male partner – the 'Educating Rita' syndrome. Women who are more likely to be employed part-time, may be less aware of opportunities stemming from the workplace, and have more domestic and childcare responsibilities, and generally poorer transport facilities, and, therefore, face many threats to participation. The most vulnerable women from the most disadvantaged backgrounds face the most barriers (Burstall, 1996).

The institutional barriers to training often come from the procedures of the providing organisations, in terms of advertisement, entry procedures, the timing and scale of provision, and a general lack of flexibility (Bowl, 2001). Colleges of further education, for example, still sometimes assume a 17-year-old norm that is fast changing, and they need to adapt to flexible opportunities for learning. Similarly, higher education institutions have been accused of being unresponsive to the needs of non-traditional students. Older people differ from young people in many ways, but adapting to having them in a class could benefit the youngsters, since the adults can have a wealth of relevant experience. People want to fit learning around other tasks of equal importance in their lives, since they cannot always get time off (Park, 1994). They have interrupted patterns of participation and diverse progression routes (Istance and Rees, 1995). Non-completion of courses is now so high that it must be partly seen as an indictment of the quality of provision at all levels, schools, further and higher education, and training.

Drop-out is commonly caused by people discovering that they are on the wrong course, with nearly half of students in one survey feeling they had made a mistake (Pyke, 1996), and part of the blame for this must lie with the institutions in not giving appropriate initial guidance. Many learners are disappointed by the lack of help available in choosing a course and in staying on it. There is in general a low level of awareness of sources of information and financial incentives for training, such as the Training to Work scheme or the New Deal.

Part of the cause of lack of training is the lack of appropriate provision (Banks et al, 1992). Even those studying may not have found what they actually wanted. This is particularly true of non-work-related training and learning for leisure, and is reinforced by the current emphasis on certificated courses, heavily backed up by the incentives in the funding arrangements to provide accreditation of all adult education. Not only does this deny some people the opportunity to learn new interests and make new friends, it denies returners an easy entry route back into education, especially for women who may be more intimidated by examination demands. Even where provision is available, knowledge of opportunities may be patchy for some parts of the population (Taylor and Spencer, 1994), giving many a feeling that 'you are on your own'. In addition, an estimated six million adults in Britain may have difficulty with writing or numeracy (NIACE, 1994), and one sixth of adults have problems with basic literacy. These deficiencies appear to pass through generations of the same families, reinforcing their importance as a 'reproductive' determinant of adult non-learning.

Whatever barriers are faced, they are clearly harder for the less motivated prospective students. The lack of provision of learning for leisure and at home, with a focus only on the formal public arena, especially of work, means that potential learners may be seen as younger, better educated, and from higher income groups than they really are (Edwards et al, 1993). To some extent, this image becomes self-realising. People with these characteristics tend to be selected for learning, and so social practice becomes reproductive, and education comes to be seen as middle-class and 'not for the likes of us'. Individuals may have a poor experience of previous educational episodes that creates an obstacle for them continuing education. If initial education has not led to the creation of basic studying skills, such as numeracy, this provides a further barrier.

The influence of lack of motivation to learn may be underestimated by a literature concentrating on the more easily visible barriers, such as cost and entry qualifications (McGivney, 1990). Many people display an incorrigible reluctance to learn formally. In fact, perhaps 21% of adults form a hard core of non-participants outside all attempts to reach them (Titmus, 1994). If all the barriers were removed for them, by the provision of free tuition and travel, they would still not want to learn. They have no desire, and given greater leisure time would want to 'just waste it'. Self-identity in Britain may be more strongly linked to a job than it is in other countries, where a greater emphasis is placed on learning (Bynner, 1989). Lack of drive thus becomes the most important barrier of all, since it is seen as too easy to get a job instead, and qualifications are seen as useless anyway. Some young people do not even bother to find out what their public examination results are (Banks et al, 1992), since they are only concerned with getting a job. Qualifications may even be seen as antagonistic to getting a job, and only concerned with entry to more education.

Learning is therefore something done early in life, as a preparation, but with no relevance to the world of adults (Harrison, 1993). In an evaluation of 25 years of basic skills provision in the UK, Wells (2001) concludes that while the obvious barriers have an impact on non-participation, as does lack of the right opportunity, the challenge in overcoming basic skills deficits is more complex than that. He recalls that in 1975 simply providing the opportunities to learn was considered sufficient, then a major effort was made to advertise them, now the emphasis is on motivating individuals.

But perhaps even that will not be enough. Participation is not an end in itself. Unenthusiastic participants, and 'disaffected' learners, can be fragile in their new learner identities. They continue to need careful consideration from their teachers (Bathmaker, 2001). Even retention throughout a course, with eventual certification perhaps, is not a simple measure of success. Drop-out (or reversion to non-participation) does not have to be seen as dysfunctional and may, on occasion, be an indicator of success for that individual (Hodkinson and Bloomer, 2001).

Conclusion

This study, with its retrospective lifelong perspective, has therefore begun to answer questions that have been posed by previous studies (for example, whether training leads to better employment prospects and further training) but unanswered due to lack of a long-term perspective (Dolton et al, 1994) or the difficulty of isolating the confounding variables (Main and Shelly, 1990). In an analogous way to the fact that the most important influence determining an individual's unemployment in any year is unemployment in the previous years (Gershuny and Marsh, 1994), current policy assumes that longer initial education will lead to subsequent adult participation (Daines et al, 1982). Studies of the effect of learning/training on employment and income are relatively common – for example the DfEE (1995) estimated that one third of those leaving Training for Work schemes and half who left Youth Training in 1994 were employed six months later – but these studies seldom consider the impact of learning on learning.

The model of the social determinants of patterns of participation in adult education and training proposed in this study is a complex one. On the one hand, there are clear structural differences between the patterns observed here that emphasise the crucial role of an individual's socio-economic background in determining patterns of participation (as opposed to the more usually cited level of qualification and the accumulation of prior learning). However, there are clearly individuals who do not fit the overall pattern, and to explain these there are basically two additional components: error and omitted variables. The 'error' term may be attributable to a variety of problems including recall, reporting, embellishing, recording, coding, transcription, and statistical manipulation. All models are likely to contain an error component, and it would be unwise to expect any model to explain 100% of the variance in the observations on which it is based.

A second strong possibility is that the model does not include one or more significant explanatory variables, and so over-emphasises the relevance of those that are included. Although, perhaps by definition, it is difficult to identify candidates for variables that have been omitted, our theoretical model (set out in Chapter Two) does allow for choice by the individual. In so far as choices are predictable within those bounds, the above figures may give a reasonably full account. What is left out is the formation in individuals of a relatively stable learner identity based on their previous experience of learning, primarily at school, and affecting their view of what is appropriate participation for them in the future – either as a consolidation or a counter-reaction. In so far as qualifications and failure in examinations have a role in determining patterns of later participation, then perhaps their influence is also mediated via such an identity.

There is reasonable agreement across different research and interest groups as to the nature of current non-participants in post-compulsory education and training (Tight, 1998a). Recent government-sponsored reports, subsequent green papers, and academic studies list the unemployed and others on low incomes, the unskilled and unqualified, ex-offenders, part-time or temporary workers, those with learning difficulties or low levels of basic skills, and some ethnic groups as being the least likely to participate (Fryer, 1997; Kennedy, 1997; DfEE, 1998). A key question for policy makers and practitioners is how to encourage these individuals to respond (*whether* they should want to participate is usually taken for granted). The standard diagnosis is that education and training will give skills to the unskilled, and jobs to the unemployed and so on. The findings reported here present at least a partial challenge to that 'human capital' view by suggesting that it is socio-economic changes that are driving changes in patterns of participation rather more than vice versa.

Viewed over time, the determinants of participation have changed, but they have changed in a way that reinforces the notion that immediate and later patterns are separately determined. More people are now continuing from initial schooling, for which the leaving-age has been raised successively anyway, to further education or training. This has had the effect of making patterns of transitional participation both gender neutral and less predictable from birth. Gender is now less important than 50 years ago, while the experience of initial schooling is more so. Later patterns have not changed much, however, and sufficient time has now elapsed since the first noted increases in transitional participation to suggest that this will not necessarily increase later participation. In fact, in some respects, it may do the opposite, as observed here. Later participation is now more heavily gendered than it used to be, but despite this there are indications that for males born and living in industrial South Wales the situation is worse in absolute terms than it was in the 1950s and 1960s. Such possibilities highlight the complexities facing policy makers in creating a learning society today.

These results offer important correctives to the conventional view of participation in lifelong learning, and could explain the peculiarity noted by Field (1998) and Schuller and Field (1999) that regions, such as Northern

Ireland, with longer initial education actually have lower levels of adult participation. The standard explanation of differential patterns of participation and non-participation in adult learning is that those who participate early, participate often; and those who miss out at the start have great difficulty returning to formal learning. The findings of this study show, first of all, that patterns of participation have general determinants that predate the first episodes, and that these determine whether someone participates early.

They also suggest that the determinants of early and later participation are somewhat different, and that simply increasing front-loaded provision (increasing further and higher education, and so on) is unlikely to 'cash out' into increasing lifelong learning trajectories. This raises the crucial policy issue of where scarce resources for education and training should be directed, especially given the focus up until now on 'front-loading' investment into initial schooling. While the evidence should be treated with caution, it does indicate that shifting this balance in favour of policies addressed to the determinants of later participation would be a more efficient and cost-effective way of moving towards a learning society in the UK. Educators may also be able to make more of a difference by addressing the determinants of later participation, such as motivation, which are susceptible to change by enthusing one individual, than by addressing the determinants of early participation, such as parental class, which are not.

Although studies have shown that people generally believe that there are ample opportunities to participate in learning (Park, 1994), it is also clear that this belief is an overview, unconnected to their specific needs, and chiefly concerns opportunities for others. The position may be like that of diners in a restaurant who can see that the menu is very long, even though what any individual actually wants may not be available. The notion that the desperate need is for vocational training, the emphasis on the economy, and on qualifications, and the attempts to make current provision more open to all, may be taking attention away from other major unmet needs for education and training. Such needs may be specific and practical such as welfare rights, tenants' groups and democratic participation (Frazer and Ward, 1988) or more general self-development or everyday living (although this was not a theme that commonly emerged at interview). The long-term unemployed in this study, and those who come to the end of their working lives due to illness, clearly do not want vocational training, nor do they want qualifications.

Inequality in society will not be lessened significantly by dealing with people themselves, or training them, or more of them (Hodkinson et al, 1996). Whether they get a job depends chiefly on the businesses and the government to provide economic success. However, not everyone, nor indeed every state, can have that full 'success'. In the global market, success is relative and may be serendipitous to some extent. If the focus of economic development moves away from the North Atlantic area, as it previously did from the Mediterranean, societies here will need alternative and more mature views of education for life. Ameliorating inequalities in society directly, by redistributive taxation perhaps, will make alternative learning trajectories available to wider participation (since their determinants are primarily social). This may have a beneficial effect on training, jobs and the economy, but is surely worth doing even if not.

Educators and trainers have a role to play in such long-term societal reform, as concerned citizens and voters, but there is also an urge to act now, to decide on the best time to intervene (Maguire et al, 1993). Educators can make more of a difference by addressing the determinants of later participation, which are more susceptible to change, than the determinants of early participation. This is not to say that breaking downs barriers to participation and constraints on action is ineffective. The rise in the real cost of fees for adult education from 1976-81 was accompanied by a drop in numbers for example (Daines et al, 1982), and students were not prepared to travel as far as previously, despite more having their own vehicles. Barriers are especially important where they impede full rather than nominal participation, and these are chiefly to do with the character of the course on offer. The decision to participate or not is asymmetric, heavily loaded against participation. To decide not to participate is sufficient to achieve its objective, whereas the decision to participate must be constantly reaffirmed by action. This is one major reason why considerations of access do not lead to a complete solution. If rational thought and action are goals of adult education (Mezirow, 1990), participation is part of the goal, so that learning must come to be seen more naturally as an outcome in itself, and less as a process leading towards some half-glimpsed economic benefit.

Since 1945, there has been a growth in the proportion of each age cohort staying on in full-time education at school-leaving age, while there has not been an equivalent increase in the numbers of lifelong learners, and there has actually been a slight decrease in the numbers of delayed learners, despite all the talk of the importance of careership and multi-skilling (Jones, 1996). The current emphasis in discourse on the importance of lifelong learning is therefore a necessary and welcome relief from an obsession with front-loaded provision. In a sense, it is easy to see how to increase participation and success in education. All that need be done is improve the overall economic position of individuals in society. However, this is not simply a job for teachers and educationalists, since despite some current educational rhetoric, there is little indication that the reverse also holds, that improving education improves the economic position of society as a whole.

> We must accept that education is an ineffective form of social engineering ... if we want to distribute wealth and power in our society, we should distribute it by direct political means ... we should see education, not as a means of redistributing the cake, but as part of the cake itself. (Crombie and Harries-Jenkins, 1983, p 84)

SEVEN

The role of informal learning

with Ralph Fevre

This chapter begins by questioning the narrow definition of learning used in much present writing concerning lifelong learning, which tends to focus on the purported economic and societal benefits of prolonging and widening participation in formal education and training programmes. In contrast, much valuable and non-trivial learning already goes on, and has always gone on, outside formal programmes of instruction. This is true both at work (Fevre et al, 2000) and in leisure (Gorard et al, 1999d). If such informal learning continues to be ignored by proponents of a learning society, then the result may be an unnecessary exclusiveness in definitions of a learning society, and an unjustifiable reliance on certification.

An individual's position within the social-structure of the determinants of participation, described in Chapters Four to Six – the objective opportunities available to particular social groups at particular places and times – is located chiefly by their personal characteristics such as age, gender, and family background. A 1982 ACACE (Advisory Council for Adult Continuing Education) survey suggested that the ability to take up opportunities was affected by personal motivation and individual circumstance, as well as by individuals' knowledge of and the availability of learning opportunities (Sargant, 1996). Being a learner has therefore been described as a 'praxis' (Mezirow, 1990).

However, at least one other possibility has emerged, as there are some individuals who do not fit our more general theory of early socio-economic determinants, since their will to act comes from a crisis in their later life. Their motivation may be dispositional (Edwards et al, 1993), of the type that tends to be the most underestimated by survey-type methods (Harrison, 1993).

Although many studies have identified a vocational strand of motivation as dominant in participation (for example, NIACE, 1994), this may be as much a product of their focus as of the social reality they portray. By considering only a narrow range of formal learning, such studies may introduce variable-selection bias, making some forms of motivation appear more important by ignoring others, or by offering respondents a choice of reasons from a limited predetermined list. A study by the Employment Department, for example, necessarily focuses attention on work-related training, so that when such a study finds that the main reasons to study are to increase job satisfaction for those in work, to help get a job for those not in work, or to change their job for those prepared to fund themselves (Park, 1994), these motives must be seen as only a fraction of those actually providing adult learners with the will to act.

Much adult learning is self-planned, deliberate, and motivated by curiosity, interest and enjoyment as much as practical considerations (Sargant, 1996). Part of the reason for the apparent disagreement between the economists' view of learning and others is that 'public' learning is only the tip of the iceberg. Even more is explained by the credentialist mentality of analysts who apparently do not value adult learning unless it leads to formal qualification (Gorard et al, 2002a). National Education and Training Targets miss the point, since they are blind to informal learning that may stem from borrowing a book or watching television (THES, 1997). Many people have a vast experience of learning in different jobs, but no qualifications (although NVQs may be beginning to have an impact here).

There has been relatively little research, certainly little empirical research, into learning that does not take the form of institutionalised, accredited participation in formal education or training (but see Livingstone, 1998). The sociology of education tradition usually emphasises an individual's formal rather than 'real' level of education (Girod, 1990), and there are sound methodological and philosophical reasons for this. Informal learning does not lead to such convenient measures as participation and pass rates, for example, and once its existence has been acknowledged, it is harder to find an operational definition of learning on the continuum leading to the trivial and the commonplace (Coffield, 1997).

> In its liberal form, education is about establishing a boundary ... between itself as a 'serious' activity and other less serious or non-serious activities such as leisure. (Edwards and Usher, 1998, p 86)

With learning replacing education, the boundaries around education as a field of study are breached, since almost any activity can be seen to involve learning. Nevertheless, by effectively ignoring informal learning, writers may become confused over trends in skill formation over time (Gallie, 1988), and there is little evidence that indicators such as participation and qualification are good predictors of a person's value for employers or to society (Eraut, 1997).

This lacuna is even more marked in policy terms, where official writing about learning rarely even acknowledges the existence of informal learning. There is therefore a danger of discourse concerning the learning society being dominated by the providers, and becoming the empire of the 'schoolers', with the emphasis being as much on compulsion as opportunity (Thring, 1998; Tight, 1998b).

Eraut (1997) has argued that if learning is defined as a 'change in persons capability or understanding', then it can encompass informal 'background' learning at work without also including all changes in behaviour. One of the purposes of this chapter is to illustrate the possibility of extending this use of the term 'learning' to activities outside work, and so to rescue informal learning from the dominant educational discourse relating only to human capital (Marginson, 1993). We use a fairly broad definition of informal learning, such that it includes learning taking place as a process outside formal participation (and thus not usually encompassed by the trajectories). It is therefore similar to the notion of non-formal learning described by Eraut et al (1998) as not being constrained by 'prescribed frameworks'. Although it is probably true that much learning is 'caught not taught' even in formal episodes (Davies, 1998), the definition here does not include learning taking place in *any* participatory episodes, even where these are of a relatively informal nature; that is, informal refers here to the structure and setting rather than the style of learning (Jarvis, 1993). Therefore, we are not generally referring to non-formal episodes using the definition given by Fordham et al (1983, p 246), or to 'experiential' or 'constructivist' learning within formal episodes (Sutherland, 1997), or andragogical style (Knowles, 1990), but to "all forms of learning not included in formal and non-formal education" (Tight, 1996, p 69) which are self-directed.

As used here, 'informal learning' is very similar to non-taught learning as defined by Beinart and Smith (1998) as "deliberately trying to improve your knowledge about anything or teach yourself a skill without taking part in a taught course" (p 200). This includes non-certificated episodes, and those leading to tacit knowledge. The 1997 National Adult Learning Survey identified four types of non-taught learning, which were:

- studying for qualifications without participating in a course;
- supervised on-job training;
- keeping up to date with work by reading, or seminars;
- "deliberately trying to improve your knowledge about anything or teach yourself a skill without taking part in a taught course" (p 200).

All of these are discussed in this chapter, although the chief focus is on the last.

More crucially, informal learning encompasses learning both at work and at leisure. In this sense, talking to a technician at work about the installation of new software, or reading a weekly magazine at home about growing fruit in your garden, would be examples of informal learning. On the other hand, attending a lecture on health and safety, or learning to dance at an adult evening class would both be formal episodes. A great deal of learning goes on in work that is virtually unnoticed by researchers and even by employers, but which is vitally necessary to the organisations people work for (and perhaps also to the fulfilment of the individuals concerned) even though it is not acquired in any formal manner. In some cases the acquisition of this learning is an active process, and it does not do justice to this sort of learning to describe it as 'sitting next to Nellie'. Informal learning can be described as being acquired by proactive individuals who seek out potential Nellies, and adopt a variety of other methods in order to do their jobs. Sometimes they transform those jobs in the process. The most active informal learners may be in a process of constant transformation, both of themselves and of what they do (consider the story of a man who read on the subway for 20,000 hours, in Jarvis, 1983, p 11).

It is almost as if the best sort of learning – and not simply that very basic learning without which the organisation could not function – is often this informal type. If informal learning is ignored, as it often appears to be, then the 'learning age' may be in danger of becoming a sterile pursuit of National Training Targets or their revamped successors, and the learning society may become simply a 'certified society' (Ainley, 1998, 1999).

Leisure learning

Our systematic sample of adults aged between 16-65 were asked about all of their participation in learning 'episodes'. The attempt was made by interviewers to make the resulting list as full as possible by asking specifically about leisure learning, hobbies, and uncertificated courses as well as training at work, full-time education, participation in government schemes and so on. In summary, 31% of the respondents reported no formal learning of any kind and these are the 'non-participants', yet it is shown by analysis of the interview data that in many cases they have undergone transformations in their lives that would involve significant learning. This group, by their own definition, are informal learners. Of course, this phenomenon is also encountered in the narratives of other respondents who *have* participated in formal episodes since the end of compulsory schooling. In fact, the evidence available suggests that informal learning is even more common among some groups of participants than among the non-participants (see Table 7.1).

The only questions in the survey that directly address experiences of informal learning are to do with self-study or practice relating to a leisure interest. Table 7.1 shows a clear relationship between the answers to these questions and individuals' more formal experiences. The lifelong learners and those who have returned to education and training after leaving school at the earliest opportunity ('delayed' learners) share the characteristic of a much higher frequency of informal learning. Those who have never participated in formal adult learning, and those who moved from compulsory schooling to further

Table 7.1: Reports of informal leisure study, by learning trajectories (%)

Lifelong trajectory	% reporting informal study
Lifelong learners	27
Delayed participants	25
Transitional learners	13
Non-participants	11

education or training ('transitional' learners) both have a much lower frequency of informal learning.

Two further points can be made about these figures. First, the percentage of those still in continuous formal education or training who report such an interest (the 'immature' trajectories) is the same as for lifelong and delayed learners. Therefore, the differences between other trajectories cannot be related to age. The average age at which a new interest is reported is 29. Both groups who have experienced learning later in life (lifelong and delayed) are more likely to undertake informal leisure learning episodes, suggesting that learning could be a habit and that the boundaries between formal and informal may be unclear for such respondents. The relationship is so strong that a leisure interest is a very useful predictor of later formal participation in the two component model in Chapter Six.

In addition, the results reinforce doubts about the efficacy of simply considering opportunities and barriers in attempting to encourage greater participation for other adults. The opportunities for informal learning are already so widespread, and the barriers so few, that there must be additional reasons for non-participation. The finding that those who stay in formal education or training after compulsory schooling (the 'transitional' learners) and those who do not (the 'non-participants') are equally unlikely to have undertaken leisure study suggests that simply extending the length of initial education, the unremitting policy of successive governments in the UK, will also not be sufficient to create a 'learning age'.

Nevertheless, it must be remembered that 38 of the 342 cases described by the survey as 'non-participants' did report episodes of informal learning, and that these episodes did not include informal learning at work. Informal learning therefore exists even among those who report no formal education or training as adults. It is important to note that the present discussion only involves non-participatory education as leisure episodes. It is therefore unlikely that *self-directed* education as a leisure pursuit is as class-laden as formal classes for leisure interests have been found to be in other studies (for example, Jarvis, 1985), and this has important implications for a genuinely inclusive learning society. By only recognising formal episodes, policy may, by its very design, be excluding those that it is purportedly setting out to include.

Overall, the frequency of leisure interests has declined since 1945. An interest in local politics or history that accounted for 8% of the episodes until the 1960s, now accounts for 0% of the total (rounded figure). This interest has effectively disappeared in industrial South Wales. Similar declines are suggested in gardening (from 18% to 0%) and art and photography (from 15% to 0%). Of course, since the dates given relate to the decade in which the interest started, the decline is chiefly in those reporting a new informal interest. Many of those interested in gardening in the 1950s, may be still gardening, for example. However, it is clear that participation in sports (loosely defined), keeping pets, and using a computer have all increased from a combined total of 20% of the early episodes to 60% in the 1990s.

Since a sustained leisure interest requiring study or practice is such a clear indicator of participation in later learning (increasing the odds in a logistic regression model by 30%) it would be foolish to ignore the implications for the creation of a wider learning society. If informal learning is indeed a partial determinant of later, more formal participation in adult learning, then the decline in the evidence for such interests is a further indication of the non-linear development of patterns of lifelong learning in the UK. A genuinely liberal education has been claimed to lead to open-minded reflection and enquiry (Armour and Fuhrmann, 1993), but despite evidence that thinking skills and critical awareness can be taught, more rigid curricula means less time for critical thinking, as one struggles to learn the thoughts of others via the transmission model of education (Wales et al, 1993), while in the past, and in less formal settings, the process of learning may have been easier in some respects.

In the further interviews, we were concerned to find out about learning episodes that had perhaps not been covered in the survey stage. There were many interviewees who reported no informal learning experiences, and no leisure interests involving study or practice. In most cases, where a reason was given, this was ascribed to lack of interest, by someone who had not attended school regularly and left at the earliest opportunity, for example; or to lack of time, by someone like a consultant surgeon who had spent most of his life in formal study. In very general terms, where an interviewee described any genuine interest at length, they also described others, whether of a formal or informal nature. In a sense, as suggested by the survey findings, there are people who seek out things to learn, and people who do not.

Surprisingly, books and magazines were more frequently cited as sources of information than other people, or broadcasts or information technology. Magazines were used to learn sports like golf, the use of software such as spreadsheets, and how to build a radio transmitter. The use of books included learning musical instruments such as guitar, languages, calculus, and practical skills such as building a garage or wiring a house. It is important to recall in reading the accounts below that several of the people contacted via the systematic sampling procedure have little or no formal education after compulsory schooling.

A professional training manager from the Sandfields area tells the story of discovering that a 30-year-old worker scored very highly on an aptitude test. Initially, no one believed that the score was valid, since the man worked at a low-skill job, checking cans. He had no qualifications and no ambition to progress. However, the score was verified, and the worker was interviewed. He reported only attending school occasionally and not bothering to take any qualifications since he did not feel that he needed any to work in Port Talbot. He turned down all offers of company-provided development and training. The manager concluded:

> "I don't know what it is with Port Talbot people, they don't appear to have any ambition. Perhaps they don't fancy the school environment again."

The man in question reads widely at home, and had decided for himself when to attend school if the topic of study interested him. Thus, although not a primary respondent, this man can be used to represent one type of informal learner, who is disaffected from the process of education, but remains a 'learner'. This type of story is not common in the interviews. Generally, the informal learners are eclectic in their subjects, hungry for new experiences. If their level of formal participation is low, it is probably not because they have refused opportunities offered to them.

One man, for whom there was little separation between work and home, had taught himself pottery (with his wife), electrolysis for metallising, simple electronics, wax casting, and furniture modelling. He has a perspex-cutting room in his house, a frog that he had gold-plated in his living room, and once made a scale model of the Challenger space shuttle, which is now on the desk of a four-star general in NASA. In some cases he has been successfully employed on the basis of self-taught skills.

This story of a genuinely multi-skilled but mainly self-taught interviewee is very similar to that of a self-taught plasterer and electrician, who loved opera, but worked as a steel foundryman. He explained how he had read about the care of the 7,000 bedding plants he had in his garden.

> "Well, you see when I was doing those I used to send off for those books. Once a month you get books from them. They come in volumes. There are 12 volumes. So if ever I was stuck I look, I used to look through the books and say 'oh'. Read it up, 'oh' that's the way to do it. It's the same with the bricklaying. I ordered a bricklaying book and I read it up ... with plastering now a friend of mine is in the library and she got me a book, so ... if I got to do a job I'm not quite sure I get the book and read it up and say 'oh well' this is the way."

> "Like that wall was all different when I'd done it the first time. Then we went to Porthcawl one day and we see these walls and she [his wife] said 'yeah it's nice – could you do that on the wall?' She said 'well there's a lot of cracks there'. So we took the old wall off and I plastered it across, removed all the fittings, fitted them all in and plastered it all off and it's been there since. She likes it but then I had to do the room in there then.... Just put a couple of mouldings on the wall."

> "I like doing things. I think if you like doing something it's no hardship then. You know, time flies."

Another man reported:

> "I like to build these little things. I've got something going on here look. This is a low-powered. That's not part of it but this is a low-powered transmitter/receiver. That's the sort of thing I like doing, but that's part of a project I got out of a magazine."

Although the differences can be over-emphasised, there is a pattern in these stories in the types of skills and activities undertaken by men (as discussed) and by women (as we are about to discuss). To some extent, the gendered differences in the distribution of learning trajectories may be replicated by gendered differences in informal learning outside work. There are clear differences in the fields in which their informal learning generally takes place, but more intriguingly women may be even more likely than men to describe informal learning episodes as simply 'activities' rather than learning, and so to downplay their reporting of what must have been transformative experiences in many ways.

A woman in her forties reported taking a course in German that was uncertificated, which was how she preferred it since she was studying primarily for interest and 'tourism' and had "never taken to languages at school". This took three hours of one evening in the week. She also sews and reads a lot at home. In addition:

> "I'm very involved in my local church with the Mothers' Union and Young Wives' Group and ... I'm at the moment treasurer of the Mothers' Union.... I've been treasurer twice of the Wives' Group and secretary. I've also been secretary of the Fete committee, and as I say I was secretary of the PTA.... I'm on the social committee to do with the church, so that takes up a lot of my time."

Another woman of a similar age has taught herself to crochet and do quilting from books, building on skills in knitting and sewing she gained as a child. She organises a local 'ladies' club' and a coffee club to raise funds for her children's school. Again there are similarities with her earlier work as a book-keeper, which she undertook with no reported training, and where she taught herself how national insurance worked from pamphlets, for example. But she speaks for several respondents when she points out the pressures on her time.

> "Yes, I think when you've got a family you tend not to.... Can't seem to get around to do all the things I would like to do."

A similar story emerges from a woman in her fifties who started explaining how she taught herself to play the organ:

> "When we came here ... there were two organists and neither could play at this funeral for some reason. He said you've got to play. Fortunately there was a week in between and every day I went down, this was a very old pipe organ. I went home in tears and said 'I can't play it', it's a completely different ball game to playing the piano. You wouldn't believe it.... Middle C isn't middle C and when you take your finger off it stops. I just can't, but I did it."

She runs a sewing class for the Mothers' Union, does all the brassing for the local church, and the laundry of their linen. She is Brown Owl of the local brownie pack, and governor of her local infant school. She reports no special training to take on any of these roles, which she describes as "just inheriting".

Another woman took over the aerobics class she was attending, and is now employed as a tutor in Ogwr. The pay was so good that she gave up her job as a cashier to travel the borough providing classes. Again, no special training and no qualifications are mentioned. In fact they are explicitly denied. At the age of 53, she has gained an A grade in GCSE French, and is studying for A level, aiming for a higher qualification:

> "Then my dream is, Brian and I, we're going to – when the boys don't need us any more – we're going to get a job on a campsite in France. He's going to leave Fords. He's going to be the handyman and the person that does the garden, and I'm going to be the receptionist and I'm going to talk French to everybody."

In some cases, people's ambitions are more prosaic. One woman who was illiterate when she left school and throughout her first marriage, simply wanted to learn to read:

> "Mine started to get better really when I was having my first son. I was in hospital for nigh on six months and I mean hospital is quite boring. I started to read. I read a lot now but I find I like to go over the books a couple of times because I'm always picking up things that I've missed before."

Informal learning at work

The recent drive towards qualifying people for participating in courses was bemoaned by several respondents, but the most consistent stance on this theme emerged from consideration of the stories of the local trainers themselves. The manager of a local adult education project in Bridgend pointed out:

> "A lot of courses in the past were leisure-based with people attending for the social element. A typical profile of a learner was unqualified but interested in learning for learning's sake. Definitely not looking for qualifications out of it."

A community education manager in Blaenau Gwent made a similar comment:

> "The turning point for community education in Blaenau Gwent was the passing of the 1992 Further and Higher Education Act. This saw the end of the old ethos. We know that many of our students come to us not wanting accreditation, they have a different agenda ... who regard

this sort of provision as a lifeline ... for learning which is enjoyable in itself."

In some respects these findings reinforce the warnings made by NIACE (1994), and others, that certification is itself a barrier for some people, who might want a more relaxed return to formal learning.

In the early part of this century, informal learning can be seen as a part of the collective experience encountered as a direct result of a new wave of industrialisation. In retrospect it is somewhat alarming to discover that the growth industry in South Wales during the early decades depended utterly on a system of informal learning by which the skills and knowledge of coalmining were transferred from one group of experienced coalminers to a new group of 'want-to-be' coalminers attracted to the industry from poorly paid rural employment. In addition, this process of informal learning also applied to coalminers' families where the early socialisation of male children prepared them in a general sense for their future coalmining experience. This informal familial process of education was reinforced as son went to work with father, and brother worked with brother. This system of mentoring was in a very real sense a matter of physical well-being and even survival. What is described by respondents as 'pit sense' can also be taken to mean the lessening of potential for serious injury.

However, the educational opportunities that existed went further than coal-winning skills, for they also embraced a socioeconomic analysis of society and capitalism as its economic mode of production. Progression to more formal means of learning were not simply accidental spin-offs from these informal intellectual discussions. It is clear from the historical evidence that the mining system of mentorship also included a desire on the part of the older generation to enthuse their younger counterparts towards educational attainment.

Our survey findings suggest that most new jobs involved no training of any sort − not even half a day of health and safety. Perhaps the most common response to questions in interview about training for new tasks was that new tasks were picked up through 'common sense'. This response came from individuals in a wide variety of situations, from barristers in pupillage, to pharmacists on drug counters, to lathe operators, school teachers, sales representatives and care assistants, for example. One woman became a clerk, then an assistant to a dog-breeder, and then a small-holding farmer without any formal training at any stage. Another was trusted with the accounts of a medium-sized firm, and later set up her own playgroup for children, both without any training at all. Another respondent was a cook in the army, using only her knowledge from cooking at home for the family. The point they are making is that, in their view, formal training was unnecessary and that experience was everything, although a few complained of being "thrown in at the deep end" and not having "a clue what I was doing".

Several respondents created a problem for our trajectories based on participation in formal training episodes, by displaying a willingness and ability to learn outside of such episodes. One, a woman in her fifties, who left school at 15 with her parent's blessing and had no lifelong qualifications, had this to say of her jobs in haberdashery:

> "Once you learnt how to do things, it was more or less all the same.... What you done, you done your training for a month of how to sew and this, that and the other and used heavy machines that was it. You didn't get no more training again.... I mean the thing is I can go right through from a complete suite from the arms, backs, outside backs, cushions, front borders, seats, so I mean you know through the years I mean you know you pick it up."

A man in his 60s left school at 14 chiefly for economic reasons, like so many others. Asked why he left school at 14, he responded:

> "My father was mining underground. He had six months off, he went back for another month, and of course there was no dole or anything in those days and myself and my sister still at home.... Then I took this job. Didn't earn a lot of money but of course anything in those days was better than what we had."

He also had no lifelong qualifications, but had a very successful career in British Steel Tinplate, being promoted several times and moving between areas of work, without receiving any formal training. Another man in his fifties who worked for the same company all of his life, is genuinely multi-skilled at plastering, electrical work, welding, galvanising, and market gardening. He enjoyed his time at school but still left at 15 without qualifications. He has since had few years without either work-based training or voluntary adult education courses. On the availability of the latter formal opportunities he says:

> "I took the number, phoned the number, and yeah come on now, so I went down and found it and joined up. I think it's there if you look for them."

He does not see learning as simply to do with his job. It is also to do with his hobbies and it is here that he can be classified as an autodidact:

> "Well you come here and have a look. There are 7,000 plants down there now I've got [in back garden of terraced house].... They're all bedding plants. I like doing bedding plants.... I do have a fishpond and I like doing the garden. Give me a month's time now and all that there will ... all be full of flowers."

The role of leisure interests as the mark of a learner is an interesting one. The absence of hobbies requiring sustained study or practice correlates strongly with non-participation in education and training. One respondent told us of the demotivating input from his parents while at school. It is perhaps no surprise that he cannot comprehend the concept of learning for interest or leisure:

> "You said about education, about getting qualifications.... I might fall into something that I would really love ... but you asked me about getting education ... which I think would be a foolish thing for me to do really.... It's still a waste of time as far as I'm concerned. You seen them on the news like that woman of 70 or 80 getting a degree or something. What for, like? You know, what for? She has wasted hours ... to go and do something like that at her age is a waste of a couple of years of her life."

On the other hand, leisure interests can mark someone who has not participated in much formal institutional learning. One man who did not attend school regularly, left without qualification as soon as possible and worked in the local mine until he got 'blown up'. He describes moving from job to job – technical drawing, chargehand, airborne division, foundry, building site, carpentry, British Rail shunter, fitter, security guard – with minimal training. He is one of the 'common sense' school of learners (see following section on autodidacts), but he also clearly lied to employers about his prior knowledge and experience. An extract from his leisure interests on reading gives a flavour of his story:

> "Er, I've gone right through the Second World War, nearly every conflict or campaign that was gone through like. You see what they write and every writer has a different version of it.... I mean to say you read one book about Lord Mountbatten and how marvellous he was. When you read eight books ... the other seven there's little bits in them and when you add them together he was a complete prat."

Another man was a coal-cutter who had to give up when his local mine suffered a catastrophe.

> "There was an explosion in Six Bells – can you remember it? And there was quite a few dead. Well, we was actually working, they were working towards us from Six Bells ... and we was only a matter of from here to that wall away from them when it happened. So I thought that was enough so then, um, I came out and went to be a manager with Premier Cheques. Used to have a cheque and they could go into the shop and buy clothes. Premier Cheques it was called at that time and I was manager in Tredegar, and they moved me over to Brynmawr."

The importance of this story is that he received no training at all in order to switch from being coalminer to catalogue shop manager (apparently successfully). He states that he could have had five or six jobs, and from an era of full employment there are many such examples of what would now seem extraordinary career changes involving no retraining.

Similarly a signalman on the railways in the 1950s became a stationmaster with a staff of six "doing everything, income tax, bills, pay, everything". He learnt his tasks "just by spending a fortnight with the chap who was doing it before me ... and I'd issue all tickets". It made it difficult for him to deal with the unexpected:

> "Somebody once, I wonder if it was a put up job, brought me a bike to send to Ireland and I ended up sending it to Dudley the next station down the line because I couldn't deal with it."

An assistant in a pharmacy today found the job very difficult to start with:

> "It was about three or four months before I could really get into and know ... and knew what I was doing, but as I say I'm giving out drugs now that you don't know really what they're for and they're given different brand names. And you're not really given the generic name of the drug so there's no ... unless you ask which ... we're a very, very busy pharmacy anyway and there's not really a lot of time for training."

Another woman with several job changes has had no training despite being aged 34. She first worked as a typist in the car industry, and learnt as she 'went along', and then moved to work as a clerk for an insurance firm:

> "Well they gave me a manual to work the computer. I just learned myself. But I managed.... I had a manual to work it all out. And I wasn't computer-minded so I was right in at the deep end."

She moved to become a branch administrator for a national sports company, a move that involved added responsibility, such as installing a new networked computer system, with no training and immediate effect.

> "And, um, I had to teach the branch members how to use the computer and also my manager because he didn't really take an interest at all."

She says this job is a 'dead-end' and hopes to apply for a post in the wages department in a new Panasonic factory in Port Talbot.

Even where vocational training is apparently available, it can be in name only. A young woman made this complaint of her Youth Training, and it is clear from her later description of a 'marvellous' training course that she is able to be discriminating in her criticisms:

> "It was a complete waste of time. They didn't teach you to do anything. You had to learn it for yourself. They didn't show you what to do. It

was a case of 'here's the stuff. Have a go'.... There's supervisors walking around and foremen but all they were there for was drinking coffee and having a fag. They were a complete waste of time. [My mates] all thought the same."

Other studies have reported similar views of YT among young people and it is a moot point as to the effects that these sorts of experiences have on subsequent attitudes towards adult learning.

Sometimes people take a job with a promise of training that is not kept. One woman started at a florist's shop:

"She was going to and she promised me faithfully and they promised me this, that and the other, and when it eventually materialised like I said 'what about me signing on at the Tech?' She said 'Oh sorry, no, we can't afford to let you have the time off'. I was working 8:30am to 5:30pm six days a week."

A 30-year-old woman who started her career as a postgraduate student at Oxford University received no research-training in return for her student fees. She was also given responsibility for undergraduate teaching with no supervision and no training:

"I suppose I recognised what I thought was good in tutorials and one in particular I thought had been very successful in the way that he taught, and I tried to put together what I thought was good and rule out what was bad. All of us who were graduates spent ages sitting around talking about what constitutes good teaching and good tutorial."

On gaining a lectureship at the University of Wales, Swansea, she received only health and safety training in the form of fire drills. An 'induction day' was available, but:

"My colleagues made a big fuss – 'Why do you want to go on an induction day, it's completely useless' – and actually made it quite hard for me to go."

Eventually she was given training in how to lecture, but she had two complaints about this. First, it was too late as she had already been teaching for six years. If the training was of any value, then it would have helped six previous cohorts of her students. Second, the training was aimed at those who were completely new to teaching, but was taken by experienced tutors as a precondition of getting a permanent job. It was the archetypal 'unnecessary learning'.

Conclusion

If leisure learning is a characteristic of later-life learners, surely it is a characteristic that creators of a learning society should seek to enhance? But this self-reliance may be negated by 'the audit society' (Ecclestone, 1998). Informal learners learn at home in their spare time, not seeking certification and not linking learning to their work and they may be disappearing in association with the growth in formal participation. Although South Wales is associated with relatively low levels of training and qualification, there is a tradition of 'autodidacts' and hobbyists outside work who are not yet included in the supposedly 'inclusive' learning society of today (although they may have been picked up to some extent by the findings of the 1997 National Adult Learning Survey that while the frequency of vocational learning in Wales was very low compared to regions of England, the frequency of non-vocational learning was high: Beinhart and Smith, 1998). Do such learners have to certify their activities, or start to pay an external provider simply to gain recognition?

Our work would therefore provide strong support for a growing acknowledgement among policy makers of the significance of informal learning in the workplace, the family and community settings. The divergence between the way in which workplace training is viewed by many respondents here and that embodied in policy is a cause for concern. Certainly, this divergence appears to have been almost unaffected by the introduction of competence-based National Vocational Qualifications, as well as the other initiatives by government and firms to raise the profile of training. Some respondents may prefer non-certificated, and non-formal approaches to personal learning, and many of their stories of significant personal development do not involve formal participation as such. This finding is important, both because of the importance of providing non-threatening 'taster' courses for returners, and more importantly because of its implications for an inclusive learning society. The reality of a learning society with a far wider spread of participation than currently could be achieved by simply recognising the validity and relevance of informal learning episodes. However, this would not accord with the government policy of pursuing Lifelong Training Targets, seen as a vital indicator of the 'human capital' necessary to attract inward investment to South Wales (see Chapter Nine).

EIGHT

The learning society and the economic imperative

This chapter returns to a fuller consideration of one of the two major strands cited in the push towards a learning society (see Chapter One). This is the view that lifelong learning is increasingly necessary for work-related reasons, what we term here the 'economic imperative'. Despite rhetorical acknowledgement of the relevance of lifelong learning to issues of social inclusion, it remains the case that recent government policies in this area are rooted in this 'economic imperative' (Gorard, 2000a). This is a view based on human capital theory (or, more correctly, a rather crude version of it) that investment in education and training leads to a 'return' both for the individual and for society. It is tied up with somewhat confused notions of contingent labour, trainability, careership, and the value of human resources in a global economy. Such notions have been expressed in a variety of policy and discussion documents. The view is so pervasive it has even been cited in some NIACE publications, such as the *Learning country*, where it is stated that "lifelong learning is a means to improve economic performance".

Contingent labour

One of the main arguments underlying the need for lifelong learning, and multi-skilling, is that 'jobs for life' have gone. In this account, workers who previously worked in single occupations for their working lives, now face the prospect of several job changes. It is possible to use our individual work and training histories to assess the scale of this trend towards 'contingent labour'. If we ignore the current spell for each individual, whose length we clearly cannot measure yet, there is actually an *increase* over 50 years in the average length of work episodes, and therefore a trend *away* from contingent labour.

For a more detailed analysis, we define contingent working as a period of self-employment, or full- or part-time employment lasting less than one year before a change of state. Our 1,104 respondents reported 3,249 distinct economic episodes, distinguished solely by a change of state (for example, from government training to full-time employed, or from one type of job to another). Of these episodes 348 (or nearly 11%) were contingent in nature. These were predictably less common in full-time jobs, and more common in part-time and temporary jobs.

If we ignore the current spell, there are then insufficient episodes for reliable analysis in the 1990s. People may be more likely to have short-term jobs early in life and the sample increases in average age over time. To minimise

Table 8.1: Frequency of contingent work by decade (%)

Decade	1950s	1960s	1970s	1980s
Contingent work episodes	7	12	10	10
Male	1	5	5	7
Female	13	13	9	13

any resultant age bias, we use only episodes when people are aged 21 or over (thus also losing the figures for the 1940s). There are now only 142 contingent episodes in total, showing whatever else that contingent labour has not been a common experience for adults in South Wales. Of course, it might be argued that they are under-represented (not reported) in this retrospective study, but if this is so, it is more likely to affect older people (that is, short episodes are less likely to be reported long after the event than recent ones). This makes it doubly surprising that there is no indication of an increase in these contingent episodes over time (Table 8.1). In fact the peak was in the 1960s.

The same conclusion is reached if we consider the more entrenched situation of consecutive periods of contingent labour, where people move from one short-term state to another. When the figures are separated by gender, it appears that short-term work may have increased slightly for men after the 1950s, but has held relatively constant for women. However, the figures for men are still complicated in the 1950s by the impact of military conscription and then National Service.

What these figures mean is that we can present no clear evidence that contingent labour has increased over the period of our study. Although any increase, if it exists, may have occurred only very recently, this analysis also begins to illustrate how difficult it would be to establish this rigorously given that any analysis cannot use current episodes of work.

Whereas just over 30% of all work episodes involved some training (even if only induction or for health and safety), the figure for contingent episodes was only 13%. Given that contingent labour was more commonly reported by those who had left school at the earliest opportunity, without moving to any training, it appears that training may not be needed for flexibility. But this is not a new phenomenon, and is observable in each decade of our study. Therefore, one of the central justifications for creating this new learning society may be an illusion, but one that unduly affects the nature of that society with its policy focus on the young and the employed.

Trends in work-based training

Perhaps the next, and easiest, question to answer is 'Has work-based training increased over time?' The answer is no. The Future Skills Wales Survey (1998) reports that half of Wales' residents had undertaken some training or learning during the previous 12 months. This was mostly related to their current job, and therefore over-represents the young, full-time employed, and those already with qualifications. In this way, the survey agrees with other recent studies that characterise those liable to be participants in education or training (Fryer, 1997; Kennedy, 1997; DfEE, 1998; Tight, 1998a). According to the Labour Force Survey, work-based training (in the previous four weeks) does not appear to be increasing over time in Wales (Figure 8.1).

This conclusion is confirmed by our survey results, which show instead a decline over a longer period in substantive work-based, especially employer-funded, training in Wales. It is being replaced by state-funded, off-the-premises provision, usually immediately after the completion of compulsory schooling. In 1996, for example, only just over half of all employers in Wales provided any training at all; and it is worth recalling that however large the company, this training could be for just one employee (Welsh Office, 1995a). Most of this provision was confined to large companies (200+ employees) and to public service organisations. Therefore, there was less in areas such as Mid Glamorgan, where fewer of these companies exist.

The scale of work-based training in the UK may be relatively small, with employees averaging only seven days training of all types per year (Deloitte Haskins and Sells, 1989). However, even this average figure is misleading since in fact over half of all employees in that study received no training. There is also evidence that less training was available in 1994 than 1987. Park (1994) suggests that some 19% of the workforce aged 16-54 were involved in some vocational learning at the time of the survey, and that a further 29% had undertaken some in the past three years. Thus a total of 48% had been recently involved in vocational training and were classified as learners, so it seems that half of the population gets some training and half does not. Most

Figure 8.1: Proportion of workforce receiving work-based training during the last four weeks: Wales (%)

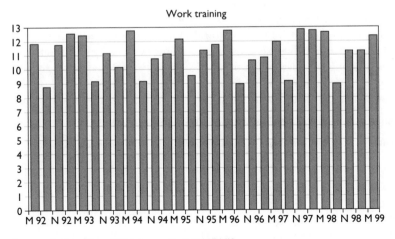

Source: calculated from LFS data supplied via NOMIS

of the learners were in work, and many of those in work were learners. Those employed in higher grades are both more likely to receive training and to be from a higher occupational class background. Trainees tend to be higher qualified and have a higher income as well as being younger (Maguire et al, 1993).

According to the OECD, job-training programmes since the 1970s have failed to stop increasing unemployment, especially in the UK and Sweden (Nash, 1999). There has anyway been a drop in the number of adults doing work-based training in Britain recently (TES, 1998a). DfEE figures for June 1998 show a drop of 8% in training (for young people) compared to the previous year. The drop is 13% down in starting training schemes, and 52% down in starting training in the three months to June. For older adults, the drop is 34% down on the previous year, and 74% down on 1994.

Employers report being aware that the skills of their employees are important, yet they are not generally prepared to pay for them (Future Skills Wales, 1998). Around 20% of employers admit to not providing adequate training, but this figure is disputed by their employees who suggest it is more like 50%. Despite the emphasis of National Targets, employers do not rate qualifications as important, and employees often see them as purely a means to get a job. Policy makers are anyway giving employers a dwindling role in the provision of lifelong learning, partly because there is actually often limited demand for higher level skills in the workplace (Keep, 2000). Despite programmes such as Investors in People, it remains the case that part-time, older, lower status, and less qualified employees, especially in SMEs, get very little non task-specific training.

In over 60% of the work episodes in our survey, the employee reported no training at all. In many cases, these employees moved from apparently unrelated jobs, such as from coalmining to shop management, with no 'training'. This confirms that a considerable amount of learning goes on in the workplace that is not reported as training (see Chapter Seven).

Most significantly the incidence of formal work-related training has not increased since 1945 (Table 8.2), remaining at around 39% of all work episodes that involved some sort of training (this lack of change is also evident when the length of employment is taken into account by dividing the number of formal training episodes by the number of months employed, for example). However, the training itself has become briefer, and the only growth in the types of training identified in the survey was in health and safety training,

Table 8.2: Frequency of work-based training by decade (%)

Decade	Any training	One day	One week
1950s	40	25	18
1960s	41	27	18
1970s	40	26	17
1980s	36	21	11
1990s	40	24	12

which has grown consistently from an occurrence in 15% of jobs in the 1940s to 28% in the 1990s. Some other types of training, such as short in-service courses (23%) and induction/initial training (18%), have remained completely constant over time. What has apparently decreased over time is the frequency of training reported by the learner as enhancing 'employability' – the type that might be considered useful by another employer. This type of training was never common, but has now declined from 9% to 7% of the episodes.

The availability of training in any episode is predictable, with an accuracy of around 80%, using similar modelling techniques to those used for the lifelong trajectories in Chapters Four to Six. Many of the socio–economic determinants of training are similar to those for general trajectories (as would be expected). The probability of training rises with an individual's level of qualification at the end of initial education, and is around twice as high for those in professional, managerial and skilled manual work as in all other episodes. Training is much more common for young males. The education and training history of family members is also a clear predictor, as is speaking Welsh, and geographic mobility. Training is more common for those with supervisory roles, in full-time jobs, within larger organisations in the public sector.

Work-related training is skewed towards jobs undertaken earlier in life, and it occurs more often in lengthy spells of employment and this is especially true of both more prolonged training and transferable training. On average, people do not receive training that enhances their employability after the age of 22. The training that is reported most recently is shorter than training in the past (and it is interesting to reflect that if this signifies a problem of recall of shorter episodes in the past, it would mean that all forms of job-related training have actually declined since 1945). There has been a relative decline in the frequency of any type of training episode lasting five or more days from 18% in the 1950s to 11% in the 1980s. This agrees, in part, with the report of the DfEE (1995) that shows that the increase in job-related training from 1980 to 1994 has been mainly in courses off-the-job on employers' premises lasting less than a week. It is also interesting that despite an overall increase in attempted certification after training, the increase has only happened in relation to short episodes lasting less than five days. In the longer episodes, there is no increase in attempted certification. When this is examined as a proportion of all work episodes it is clear that certification has declined along with substantive training (Table 8.3).

To sum up the survey results on formal training in work: health and safety training is increasing and this short employer-based course is typical of the growth in training over time. New training is often brief, prescribed by law,

Table 8.3: Percentage attempting qualification after training

Decade	1940s	1950s	1960s	1970s	1980s	1990s
Attempted qualification	10	9	9	8	6	5

non-transferable, and non-certificated (at least according to our respondents' interpretation of this term). The financial burden has shifted from employers towards government agencies (via Youth Training schemes for example). It has also shifted to the taxpayer via schools and colleges, since when the analysis is expanded to consider learning outside the workplace the chief change over time has been in extended initial education. The relative lack of substantive training in work episodes suggests that informal learning still has a key role for individuals adapting to new work situations, and that this may be becoming more important but probably less highly-regarded. Again, such an interpretation is certainly supported by many of the stories from the other phases of the project, such as those of the trainers themselves as presented in the next section.

Trainers' accounts

The introduction of a comprehensive system of nationally recognised vocational qualifications (NVQs) and the development of Modern Apprenticeships have reportedly made training more attractive to employers. Initially, many employers were suspicious of their worth, while training officers complained that the system was still too bureaucratic. One employer said "the customers like to hear about it but it hasn't made any tangible difference to our workforce". Her specific comment on NVQs was "it looks good on paper but hasn't delivered the sort of workforce we are looking for". Several respondents referred to local or national 'scandals' in accreditation of NVQs, and one trainer described how the first that one batch of 50 workers heard of NVQs was when they were photographed receiving their award for the local press. He felt that with only one NCVQ visit per year many companies would take the risk of 'sharp-pencilling', in order to be able to say that they were competent. Some employers felt that the particular training routes offered did not suit their own training requirements. However, in a constantly changing working environment NVQs constituted a convenient method of retraining workers that also attracted government funding.

Employers stressed that it was becoming progressively harder to recruit young people into manufacturing and industry. It was difficult to get schools to promote careers in industry, which is perceived as 'dirty' and 'old fashioned'. Whereas, in the 1950s and 1960s, the brightest working-class males went into apprenticeships, this was no longer the case in the 1990s. This cohort is more likely to go on to further and higher education, and industry has found it increasingly difficult to attract the 'middle ability' band.

The demise of the Manpower Services Commission was not welcomed. Personnel from the subsequent Training and Enterprise Councils (TECs) were perceived as too Civil Service orientated with little understanding of the training needs of industry. Their financing of training was seen as inflexible, particularly in relation to age criteria, and favouring the young. It remains to be seen whether, with the demise of the TECs and their replacement by ELWa (Education and Learning, Wales), this improves. In many cases TECs did not even provide information. A training manager in a Neath company repeatedly sought contact on the New Deal. The problem was they took his name, promised to get in touch and he heard no more.

> "That worries me.... I would have thought the TEC would be clamouring for organisations such as this size to help out, but when they don't even bother to return the phone call. It makes me wonder really. A lot of hype but you hear nothing."

Many jobs, perhaps most jobs, do not require multi-skilling or even mono-skilling. They remain low-skill jobs on the shopfloor, open to anyone without qualifications. A training manager for a manufacturing company near Neath points out how easy it is to get workers:

> "The people who apply are predominantly female, and when I say apply there's a lot of word of mouth from the people who work here. They tell their mothers or their sisters or their cousins. 'OK there's jobs going at XXXX' and that's the way we tend to recruit.... I mean we have entire families working here.... The people we employ on the shopfloor they don't particularly need any skills to get the job. What we're looking for here is ... a positive attitude to work. It is very repetitive work. At most an operative will do three minutes of work and then do it again.... The fact that they're working here probably means that they didn't achieve that much at school. In general, they are people who would have left school with the minimum level of bad GCSEs."

Needless to say, this company does not experience a skills shortage, although a few engineers have left for larger rivals and higher pay.

Another respondent who does not recognise the apparent skills shortages he reads about in monthly bulletins from head office is on the Training Board for the construction industry. Companies like British Steel (as it then was) had "in excess of 700 applicants every year across the two sites for 40 odd positions. So that means you can really pick and choose.... It gives us the opportunity to take the best". An engineering firm from Neath still runs a traditional apprenticeship scheme. According to the manager, this is relatively unchanged in style since 1946. They have tried the modern scheme with one trainee but do not intend to continue:

> "Because we're not convinced about sending someone to college for a year. We can usually set apprentices something useful to do from the first week.... Once we take on an apprentice as an improver and ultimately as a craftsman [no women], they stay with us. The reason for that is because the apprentices we get here in the first place have nearly always been rejected by Sony or some bigger outfit."

The view of work-based training from outside industry is somewhat different. A local college principal believes that firms are actually doing less training now than in the quite distant past, and the reason is that they are unwilling to pay for it:

> "They don't pay, they're not as willing to pay as they used to be going back a long time age, since the Training Boards were closed down things have been far more difficult.... A lot of them [small and medium-sized firms] are really working at the margin.... You know the exporting firms locally on the trading estate are finding it very, very hard going because of the strength of the pound at the moment. Most of them are losing money but they hope that the tide will eventually turn. Well at that stage, as I'm sure you're aware, training is often the one that goes, gets the lowest priority.... One of the [problems] is the high turnover of companies on the industrial estate ... there was that period when firms used to come into South Wales for the grants. Pick up the grant and at the end of four years just go back to wherever they came from."

All trainers commented on the 'quality' of trainees. One said "the problem now is that people want is to train kids but the calibre of trainee just isn't coming forward". Numeracy and literacy levels were low and were perceived as getting worse. The consensus was that this was largely because training was seen as a second class option compared to going on to further education. Sixth forms, colleges and the Modern Apprenticeship Scheme, for example, are all seen as competing for the same batch of students in each cohort, with the students often deciding on grounds of prestige rather than long-term outcomes or suitability. Consequently, training organisations tend to attract the lowest achievers. By and large, they are also excluded from promoting training in schools, and their material is frequently discarded or returned. This was put down to the financial pressures on schools and colleges to retain their numbers on roll.

Some trainers are 'bitter' about these developments. They see colleges as unable to deliver 'real' work-based training but better able to attract TEC funding. TECs (now part of ELWA) are seen as 'out of touch' with the needs of training and unwilling to listen to trainers. Some trainers saw the fault lying more with the Welsh Office (now the National Assembly for Wales). Even those youngsters who start off in training are often attracted away from the scheme by the salaries available from a short-term contract at an employer such as Bosch or Sony. Some employers may be using the training schemes as a subsidised selection process, and the trainees come from a culture in which parents see training as purely a 'stepping stone to a job'. So if a job is available, why train? Short-term economic benefits to the family may be paramount. This view is reflected in our historical analysis, in which work and training were seen to be mutually exclusive alternatives. Training was only considered until a job was available.

Another adviser feels that some trainers are inadvertently doing a disservice, especially when dealing with a certain kind of factory, perhaps using low-skill, low–wage workers.

> "Some local firms have a pattern of advertising jobs just at the time the CoE kids leave at Easter. The kids take the job but I know for a fact the week before Christmas those kids will be back with us right? It's a pattern. Another problem we're getting is like with the training centre up there ... young persons will go and work with factories like that, and then they [trainers] will go into the factories and say 'Have you got a young person starting?... Well can we sign them up for NVQs?'... Well at the end they'll drop them off and say 'Well you've got your qualification' and that's it. An NVQ and they don't want them any more, so what do we do then? Because they've already been on a scheme, got an NVQ2, there's nothing more we can do for them.... They [policy makers] say we want everyone on the workforce NVQed, so the trainers are going out and looking for them.... If the Training Centre didn't do that ... or if there was a problem and they dropped out ... and were made redundant ... at least you've got the training to put them on.... The trouble is it gets training a bad name with people. They only remember the bad things."

Another view from a trainer was that the training system was riddled with widespread corruption. Students were being 'signed off' for NVQ modules when they had not completed the units, and encouraged to copy other students' workbooks, and this means that although some "would have made it eventually", some are "not up to it". "At the very least there should be witness testimony". This trainer has very strong opinions on the value of current vocational qualifications, arguing that NVQs are meaningless as a guide for recruitment because "they can't be trusted". Presumably he would make the same comments about apparent progress towards National Training Targets, and he would be supported in this by the views of the principals of local further education colleges.

The further education colleges themselves were under the same sort of pressures. College Principals all agreed that their biggest problem was finance. Every year they were expected to recruit more students and widen their range of courses, while having their funding constantly cut back by the TECs. The 1990s have therefore been characterised by constant expansion in the face of increasing financial uncertainty. This has led to criticisms, especially from local careers advisers, that colleges are totally dominated by 'bums on seats', taking anyone willing to come, even if this is not the most appropriate move for the individual. Few actively engage with the learning process or find employment afterwards, and this has an effect on those who might gain from the courses available:

> "They get on the bus on their first day of college and they find the same 'louts' on the bus, performing and shouting, that they had to put up with every day of their school careers. And when they come back to

me and ask me why this is I can't give them an answer. They've had enough of them in school holding them back ... most kids who go to college end up on the dole. It's a generational cycle that they are caught up in."

The economic imperative

There are, it appears, two major problems with the economic imperative underlying the learning society. As we have seen, it is based on at least one false premise, is not working out in practice, and appears to be in conflict with the social inclusion motive. Policy documents such as the Dearing, Kennedy and Fryer reports give priority to vocational learning, putting the blame on non-participants, and threatening them with social/economic exclusion (Tight, 1998b). In 1998, a mature student, who returned to education aged 50 to take a degree, applied for teacher training. He was refused a loan by the Student Loans Company because he was too old, presumably having too little of his working life left to be 'worth' the human capital investment (TES, 1998b). Stories such as these illustrate better than any argument the failings of the economic argument in terms of social inclusion.

For the individual, there is some doubt whether education and training pay off in strictly economic terms. Although a common goal of many economic studies of training is to relate learning to earnings, their findings are not clear-cut (McNabb and Whitfield, 1994). In the short term, the employment rates of those staying on in post-compulsory education, or undertaking Youth Training are no better than those making a traditional transition to the labour market at 16 (Roberts et al, 1991). Most vocational qualifications, and academic examinations such as GCSEs taken after the age of 16 produce no return on the investment of time and opportunity costs. There is no personal economic return on any qualification less than HNC/ HND compared to those with no qualifications (NIACE, 1994), and no lifelong return in earnings on any vocational qualification at all. In fact, Greenhalgh and Stewart (1987) estimate that training only has any impact for the first four weeks after its completion in terms of individual earnings and promotion. The value of training depreciates rapidly over time anyway, and the quality, level and duration of much training remains very low (Keep, 1997).

Part of the reason for these findings may be that British employers undervalue vocational training, still preferring to use academic prowess as a predictor of 'trainability' (Whitfield and Bourlakis, 1991). Those who have been successfully educated in the past should be cheaper to train in the future, and since employers see training as an overhead, they concentrate their efforts on the immediately applicable future (Deamer, 1996). Selection for employment is therefore not based on technical competence as much as social attributes such as age, gender and ethnicity, and on the applicant's attitude to work as far as it can be judged (Rees et al, 1992).

There has been a growth of semi-skilled and unskilled jobs in South Wales, such that most manufacturing jobs now require only very limited skill. Almost anyone would be capable of doing them after a brief period of on-the-job training. Claims of skill shortages by employers should anyway be treated with caution. It is not always possible to distinguish between a shortage of skilled applicants for jobs because they do not exist, or because no one with the appropriate skills wishes to apply for the conditions on offer. The skills needed to get a job now encompass the behaviour of labour, including punctuality, reliability and commitment, but these are not the kinds of skills that usually spring to mind when politicians and economists talk of skills shortages. Few firms find much weakness in the basic education of their recruits that needs correcting for them to work effectively (Pettigrew et al, 1989). Almost as many British employers are worried about providing their workers with transferable skills and so running the risk of losing them to competitors, as report being prompted to train workers in order to maintain competitiveness in their market (Deloitte Haskins and Sells, 1989).

When Siemens and Samsung opened plants in North East England, or LG invested in South Wales, they chose areas of the UK that had three characteristics in common: high unemployment/cheap labour, relatively low qualifications in terms of the UK population, and substantial incentives in the form of regional grants. When Siemens and Fujitsu pulled out of the North East, and LG threatened to pull out of Wales, they did not do so because their potential workforce was not educated enough, and they did not move their investment to an area with greater human capital. In time of recession (in this case in the Pacific), the factories close. It is a myth 'that education alone can create economic prosperity and social justice for all' (Coffield, 1998). So for any community there must be considerable doubt whether a highly qualified (and perhaps highly paid) workforce is actually attractive to many investors.

In the ETAG report (now accepted as the basis for policy by all four main parties in the National Assembly for Wales) the purported evidence for skills shortage in Wales is presented first in terms of the relative lack of qualifications (ETAG, 1998, p 11). Of course this is a nonsense. Skills are not the same as qualifications and, as we have seen, there are considerable numbers of unqualified but skilled and even multi-skilled people in Wales. The key logical error underlying this plan is exposed in paragraph 6, page 12. It says "people who are better qualified are more likely to be employed and earning higher wages.... Lifting qualifications is therefore a vital ingredient in increasing prosperity within Wales". While there is plenty of evidence from our study and others that socio-economic class is a key determinant of participation in education and training, the plan insists that it is the education/qualification that leads to an individual's economic success. Nowhere is there much evidence for this proposition. In fact, as we saw in Chapter Four, when potential explanatory variables are entered into models of participation in the order that they occur in life (gender and year of birth before level of schooling before area of residence and current occupation and so on) then an individual's level of qualification and economic success can both be predicted very accurately using information only about their parents.

A second problem also appears at this stage, since the plan admits that 'competitor' economies are increasing their level of qualifications as well. The implication in the plan is that it is actually the *relative* qualification of Welsh workers that is crucial. A moments thought here reveals the contradiction in this reasoning. It might be possible for all of the alleged deficits to be overcome in Wales (for example, all students gain NVQ level 2) but for Wales still to lag behind its competitors in terms of paper qualifications.

When the plan speaks of 'skills shortages' the reader tends to think of a shortfall in technical and scientific areas. These are the shortages used at the start of the section (p 12). Terms used include 'electronics', 'aeronautics', 'engineers and technicians', 'design and research teams', and 'high value manufacture'. These all sound plausible areas for shortages, and many readers will have heard evidence of poaching of skilled craftspeople by new companies since there are, almost inevitably, insufficient numbers of these in the area when the new company first arrives (since highly skilled workers are unlikely to remain unemployed in one area when they have the choice of moving to a job elsewhere). On reflection though it is not clear why commentators would expect excess skilled workers to stay in an area with no appropriate job in the hope that a new firm may require them. As has always happened in Wales (as elsewhere), people who are trained for jobs that are not available locally will simply move elsewhere. In the same way, as the plan admits, temporary skills shortages in Wales are addressed by moving people here from England or further afield. As the plan accepts on page 13, the mobility of labour within the EU is increasing and so the phenomenon of skills following skilled jobs is likely to grow. It is certainly more likely than that a high density of skilled people can be maintained in one area without work to tempt potential investors.

The report then introduces the results of the 'Future Skills Wales' project, and in doing so destroys the 'skills shortage' argument being built up (such as it is). As shown by this large-scale survey of employers in Wales, employers do not actually want 'skills' as the average reader might interpret them, and as they have been introduced above. In fact, the top six skills cited are not technical at all (but things like 'team-working', and 'reliability'). Of course, this finding could represent a flaw in the research, which is that by aggregating responses it presents the lowest common denominator. Or, it could be that employers tend to emphasise not the skills they require but those they are currently most critical of (Hesketh, 1998). Or it could be that employers are not good judges of their own future skills requirements (Spielhofer, 1996; Stasz, 1997). Or it could be that the prognosis on page 12 was simply wrong and the employers are right. Perhaps there are enough skilled craftspeople in Wales, but not enough employees able 'to follow instructions' (p 13). Whichever version is preferred, the notion of skills shortages becomes much more complex than is portrayed in the plan. Different groups are talking about different things, and nowhere is this addressed or even acknowledged. It is clear that qualifications do not impress most employers, and are rated as second to last in order of importance, but again the plan that otherwise makes so much of the importance of qualifications does not even acknowledge this contrary evidence.

Conclusion

This chapter is not able to present much clear evidence in favour of the economic strand of the learning society. The initial condition of needing more flexible labour does not seem to have materialised. Work-based training is not rising, is not being funded by employers in the main, and is predictable to a large extent from long-term social and family characteristics of each individual. Using the accounts of local trainers themselves we have seen how successive policies have not actually been conducive to real increases in training opportunities (at least for those currently excluded), and a case study of policy making from documents tends to support this view. In the next chapter we look in more detail at two major policies intended to increase participation in lifelong learning.

It can be argued that the current economic focus of adult learning detracts from its potentially transformative nature for the individual, and for society, regardless of later financial reward. In a sense, the call for lifelong learning has been reduced to the simple claim: education and training are good because they earn you money. This is in contrast to the more complex, and perhaps more realistic, education and training are good because they are fulfilling (and they *could* earn you money).

NINE

The impact of policies to widen participation

with Neil Selwyn

This chapter outlines our emerging evidence on the impact of a range of current policies to deal with the problems in patterns of participation, as they have been described so far. One group of these policies relies heavily on increased use of technology. They argue, in essence, that information and communications technologies (ICT) allow learning opportunities to transcend the physical barriers to access, such as time and space (Selwyn et al, 2001). Another group of policies is based on setting and working towards national targets for participation in lifelong learning.

In some ways, these two examples of policy initiatives are illustrative of the wider approach that is currently being adopted towards the fostering of lifelong learning in Britain. Hence, in both instances, the 'problem' of relatively low levels of participation in adult learning is seen to lie in facilitating or encouraging the activities of individuals. If 'barriers' to participation can be removed and the 'pay-off' in qualifications made more transparent, then – it is presumed – the 'problem' will be removed, or at least substantially ameliorated.

There is, of course, some truth here. Certainly, the emergent evidence with respect to the two policy initiatives discussed in what follows suggests that their impacts are generally positive. However, what is equally clear is that they fail to address the fundamental determinants of patterns of participation in adult learning, as these have been analysed in the preceding chapters.

The technical fix

If the large-scale non-participation in lifelong learning described in previous chapters is caused chiefly by physical barriers (as described in Chapter Six, for example), then overcoming those barriers will lead to a widening of participation. Some policy makers now propose to overcome the barriers of time, travel and opportunity at a stroke and universally by using technical means, such as digital broadcast and the Internet. Learning in the new 'information age' is seen to be very different from before. This is the thrust being taken by the New Labour government through initiatives such as the University for Industry (UfI) and learndirect, as well as the many more localised and specialised ICT-based learning solutions, such as the Digital College of Wales (Gorard et al, 2000a). If their claims are to be believed, the information revolution is to be primarily a *learning* revolution. For example:

> ... the University for Industry will help deliver the widest available access to new forms of learning. The new opportunities of the new information age must be open to all – the many, not just the few. (Central Office of Information, 1998, p 1)

Although other media such as the telephone, fax and paper-based materials were intended as integral parts of the programme, the dual use of digital television (DTV) and the internet were presented as fundamental to the successful implementation of the Digital College of Wales (WDC) in its official launch literature:

> Anyone interested in learning new skills – vocational or non-vocational would be able to benefit and exciting and effective access procedures would be put in place to attract and support traditionally non-participating groups such as the young unemployed and adult returners. Television is a powerful medium and can prove an effective access point. It was foreseen that the service would be particularly useful for job-seekers, those seeking new directions and challenges early or late in life and those seeking open learning opportunities. (Wales Digital College, 1998, p 15)

As Professor Bob Fryer (a member of the UfI Board) exhorted at the business launch of the WDC, in attracting adult learners the initiative could not be seen to merely recruit the "usual suspects ... this would not only be a failure but deeply hypocritical" (Fryer, 1999).

Our study of these initiatives suggests that such a failure is only too likely, reinforcing our belief that the actual role of physical barriers to participation may be much less than in the popular and, indeed, policy makers' imagination. In our empirical research, we have identified a number of reasons for the early failure:

- The initial marketing of these schemes as virtual 'colleges' and 'universities' has done little to encourage those for whom the formal structures of education hold no appeal.
- There has been a 'turf war' between the actors involved in setting up the various components of the whole.
- The ICT model of learning has been primarily about information transmission and the registration of users, rather than genuinely transformative experiences. Users feel that they miss out on the vital 'social' and 'face-to-face' elements of adult education.
- Many of these problems stemmed in part from technological difficulties,

caused by 'over-hyping' of capability and the need to have schemes up and running quickly.

- These technical problems extended even to the telephone advisory systems.
- None of the organisations we studied had made any serious attempt to measure their success in widening participation (not even recording basic user characteristics such as gender and occupation in some cases). They measured their own success primarily in hit rates and viewing figures.
- There was a widespread ignorance within the organisations of the actual living conditions of those they were intending to include (as exemplified by assurances that second telephone lines are cheap to install when most of those currently not participating in any education or training do not even have access to a shared payphone at their home).
- These initiatives were anyway overlaid onto existing structures of educational provision, partly as a result of the turf wars over funding mentioned earlier. Our respondents felt that the policy of drop-in centres and distributed access learning was a sham. However it had started, it was being used by traditional colleges to attract traditional paying students, rather than as a valid learning experience in its own right.
- Above all, what is clear from our survey and interviews is that ICT approaches to learning are simply recycling existing users of further and higher education. In our case study of an online training course, for example, all of the registrants had a degree, many had higher degrees, most worked in the computing industry anyway, and *all* were already lifelong learners using our classification from Chapter Four.

The future for the technical fix

The policy approaches outlined here are forming the basis of long-term 'information age agendas' for politicians and educationalists alike. We can, therefore, be certain that the virtual education approach is here to stay, if for no other reason than that ICT-based education is now proving to be big business around the world. In the US alone, it is predicted that over two million students are taking online courses as part of a worldwide online learning marketplace expected to be worth US$50 billion by 2005 (Dumort, 2000). With multinational corporations such as Microsoft actively involved in such programmes, virtual education does not look set to fade away quietly just because it may not be fulfilling its socially inclusive aims.

Too much time, effort and resources have probably already been invested in ICT-based lifelong learning for future governments of any political persuasion to deviate substantially from the approaches described. While the New Labour government regularly proclaim their new ICT policies to be 'breaking new ground' (Blair, 2000) the political predilection for using ICT as primary means of establishing a learning society was, in fact, already set. The continuity in both theoretical approach and intended outcome can be seen in the latest raft of lifelong policies in 2001. For example, while the aim of the Learning and

Skills Council is to "overcome the false divisions between our foundation learning and the post-compulsory system" (National Skills Agenda, 2001, p 5), their logic remains firmly that of simple human capital theory. Apparently "higher skills lead to higher earnings" (p 5), "matching people's aspirations to the skills employers need will be a key priority" (p 6), and we need "to strengthen the link between learning and employment" (p 6). Yet the same plan argues that ICT-based developments such as the UfI "will offer flexible, accessible opportunities to learn online to a wide audience including some of our most disadvantaged communities" (p 7).

> ICT can play a key role in breaking down the barriers to learning that people face, offering new opportunities to access learning for the most disadvantaged and those who have not traditionally taken up learning opportunities. (New Opportunities Fund, 2000, p 5)

We are confident that, as they stand, these initiatives face more or less the same enduring problems and the limited success in widening participation as the examples examined in this book. We know that participation in adult learning has not improved over past years, despite considerable political activity intended to promote lifelong learning (NIACE, 2000). More than half of the respondents in the most recent NIACE survey of lifelong learning stated that they were not likely to take part in any formal learning in the future, and the systematic differences between these non-participants and the likely participants is growing in terms of occupational class, employment and prior education. Thus, as we have illustrated, whether ICT-based or not, the problems of establishing an inclusive learning society in the information age are deep rooted and stretch far beyond issues of accessibility, time and distance.

The sheer technical scope of establishing and operating an ICT centre in the South Wales valleys, for instance, having to rely on sporadically reliable network connections and not always perfect software, belies the rhetoric of the seamless 'network society' and the provision of 24-hour online learning 'anytime, anyplace, anywhere'. As always, ICT is not perfect and, despite inevitable improvements these will lead to further teething troubles. Audience demand for DTV has anyway remained low throughout the 1990s and into the first years of the 21st century; replicating the previous failure of satellite and cable television to establish more than a minority hold in the UK marketplace. Thus, as Corcoran (1999, p 67) observes:

> ... on the face of it, DTV would seem to be a technology for which consumer demand is weak at best. As a production, delivery and display innovation, its deployment is more obviously driven by a technological rather than audience imperative.

The impact of technical shortcomings were amply illustrated in our interviews with those learners already using ICT-based provision. Faced with the considerable limitations of a real-life website via a real-life Internet connection on a real-life computer, the promises of constantly streamed video footage and interactive access to online tutors suddenly appeared rather naive. Similarly, the technical problems faced by those learners in distributed learning centres (such as the learndirect centre where the same learner had to use the same computer every day in order for the system to work, where the online tutoring system was unavailable, and where many of the advertised modules did not work), often led to dissatisfaction and disengagement with the learning process (Selwyn and Gorard, 2002).

Significantly, for example, the data within the National Assembly's (2001) Cymru Ar-Lein consultation document show clearly that areas of Wales with low rates of qualification among the population, also have low rates of training and reported learning, and low use of and access to computers. Areas that stand out from comparison across several of these maps are Blaenau Gwent and Neath-Port Talbot (two of the sites for our principal empirical study). It is important for the authors of Cymru Ar-Lein, and the relevant Assembly members, to realise that simply altering one of these problems will not lead to amelioration of the other. The results we have presented in this book do make one thing clear. Simply increasing the availability of computers (and other digital media) will not lead to changes in training and qualifications among current non-participants. What these maps actually show is that ICT is simply replicating, and thereby reinforcing, the existing barriers to inclusion in Wales.

The National Targets for Lifelong Learning

The National Targets for Education and Training in England and Wales include indicators for lifelong learning, and the progress towards the targets set for these indicators has been lauded by politicians and other observers. However, our work in this area reveals how weak the claim is that we can ever adequately measure even the relatively simple, quantitative output targets favoured by UK policy makers (see Gorard et al, 2002a). As far as we can assess, much of the apparent progress towards these targets is actually accounted for by changes in these same indicators at Foundation (school-age) level. In fact, once this is accounted for, there is then very limited evidence that Lifelong Learning targets have had any impact at all (Gorard et al, 2002b).

A coherent and strategic drive towards a comprehensive nationwide system of educational targets began to emerge in the UK from the end of the 1980s and the setting of the National Targets for Education and Training (NETTs). The NETTs were first suggested in the 1989 CBI document *Towards a skills revolution*, which focused on improving the perceived characteristics of the British workforce as "under-educated, under-trained and under qualified" (CBI, 1989). In 1993 an independent employer-led body – the National Advisory Council for Education and Training Targets (NACETT) – was founded to oversee the NETTs, charged with monitoring progress towards achieving the targets, advising the government and 'providing business leadership'. The targets themselves were revised in 1995, and again in 1999 in

Wales. This latter task was given to the Education and Training Action Group for Wales (ETAG). ETAG's *Education and training plan for Wales* (1999) proposed a range of outcome targets for both pre- and post-16 education and training in Wales, building on previous sets of targets suggested in *A bright future: The way forward* (Welsh Office, 1995c), *A bright future: Beating the previous best* (Welsh Office, 1997) and *Learning is for everyone* (Welsh Office, 1998).

In particular, the following qualification-based Lifelong Learning targets were recommended in the 1999 ETAG plan and accepted by the National Assembly for Wales:

- The proportion of adults of working age without qualifications to reduce from some one in four in 1996 to one in seven by 2002 and to fewer than one in eight by 2004.
- The proportion of adults of working age with an NVQ level 2 or equivalent to increase from over five in 10 in 1996 to seven in 10 by 2002 and over seven in 10 by 2004.
- The proportion of adults of working age with an NVQ level 3 or equivalent to increase from some three in 10 in 1996 to approaching five in 10 by 2002 and over five in 10 by 2004.
- The proportion of adults of working age with an NVQ level 4 or equivalent to increase from some one in five in 1996 to over one in four by 2002 and approaching three in 10 by 2004.

School-level indicators derived from the school census, key stage tests, and the public examination boards are used to determine progress towards the foundation targets. There is no equivalent source for the lifelong targets. All of the figures cited in relation to these targets are estimates derived from the Labour Force Survey. There are serious doubts about the comparability of examinations at school between subjects, years, boards and modes (see Gorard, 2001b). Given that the range of supposedly equivalent qualifications in the post-school system is far greater – the UK currently has around 17,500 publicly funded qualifications from 250 awarding bodies – the situation is even worse. The equivalence between different qualifications, such as is used to define the 'levels' of equivalence to NVQs for targets, therefore requires judgement and considerable guesswork (Robinson, 1995).

In the Labour Force Survey (LFS), as in any survey, some respondents reply 'don't know' or 'no answer' when faced with a question about their highest qualification. If these responses are assumed to come equally from all possible responses, and are divided proportionately between the remaining categories, the likely outcome is a bias towards higher qualifications. This is because a contrary assumption would be that those with PhDs, or postgraduate certificates, are more likely to respond and more likely to know what their qualifications are than those with level 1 or no recognised qualifications. For the same reason, if these responses are simply ignored, then the same effect results, since if they had answered the 'don't knows' might have been more common among the lower-level qualifications. If, on the other hand, the assumption is made that 'no response' is equivalent to 'no qualification', the overall population estimates will be biased towards the lower level of qualification, since at least some of the 'no responses' will actually have qualifications. There is no clear basis on which to partition the null responses between these three alternatives. Perhaps the safest assumption is that null responses all represent qualifications below level 2, and should be partitioned between none and level 1 in proportion to the existing frequency of those categories. Official sources currently allocate them proportionately to all other categories (so that at least some of those who do not know are 'awarded' a PhD).

Similar comments can be made about the much larger group (7% of base) classified in the Labour Force Survey as 'other qualifications' (that is, not one of the other named 46 qualification categories). In total as many as 20-25% of cases in the LFS are somewhat arbitrarily allocated to an NVQ equivalent. The potential impact can be seen in Table 9.1 that shows the proportion of the working-age population with level 2 and 3 qualifications according to the LFS. In each case, the first row uses all operational governmental assumptions about non-response, other qualifications, trade apprenticeships, and Scottish qualifications. The second row treats other qualifications as level 1, and non-response as level 1 at best.

Progress towards the targets

We have shown elsewhere how progress towards current targets for lifelong learning is problematic for all indicators (Gorard et al, 2002b). Here, we consider the level 3 target as an exemplar. There has been significant growth towards the level 3 target, but despite previous downwards adjustment as a result of the 1995 and 1999 revisions, the figure for attainment is still a long way short of the proportions envisaged even for 2004 (Figure 9.1).

Even so, using our notion of the two dimensions of time from Chapter Six, if we separate out the improvement due to the training of adults as adults, and the passing of qualified young persons into the workforce we see that it is the latter that accounts for most progress. The proportion of school-leavers with any level of qualification up to level 3 is higher than in the population as a whole and is rising every year. Moreover, the proportion with any level of qualification is lowest among the older age groups. Since 'working-age' is

Table 9.1: Testing the impact of assumptions

	1996	1997	1998	1999
Level 2a (WO)	54.1	55.9	58.9	59.9
Level 2b	48.2	52.0	55.4	56.1
Level 3a (WO)	32.0	33.1	36.7	36.4
Level 3b	29.8	32.1	35.8	35.5

Figure 9.1: Percentage of working-age population with level 3 qualifications

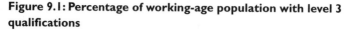
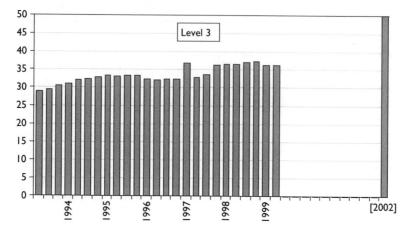

Source: calculated from LFS data supplied via NOMIS

defined as 16-59 or 64, significant 'progress' towards the lifelong targets is being achieved without a single extra adult participating in education or training and gaining qualifications, simply as a consequence of adding qualified school-leavers to the adult population, and losing less qualified adults to retirement. This is what we have called the 'conveyor-belt' effect.

It is also possible to question the actual impact of targets on the growth of related indicators, and to estimate this impact by comparing progress before and after the creation of the NETTs in 1991. Although it is clear that other factors than the targets also differ pre- and post-1991, it is certainly not clear that these policies and interventions since 1991 have been any less, or any more effective (Gann, 1999). Therefore, it is fair, in the first instance, to assume that if the policy of setting targets has been a useful one, then this will be reflected in improved progress in terms of levels of qualifications since the targets were introduced. For example, NACETT (1994) have claimed that 'We have made real progress since the National Targets were launched in 1991', but without making clear against what criterion this progress was measured. In this context it may be noteworthy that the lowest annual growth in the indicator for the original Lifelong Target 3 is in 1996 (actually negative), and the growth in 1998 is otherwise the lowest since 1991 (Table 9.2). The

Table 9.2: Percentage of 21-year-olds with level 3 qualifications: Britain

	1988	1989	1990	1991	1992	1993	1994	1995	1996	1997	1998
L3	27.5	28.6	30.5	30.7	34.7	37.6	40.9	45.0	44.3	48.8	50.3
Change	–	4	7	1	13	8	9	10	-2	10	3

Source: NACETT (1998)

average growth since 1992 has been 7.5% per year, but the average growth until 1992 was 8.7%. Overall then, it is likely that not much has changed as a result of target-setting, but whatever has changed is apparently in the wrong direction.

Progress towards several of the National Targets for Lifelong Learning is slow, and anyway stems from growth in school-based qualifications. The progress that has taken place appears to be unimproved by the setting or monitoring of targets. On the other hand, the targets miss out a great deal of the learning that actually occurs among the adult population, in consequence of their focus on certificated education and training (see Chapter Seven). In part, of course, this reflects the paucity of data. Similarly, there is no strong rationale for the continued exclusion of individuals past the conventional retirement age from the targets, although again data are not readily available. In addition it would be useful to consider ways of rephrasing some targets so that they are expressed as average qualification (or participation) per resident, rather than a proportion meeting a certain threshold (Tymms and Stout, 1999). As currently designed, for example, if an educator and a student work hard together to obtain three GCSE passes rather than two, there is no impact on progress towards achieving targets. If the targets have an impact on qualifications and participation, the current set appear to encourage a focus on those who are on the 'cusp' (for example, between grades D and C at GCSE). The setting of thresholds may also serve progressively to exclude those furthest from it. As any indicator, such as the proportion qualified to level 1, approaches 100% its possession means less and less, while its non-possession can mean more and more. Ironically, progress towards that target then becomes progress away from an inclusive learning society.

Our findings suggest a rather stark disjuncture between the appearance and reality of target-setting in current British educational policy. On the one hand, the seeming strength of the targets as a policy instrument derives precisely from the 'scientific' certainties expressed in their exclusively quantified form (van Herten and Gunning-Schepers, 2000). It may be that the greatest impact of adopting the National Targets has been in the presentation within the public sphere of changes in the educational system, rather than any direct measurement of them. Successive administrations have therefore been able to use the National Targets as an apparently unambiguous (because quantified) vehicle for presenting a generally (but by no means exclusively) positive picture of rising levels of educational attainment, although the measures embodied in the targets are in fact only partially rooted in the reality of actual educational change. Like the technical fix, simply setting and monitoring targets has not provided a ready solution to the problem of widening participation.

Conclusion

What our brief analyses of these policy initiatives demonstrate are the limitations of current approaches to the creation of a learning society. Clearly, it would be unwarranted to suggest that their impacts are wholly negative.

Undoubtedly, there are people who will take part in adult learning and gain further qualifications in response to these initiatives. However, the overwhelming impression that derives from our analysis is the restricted scope of what is being attempted. Certainly, it is difficult to conclude that policies such as these will bring about the transformations in patterns of participation in adult learning that would be required to produce a learning society.

More significantly, however, the reasons for this lack of ambition in current policy lie in an apparent failure to appreciate fully the nature of the problem that is to be addressed. So long as non-participation in adult learning is conceived of as the product of the 'barriers' that individual learners face or the lack of adequate transparency in the acquisition of qualifications by individuals, then the policy responses are likely to remain relatively shallow. Political pressures to produce a 'quick fix' reinforce this tendency.

Our empirical analysis of the determinants of participation and non-participation in adult education and training paints a very different picture. Here, non-participation is seen to be the outcome of quite fundamental social processes that derive from people's early experiences in their families, schools and wider communities. The 'learner identities' that are created through such early social experience have powerful impacts on subsequent learning. In particular, individual dispositions towards later-life learning (after the immediate post-school phase of transitional participation) reflect the impacts of experiences gained much earlier in people's lives.

This analysis, therefore, suggests the need for a much more thorough-going approach to policies for the development of lifelong learning. In particular, the *continuities* between the ways people experience learning during different phases of their lives needs to be prioritised. Quite simply, it is unhelpful to distinguish, in terms of curriculum and pedagogy, school-based learning from that which takes place during later phases of life (as happens currently). Moreover, fostering learning among adults needs to be seen as one element within a wider range of policies that address issues of social and economic disadvantage. The extent of non-participation is such that unless it is approached in this way not only will policies fail to bring about much greater social inclusion, but also the economic objectives of lifelong learning policies will not be achieved either.

TEN

The prospects for a learning society

The principal aim of this study was to develop a better understanding of the determinants of participation and non-participation in lifelong learning. This involved a close analysis of changes in individual trajectories of participation over time, as well as the detailed consideration of the impacts of regionally and locally specific patterns of social and economic development. While our analysis is, of necessity, based in one economic region it is quite clear that most of the lessons we have drawn for policy making are more generally applicable to the UK and beyond. Our understanding of the role of local factors allows us to separate their impact on lifelong participation from the impact of more general determinants and of individual choices. It is this complexity that would be missed in attempts at explaining the ensuing patterns via individual narratives or universal 'rules' (such as those of simple human capital theory).

Overview of main findings

It is significant that 'non-participants' account for almost a third of respondents, neatly balancing the number of 'lifelong learners'. For this substantial minority of respondents, their experience of lifelong learning ended with initial schooling, which confirms previous accounts of the size of the task confronting policy makers seeking to promote lifelong learning. The full model used to explain the five patterns of participation in lifelong learning includes over 40 independent variables, but the sense of these can be summarised in terms of five broad factors, all of which reflect characteristics of respondents which are determined relatively early during the life course.

Time

When respondents were born determines their relationship to changing opportunities for learning and social expectations. It is significant that respondents with similar social backgrounds from different birth cohorts exhibit different tendencies to participate in education and training.

Place

Where respondents are born and brought up shapes their access to specifically local opportunities to participate and social expectations. Those who have lived in the most economically disadvantaged areas (such as Blaenau Gwent) are least likely to participate in lifelong learning. However, those who have moved between regions are even more likely to participate than those living in the more advantaged localities.

Gender

Men consistently report more formal learning than women. Although the situation is changing, these changes are different for each gender. Women are still less likely to participate in lifelong learning, but are now more likely to be 'transitional learners'.

Family

Parents' social class, educational experience and family religion are perhaps the most important determinants of participation in lifelong learning. Family background is influential in a number of ways, most obviously in material terms, but also in terms of what are understood to be the 'natural' forms of participation.

Initial schooling

Experience of initial schooling is crucial in shaping long-term orientations towards learning; and in providing qualifications necessary to access many forms of further and higher education, as well as continuing education and training later in life. There are important age effects here, however, relating especially to the reorganisation of secondary schooling in the maintained sector.

These results have important implications for policy development. Hence, non-participation is largely a product of the fact that individuals do not see education and training as appropriate for them and these views, in turn, are structured by factors that occur relatively early in life. This suggests that policies that simply make it easier for people to participate in the kinds of education and training that are already available (for example, removing 'barriers' to participation, such as costs, time and lack of childcare) will have only limited impacts. Where a model is constructed to distinguish between those forms of participation that occur immediately after compulsory schooling and those that occur later in life, different factors are highlighted. These results offer important correctives to the conventional view of participation in lifelong learning, and also raise the crucial policy issue of where scarce resources for education and training should be directed, especially given the focus up until now on 'front-loading' investment into initial schooling. Shifting this balance in favour of policies addressed to the determinants of later participation would appear to be more efficient and cost-effective.

The changes over time in patterns of participation raise questions about conceptualisations of the 'learning society' exclusively as a desirable future state, yet to be achieved (as is most commonly the case in contemporary discussions). They discount the possibility that elements of past practice in education and training were superior to the present; or that the development over time of participation in learning may be distinctly non-linear, especially for particular population groups. Certainly, for those men who left school in South Wales during the 1950s and 1960s – a period of full employment, relative affluence and settled welfare state provision – their situation with respect to lifelong learning was significantly better not only than that of their female contemporaries, but also than that of those who have left school during the 1980s and 1990s.

The proportion of the population continuing their full-time continuous education past the minimum school leaving age has increased significantly since 1945, and this has led to a proportionate increase in post-16 qualifications. The proportion of the population not participating in any education or training after 16 has declined, but the proportion returning to education or training after age 21 has also declined in tandem. The frequency of all work-based training has remained relatively constant since 1945. The frequency of employer funded training, training lasting more than four days, and training involving a qualification has declined significantly since 1945. These types of training have been replaced by government funded training, and short uncertificated courses especially in Health and Safety.

Future research

Our findings have already fed into important policy developments, most notably in the formation of a prospective education and training policy agenda for the new National Assembly for Wales, via the researchers' work with the Institute of Welsh Affairs, and links with the then Welsh Office, NIACE, the Digital College of Wales, the then local TECs, and the Welsh Education and Training Action Group. The results have also had a wider dissemination both nationally, to the Treasury for example, and overseas.

Three priorities for future research may be highlighted. First, this study has, we believe, demonstrated the fruitfulness of statistical modelling of the determinants of participation in lifelong learning. These approaches could usefully be applied to the larger data sets that are derived from very large-scale, national panel surveys. Second, this study has emphasised the complexities associated with workplace learning. Detailed studies, preferably based on direct observation, would immeasurably improve understanding of the processes involved here. Third, given the importance of place and mobility as evident in these findings it will be interesting to monitor the impact of new technologies in engaging those who were previously disaffected from the process of education and training. If the conventional view of barriers is correct then access to learning via the University for Industry and others will go a long way to solving the 'problems' of current non-participants, but there are already indications that this may not happen. If so, the fault may not lie with the providers but with the conventional notion of barriers to access.

The learning society: are we nearly there yet?

A learning society is generally seen as a future ideal state, one towards which Britain is or should be striving. However, advocates of greater educational equality and industrial competitiveness are not new (Cropley, 1977). The standard learning society analysis may be too simple, suffering from what Yeomans (1996) calls 'historical amnesia'. We have been here before, as early as blaming the loss of industrial pre-eminence on a failure of the education system in the late 19th century (Rees, 1997). In Britain, many of the policy components of a learning society were described and advocated by the 1919 Smith Report (Lowe, 1970), although few were implemented, perhaps because lifelong education proposals often seem idealistic rather than practical to educational planners (Furter, 1977). Lifelong learning was not perceived as having the economic benefits claimed by some more recent writers. For the 1917 Adult Education Committee, education was the key to a better society. Although there was some emphasis on the economic benefits of learning, a special concern was that education was not simply for personal benefit alone but for the common good. Education should have a collective purpose. However, the report wisely accepted that educational progress does not come from educational reforms alone – in today's terms a learning society cannot be created just by providing more learning – and its recommendations included more leisure time for all, through longer holidays and shorter working hours, sufficient wages, better living conditions, and holidays with pay. It was perhaps when society came closest to achieving these worthwhile goals, in the aftermath of the post-war settlement that South Wales came closest to becoming a learning society. In some respects, change may have been retrograde since.

What emerges very clearly from our study is that the model that currently underpins official versions of the learning society in Britain is not compatible with the realities of actual patterns of participation in lifelong learning and their determinants. Certainly, people make choices about their participation in education and training after school. However, these are not framed exclusively in terms of the economic benefits that will accrue from such participation. Rather, they reflect deep-seated attitudes towards learning in formal settings, such as educational institutions and workplaces. These 'learner identities', in turn, are predominantly formed early in life through the influences of family and the experiences of compulsory schooling.

The high level of predictability about patterns of adult participation suggests that barriers and obstacles to learning such as cost, time and lack of childcare, while genuine, will not be overcome in an ad hoc way. The fact that an individual's social and family background at birth has such an impact on their later life suggests that policy makers may be advised to concentrate on reducing inequalities in society, rather than simply trying to increase the opportunities for everyone to learn. In summary, it is perhaps more likely in trying to create a learning society, that a just society will lead to an increase in participation, than that an increase in educational participation will lead to a just society.

This also suggests, of course, that lifelong learning should mean precisely that. The relationships between initial education and training and developing lifelong learning are highly complex. We have seen, for example, that the considerable growth in participation immediately after the completion of compulsory schooling has not been paralleled by the expansion of continuing participation through life. Whether this changes in the future is dependent on the development of learning careers that extend 'from cradle to grave'. Accordingly, it follows that priority should be given to the facilitation of lifelong progression routes, rather than focusing on *either* initial or continuing education and training (and reflecting this in the organisation of the Civil Service, where 'lifelong learning' actually refers to post-16 formal provision only). Certainly, the current front-loading of public investment into initial schooling is called into question, if the objective is to produce a learning society based on lifelong learning. Moreover, major questions are raised about the appropriateness of a curriculum and associated teaching methods that are driven by criteria of raising standards measured in terms of formal qualifications, if the objective is to produce self-motivated and self-directing learners equipped to participate in learning through adult life.

In addition, our study uncovered a vast amount of learning taking place wholly outside of the formal arena of education and training. It is true there are some indications of a growing acknowledgement among policy makers of the significance of informal learning in the workplace, the family and community settings (for example, Fryer, 1997). However, for these insights to be fully integrated into policy development would require the adoption of a vision of the learning society that continues to encompass the needs of individuals to engage effectively with the world of work, but that extends beyond the current preoccupation with the purported role of human capital in ensuring economic competitiveness.

The two components of participation

Initial post-compulsory participation in education or training appears to be determined to a large extent by an individual's background, more than their experience of initial education. Therefore a particularly good or bad experience of schooling, including success or failure in examinations at 16 or 18, does not seem to make any difference to what is effectively already an individual's learning 'trajectory'. More simply, early educational experience can affect what one participates in between the ages of 16 and 21 but not *whether* one participates. Some people stay on in full-time education after school-leaving age, or move to a job with related training and others do not. It is possible to predict which is which with considerable accuracy simply on the basis of what is known about them when they are born.

On the other hand, later formal learning experiences (such as retraining, mature studentship, or adult education) are more dependent on schooling, perhaps due to the nature of motivation or a learner identity forged by that experience. Many people who 'stay on' in education at 16 never have any further experience of education or training, while many who leave school at 16 but receive no immediate training, still experience formal participation later on in their lives. Although it is true that those who participate at any age are more likely to participate at any other, the link between the stages is a relatively weak one.

What appears to have happened in the 50 or so years since the 1944 Education Act is that initial education has been extended, so that the majority of students continue to participate after the age of 16, and a substantial proportion would now expect to continue to higher education aged 18. However, this has made little discernible difference to their *lifelong* patterns of participation. To some extent, extended initial education has replaced formal job-related training, and to a larger extent, extended education now involves those who in previous generations would never have experienced any formal adult education or training. Unfortunately this experience of extended education is not sufficient by itself to encourage later participation.

By 'extended initial education' we refer to initial schooling and consecutive near-continuous episodes of post-compulsory education or training. The latter includes further and higher education courses taken at the traditional age (with or without a 'gap' year), trade apprenticeships and induction training taken on entering the workforce for the first time, and government programmes for school-leavers such as the New Deal and its predecessors. In this way we hope to distinguish it from later episodes of adult education or training, such as adult evening classes, second- or third-age returners to education, and the in-service training of established workers (to follow).

Despite what we have termed elsewhere the ongoing 'crisis account' of British schooling (Gorard, 2000c) and without wishing to produce an overly complacent attitude, it remains the case that initial education shows significant changes for the better. Progress in the 20th century has led to considerable improvements in social inclusion and opportunities by gender, ethnicity, and class, and these improvements apply to education as much as any other social phenomenon (Mackay, 1999). To admit these improvements is not to deny the existence of the remaining problems, but to help describe the current situation more precisely and so define those problems more closely.

By 'later learning' we refer to episodes of education or training taken after a break from continuous education and training following school-leaving age. The situation here is very different to that in extended initial education. Whereas initial education has grown in length, scale and funding since 1944 and still receives the bulk of political attention in Britain, later participation in education or training has not and does not. Formal adult participation in learning is now less prevalent, and less equally distributed between social groups than it was in the recent past. The decline of adult learning is not immediately obvious to all commentators, and may even be disputed in some quarters. One reason why this relatively simple picture is obscured stems from our notion of the two dimensions of time. Each successive age cohort leaving initial education tends to have a longer education and a higher mean level of qualifications. However, each age cohort also tends to simply retain, rather than improve, their initial education over the remainder of their lives.

Among those aged 38-65, men were three times as likely as women to have completed further study immediately after school, but no more likely to have undertaken any study thereafter. Among those aged 21-37, men were no more likely than women to have completed further study after school, but over four times as likely to have undertaken study thereafter. Therefore over time, initial participation in South Wales has become gender neutral, while later participation now considerably over-represents men. This asymmetry also leads to interesting speculation on the relationship between the two types of participation. It is a commonly held view that later learning episodes are contingent on earlier ones – the accumulation thesis implies that somehow increasing extended initial participation will itself lead to greater participation in later learning. The above finding, and others like it, show that this is not so. Many episodes of extended initial education are instead of, not additional to, the episodes of later-life learning that occurred in previous generations. An unjustified belief in the accumulation thesis may be part of the explanation for the political concentration on initial episodes of learning, and this belief is fostered and reinforced by many practitioners as well as academic researchers.

Overall, the reasons for the discrepancies between initial and later learning may be due to political attention and funding (for example, Low, 2000). Policies to improve education, even those to improve adult education, generally concentrate exclusively on one dimension of time (that is, changes between successive age cohorts). The concern is for 'young people' and their future, and progress stems from the fact that the qualifications of each cohort are better than previous cohorts. Very rarely are major policy initiatives, and even more rarely funding, designed to improve the education of adults while they are adults (but only to make sure that future adults are better educated). And even on these rare occasions then the focus is on the employed and the employable, rather than the life course. One such recent 'big' national policy for lifelong learning has been the creation of, and attempted progress towards National Targets for Education and Training. The targets in England and Wales include several for lifelong learning, and much has been made of the apparent progress towards them. However, on closer inspection it can be seen that this 'progress' consists almost entirely of passing young people with extended initial education into the category of 'working-age' and passing older people with few episodes of participation or qualification out of it. Once this is taken into account the impact of the policy is non-existent. In fact, despite the calls for lifelong learning, adults may now be less likely to take part in learning *as adults* than they were 20 or even 50 years ago. The incidence of education among those past retirement age is no longer targeted, and consequently ignored in policy terms. The disastrous impact of this on third-age patterns of participation can only come from disentangling within- and between-cohort changes over time.

However, those of us working in the area of lifelong learning must also bear some of the responsibility for problems, through our apparent obsession with supply and with overcoming barriers to access. Providing extra places and courses, and making participation easier and cheaper are certainly necessary precursors to improving rates of participation among adults. Are they sufficient? There is an air of compulsion in some writing about a learning society, suggesting that non-participation in formal learning cannot be a lifestyle choice and is somehow deviant. This underplays the role of motivational factors that are crucial to later learning (the second component of lifelong learning). The above analysis ignores a major part of non-trivial learning that takes place that is 'informal', and which is now being cited as a potential area for greater recognition (Skills Task Force, 2000). This move is welcome and overdue. Unfortunately, informal learning is not generally recognised by policy makers, nor included in National Targets for participation, and therefore too readily ignored by all of us as immeasurable. This is especially true in official discourse where skills and qualifications have become almost synonymous (for example, in ETAG, 1998). The privileging of the visible in target-setting, and funding arrangements based on certification, actually discourage this valuable area of learning. It is perhaps no surprise that as far as it is possible to assess, such informal learning is decreasing among adults. Yet this self-directed learning for its own sake could be at the heart of a true learning society.

A recent typical, but innovative, attempt to widen participation by overcoming barriers has been the attempt to harness digital technology in the form of virtual and distributed colleges. The argument is that digital broadcasting, the Internet and so on overcome barriers of space, inflexibility and travel by bringing learning experiences to the home or near-neighbourhood of those currently excluded. What appears to be ignored in this plan is that access to the relevant technology and expertise is unevenly distributed in society, and that those without access are also more likely to be those currently not participating in more traditional episodes. Around one third of the adult population left school at the earliest opportunity and have received no education or training since. There are systematic social and economic differences between these individuals and those characterised as lifelong learning participants, which have been confirmed in many reports. Non-participants are generally older, less economically active, less geographically mobile, still more likely to be female, from less-educated families, and of less prestigious occupational class. They are therefore identical in summary to those currently excluded from access to the Internet. Around one third of the adult population in Wales does not have access to a home telephone, and around two thirds do not have access to any form of computer. Needless to say, these figures will decline in the future but the technology will also change (obsolescence every 18 months is a recent estimate, Gorard and Selwyn, 2001). Those currently without suitable technology are likely to still be playing catch up.

Balancing the 'economic imperative'

A fundamental dichotomy that runs throughout current lifelong learning policy-making is that between increasing social inclusion and increasing economic competitiveness. Beyond broad statements of intent, it is clear that the present lifelong learning agenda is almost exclusively economically focused in practice, and that any concern with the socially excluded can be more accurately seen as a concern with the economically excluded (Bynner, 1998).

This prioritising of the economic over the social characterises current government policy-making in general (Levitas, 1996; Byrne, 1997; Preece, 2000). A 1999 budget announced that vocational tax relief was to be phased out and with it public support for non-vocational courses. Learners therefore receive no help from the Treasury unless their learning is apparently of immediate economic benefit (Tuckett, 1999). As Barry (1998, p 9) observes, social exclusion would appear to be "culturally defined, economically driven and politically motivated" and initiatives such as the UfI reflect a wider new work ethic that is underpinning the current New Labour policy agenda. "Increasing participation in the labour market is at the heart of the current government's social policy" (Holden, 1999, p 529).

The conventional wisdom that governments should prepare 'all' citizens for highly skilled employment in a 'high tech' economy ignores the actual widespread lack of 'high-skill' jobs (Robins and Webster, 1999). As Apple (1997) points out, the majority of jobs in high tech industries do not require a substantial knowledge of technology, with only the relatively few individuals in high tech occupations needing technological skills. Furthermore, a trend in technological deskilling looks set to continue as ICTs become more sophisticated and the need for knowledge to use them declines. Thus, as Neill (1995) contends, buttressing social-policy reform by pointing to the presumed high-skill information economy ignores the fact that most workers may require little more than a 'MacDonald's level' of familiarity with technology, primarily consisting of lower order data-entry and limited problem-solving skills.

Recognising the importance of informal learning

Significant learning goes on in work that is virtually unnoticed by researchers, and even by employers. This oversight has simply been replicated by ICT initiatives according to Bob Fryer (McGavin, 2000a). The emphasis of the Learning and Skills Council is still too much on the supply of courses, and provision for the young, with little consideration of the role of motivation, according to the Director General of the British Chamber of Commerce and Chair of the Skills Task Force (McGavin, 2000b). Informal learning may be vitally necessary to the organisations people work for (and perhaps also to the fulfilment of the individuals concerned), but the degree of importance attached to informal learning as opposed to formal learning has changed. While no definitive answer to the question of whether people were more likely to acquire necessary knowledge and competencies in a formal way is provided here, our study has produced evidence that would tend to suggest that this is not so. Perhaps largely as a consequence of credentialism, increased formality has also increased the proportion of unnecessary learning that is undertaken while necessary learning continues in informal and uncertificated settings.

An inclusive learning society cannot be encouraged simply by more pressure to conform to the existing set up. It may be necessary to overcome real barriers to participation, to make people more aware of opportunities available, but three other changes are also, and perhaps more clearly, needed. Changes are needed in the nature of opportunities available, since even in a system of rationality that is seen as heavily bounded by socioeconomic constraints, it seems that there are many people who do not want to take part in the courses that are available to them. Progress is necessary towards economic and societal justice other than through increased education. We now also argue that it is possible to recognise wider existing skills cheaply. Greater inclusion in a learning society may come more easily from greater recognition of tacit knowledge than more participation. Unfortunately this recognition of the value of informal learning and of individual autonomy (Strain, 1998), with its tradition of self-reliance, does not link up with the economic imperative and its human capital approach to systems of education and training. It is therefore less than surprising that recent green papers on lifelong learning do not really address any of these issues, any more than they address the decline in substantive training financed by employers. They do not start from the premise that informal learners are involved in a lifelong process. Their simple answer is to leave society as it is, and to encourage learning chiefly through publicly or individually financed episodes of certificated formal learning.

Alternative paths to a learning society

Actual opportunities for participation change over time because social mores, national policies, expenditure by government and employers, and the economy, also change. The closure of coalmines in South Wales may have had as much impact on male participation in work-based training as the closure of textile plants in Rochdale has had on participation in employment (Penn et al, 1990), for example. Devising a new educational scheme or policy cannot by itself transform patterns of participation, in the form of widening as well as merely increasing access, or reducing inequality and social stratification (NIACE, 1994). Such changes also require consideration of the barriers that people face and their motivation to overcome them in order to take part. For the government, one of the advantages of this may be that it appears to shift the responsibility for non-participation to the individual, whereas there are many indications that opportunities are only relevant within a framework provided by an individual's social background and previous experiences. "Career routes have origins much deeper in the structure of society than in the employment opportunities on offer in the particular locality or in the credentials young people acquire ... from the education system" (Banks et al, 1992, p 43).

Participation in lifelong learning would be made more attractive to the excluded one third of the population of Wales by introducing something similar to the Education Maintenance Allowance pilot scheme in England that has proved successful in retaining students at age 16, and increasing completion rates (Piatt, 2001). If this was extended to older age groups, and to regions other than England, it could be very effective. We have known for some time what the factors are that would genuinely encourage wider participation (for example, McGivney, 1992). There is, perhaps surprisingly for educational research fields, almost unanimity on these. As has been illustrated in our own research 'individuals do not wish to engage in activities that are not perceived as normal within their peer and reference groups'. Therefore, we need to target outreach work, provide counselling support, encourage group formation to overcome feelings of isolation, and help to establish a work routine. Time, cost, distance and so on are only barriers if there is motivation, and ironically our historical analysis suggests that where there is motivation the role of barriers is less.

A learning society is not simply a desirable future objective, or an ideal towards which we progress in a smooth fashion (Gorard et al, 1998b). Nor, as evidenced by the increased rate of library loans during the Great Depression for example, is it necessarily related to the economic health of the country. If it is a social and cultural phenomenon and not simply a normative concept of inclusiveness or product, then understanding the learning society involves a better understanding of what has gone before. This is made more complex because the determinants of historical patterns of participation in education and training – family, industry, availability – are likely to be subject to geographically specific variations. A learning society is based on real, rather than ideal, institutions and the social connections within and between them. Developments in education and training may be non-linear and retrograde in some respects for particular groups. Thus, insights might be gained from an analysis of the way in which contemporary patterns of participation have emerged from previous ones, and these could also give a clue to the future.

Markedly different interpretations of the term 'learning society' are in common use among politicians, economists, policy makers and educationalists, but to some extent 'learning society' is used as a term of convenience. It is an ideal notion (but one with very prosaic targets couched in terms of certification) that may help mask the lack of real progress in some respects towards an 'educated public'. While most people agree that society benefits from a well-trained workforce, there are currently tensions in relevant writing between an economic imperative and an inclusive definition of a learning society, which may on analysis be found to be in conflict. Some commentators want more money spent on initial or higher education, others wish to put the money into compensatory literacy schemes for example. Either way the pressure is to spend more and more money on education. Another tension lies in the false dichotomy of academic and vocational knowledge, which ignores the "really useful knowledge ... calculated to make you free" (Johnson, 1993, p 23). A more radical, some might say realistic, agenda requires more than educational change. It entails social and labour market reform as well. Instead, education is generally accepted as what it is, even though standards may be decried, and the growth of it is encouraged. Non-participants are therefore seen merely as a pool of potential clients for the existing set-up who must be enticed in without eroding quality. Non-participation is seen as the problem, and the fault lies with the client or the institutional marketing, or perhaps the barriers outlined already, not with the opportunities on offer.

The good news is that, whatever progress remains to be made, long-term indicators from extended initial education are moving in the right direction. Participation and qualifications are improving, while the differences between sectors and social groups are declining. These changes mean that the same indicators are also moving slowly in the same direction for the adult population, as people leave initial education for the workforce. However, once these 'conveyor belt' changes are separated out, there is no progress in participation and qualifications for adults while they are adults, and the differentials between some sectors and social groups are actually increasing over time. Current initiatives to deal with this problem suffer from one or more of the following defects: they are output-driven, they replicate and reinforce existing inequalities, and most importantly they deal almost exclusively with improvements in formal initial education or training. The standard human capital thesis that education and training are valuable for the economy (rather than valuable in their own right) is far from convincing anyway, but especially so when employers appear unconvinced of the need to invest in the skills of their own employees. Perhaps one ameliorative step would be to weaken the link between education and models of 'investment', and foster instead a vision of lifelong learning that is valuable for its own sake and that may have economic benefits as well.

References

Ahleit, P. (1994) *Taking the knocks:Youth unemployment and biography – a qualitative analysis*, London: Cassell.

Ainley, P. (1998) 'Towards a learning or a certified society? Contradictions in the New Labour modernization of lifelong learning', *Journal of Education Policy*, vol 13, no 4, pp 559-73.

Ainley, P. (1999) *Learning policy: towards the certified society*, London: Macmillan.

Antikainen, A., Houtsonen, J., Kauppila, J. and Huotelin, H. (1996) *Living a learning society: Life histories, identities and education*, London: Falmer.

Apple, M. (1997) 'The new technology: is it part of the solution or part of the problem in education?', in G.E. Hawisher and C. Selfe (eds) *Literacy, technology and society: Confronting the issues*, New Jersey, NY: Prentice Hall.

Armour, R. and Fuhrmann, A. (1993) 'Confirming the centrality of liberal learning', in L. Curry, J. Wergin and Associates (eds) *Educating professionals*, San Francisco, CA: Josey-Bass.

Ashley, R. and Walkley, S. (1996) *Education for employability*, Occasional Paper, London: Coutts Career Consultants.

Ashton, D. and Green, F. (1996) *Education, training and the global economy*, Cheltenham: Edward Elgar.

Ashton, D., Spilsbury, M. and Maguire, M. (1990) *Restructuring the labour market: The implications for youth*, London: Macmillan.

Ball, S. (1990) *Politics and policy making in education: Explorations in policy sociology*, London: Routledge.

Ball, S., Maguire, M. and MacRae, S. (2000) *Choice, pathways and transitions, post-16: New youth, new economics in the global city*, London: Falmer.

Banks, M., Bates, I., Bynner, J., Breakwell, G., Roberts, K., Emler, N., Jamieson, L. and Roberts, K. (1992) *Careers and identities*, Milton Keynes: Open University Press.

Barry, M. (1998) 'Introduction', in M. Barry and C. Hallett (eds) *Social exclusion and social work*, Dorchester: Russell House.

Bathmaker, A. (2001) '"It's a perfect education": lifelong learning and the experience of foundation-level GNVQ students', *Journal of Vocational Education and Training*, vol 53, no 1, pp 81-98.

Becker, G. (1975) *Human capital: A theoretical and empirical analysis*, Chicago, IL: University of Chicago Press.

Beinhart, S. and Smith, P. (1998) *National Adult Learning Survey 1997*, Sudbury: DfEE Publications.

Blaenau Gwent (1996) *Official guide and street plan for the County Borough*, Ebbw Vale: Blaenau Gwent County Borough.

Blair, A. (2000) Speech at the Knowledge 2000 Conference, 7 March [http://www.number-10.gov.uk].

Bloomer, M. (2001) 'Young lives, learning and transformation: some theoretical considerations', *Oxford Review of Education*, vol 27, no 3, pp 421-47.

Boddy, M., Fielder, S. and Rees, G. (1990) *The institutional determinants of employers' training strategies: Local labour market profiles*, ESRC Project Paper 2, Cardiff: University of Wales, Cardiff.

Bosworth, D. (1992) 'The extent and intensity of skills shortages 1990', *International Journal of Manpower*, vol 13, no 9, pp 3-12.

Bowl, M. (2001) 'Experiencing the barriers: non-traditional students entering higher education', *Research Papers in Education*, vol 16, no 2, pp 141-60.

Bowman, H., Burden, T. and Konrad, J. (2000) *Successful futures? Community views on adult education and training*, York: York Publishing Services.

Burge, A., Francis, H., Trotman, C., Rees, G., Gorard, S. and Fevre, R. (1999) *In a class of their own: Adult learning and the South Wales mining community 1900-1939*, Working Paper 16, Cardiff: School of Social Sciences, Cardiff University.

Burstall, E. (1996) 'Second chance stifled', *Times Educational Supplement*, 22 March, p 27.

Butler, L. (1993) 'Unpaid work in the home and accreditation', in M. Thorpe, R. Edwards and A. Hanson (eds) *Culture and processes of adult learning*, London: Routledge.

Bynner, J. (1989) *Transition to work: Results from a longitudinal study of young people in four British labour markets*, ESRC 16-19 Initiative Occasional Papers, No 4, London: City University.

Bynner, J. (1998) 'Youth in the information society: problems, prospects and research directions', *Journal of Education Policy*, vol 13, no 3, pp 433-42.

Bynner, J. and Parsons, S. (1997) *It doesn't get any better*, London: Basic Skills Agency.

Byrne, D. (1997) 'Social exclusion and capitalism: the Reserve Army across time and space', *Critical Social Policy*, vol 17, no 1, pp 27-51.

CBI (Confederation of British Industry) (1989) *Towards a skill revolution*, London: CBI.

Central Advisory Council for Education (Wales) (1967) *Primary education in Wales*, London: HMSO.

Central Office of Information (1998) *Our information age: The government's vision*, London: The Stationery Office.

CERI (1975) *Recurrent education: Trends and issues*, Paris: OECD.

Cervero, R. and Kirkpatrick, T. (1990) 'The enduring effects of pre-adult factors on participation in adult education', *American Journal of Education*, vol 99, pp 77-94.

Chambers, P., Gorard, S., Fevre, R., Rees, G. and Furlong, J. (1998) *Changes in training opportunities in South Wales 1945-1998: The views of key informants*, Working Paper 12, Cardiff: School of Education, Cardiff University.

Coffield, F. (1994) *Research specification for the ESRC Learning Society Research Programme*, Swindon: ESRC.

Coffield, F. (1997) 'Nine fallacies and their replacement by a national strategy for lifelong learning', in F. Coffield (ed) *A national strategy for lifelong learning*, Newcastle upon Tyne: Department of Education, University of Newcastle upon Tyne.

Coffield, F. (1998) 'Easy come, too easy go', *Times Educational Supplement*, 18 September, p 15.

Coffield, F. (1999) 'Breaking the consensus: lifelong learning as social control', *British Educational Research Journal*, vol 25, pp 479-500.

Coffield, F. (2000) 'Lifelong learning as a lever on structural change? Evaluation of White Paper: *Learning to succeed: A new framework for post-16 learning*', *Journal of Education Policy*, vol 15, no 2, pp 237-46.

Coffield, F., Borrill, C. and Marshall, S. (1986) *Growing up at the margins: Young adults in the North East*, Milton Keynes: Open University Press.

Coleman, J. (1990) 'Choice, community and future schools', in W. Clune and J. Witte (eds) *Choice and control in American education*, London: Falmer Press.

Corcoran, F. (1999) 'Towards digital television in Europe: a race or a crawl?', *Javnostó-The Public*, no 6, p 3.

Crombie, A. and Harries-Jenkins, G. (1983) *The demise of the liberal tradition*, Leeds: Department of Adult and Continuing Education, University of Leeds.

Cropley, A. (1977) *Lifelong education: A psychological analysis*, Oxford: Pergamon Press.

Cross, K. (1981) *Adults as learners: Increasing participation and facilitating learning*, San Francisco, CA: Josey Bass.

Crouch, C., Finegold, D. and Sako, M. (1999) *Are skills the answer? The political economy of skill creation in advanced industrial countries*, Oxford: Oxford University Press.

Croxford, L. and Raffe, D. (eds) (2000) 'The education and training systems of the UK: Convergence or divergence?', Papers from a seminar 'A Home International Comparison of Education and Training Systems in the UK', Edinburgh: Centre for Educational Sociology, University of Edinburgh.

Cutler, T. (1992) 'Vocational training and British economic performance: a further instalment of the "British labour problem"', *Work, Employment and Society*, no 6, pp 161-84.

Cymru Ar-Lein (2001) 'Online for Better Wales' [www.wales.gov.uk/cymruarlein/, accessed 10/3/01].

Daines, J., Elsey, B. and Gibbs, M. (1982) *Changes in student participation in adult education*, Nottingham: Department of Adult Education, University of Nottingham.

Dale, A. and Davies, R. (1994) *Analyzing social and political Change: A casebook of methods*, London: Sage Publications.

Dave, R. (1976) *Foundations of lifelong learning*, Oxford: Pergamon Press.

Davies, P. (1998) 'Formalising learning: the role of accreditation', Presentation at the ESRC Learning Society Programme seminar on informal learning, Bristol.

DE (Department for Education) (1994) *Competitiveness: Helping business to win*, London: HMSO.

Deamer, I. (1996) 'Implications of unconscious learning for organisationally-based training', *Research in Post-Compulsory Education*, vol 1, no 1, pp 65-75.

Dearing, R. (1997) *Higher education in the learning society*, London: National Committee of Enquiry into Higher Education.

Deloitte Haskins and Sells (1989) *Training in Britain: A study of funding, activity and attitudes*, London: HMSO.

DfEE (Department for Education and Employment) (1995) *Training statistics 1995*, London: HMSO.

DfEE (1996) *Skills and Enterprise Executive Issue 2/96*, Nottingham: Skills and Enterprise Network.

DfEE (1997a) *Labour Market Quarterly Report*, Nottingham: Skills and Enterprise Network.

DfEE (1997b) *Meeting the challenge of the 21st century. A summary of 'Labour Market and Skills Trends 1997/98'*, Nottingham: Skills and Enterprise Network.

DfEE (1998) *The Learning Age: A renaissance for a new Britain*, London: The Stationery Office.

DfEE (1999) *Learning to succeed: A new framework for post-16 learning*, London: The Stationery Office.

Dolton, P., Makepeace, G. and Treble, J. (1994) 'Measuring the effects of training in the Youth Cohort Study', in R. McNabb and K. Whitfield (eds) *The market for training*, Aldershot: Avebury.

Downs, S. (1993) 'Developing learning skills in vocational learning', in M. Thorpe, R. Edwards and A. Hanson (eds) *Culture and processes of adult learning*, London: Routledge.

Dumort, A. (2000) 'New media and distance education: an EU–US perspective', *Information, Communication & Society*, vol 3, no 4, pp 546-56.

Eaton, G. (1987) *A history of Neath*, Swansea: Christopher Davies.

Ecclestone, K. (1998) 'Care and control: defining learners' needs for lifelong learning', Presentation at BERA Annual Conference, Belfast.

Edwards, R. (1997) *Changing places? Flexibility, lifelong learning and a learning society*, London: Routledge.

Edwards, R. and Usher, R. (1998) 'Lo(o)s(en)ing the boundaries: from "education" to "lifelong learning"', *Studies in Continuing Education*, vol 20, no 1, pp 83-103.

Edwards, R., Sieminski, S. and Zeldin, D. (eds) (1993) *Adult learners, education and training*, London: Routledge.

Ellis, T. (1935) *The development of higher education in Wales*, Wrexham: Hughes and Son.

Employment Department Group (1994) *Training in Britain: A guide*, London: HMSO.

Eraut, M. (1997) 'Perspectives on defining "the learning society"', *Journal of Education Policy*, vol 12, no 6, pp 551-8.

Eraut, M., Alderton, J., Cole, G. and Senker, P. (1998) *Development of knowledge and skills in employment*, Final report of ESRC project, Brighton: University of Sussex.

ETAG (Education and Training Action Group) (1998) *An education and training action plan for Wales: Consultation*, Cardiff: ETAG for Wales.

ETAP (Education and Training Action Plan) (1999) *An education and training action plan for Wales*, Cardiff: Welsh Office.

EC (European Commission) (1996) *Teaching and learning: Towards the learning society*, Luxembourg: Office for Official Publications of the EC.

Evans, L. (1971) *Education in industrial Wales 1700-1900*, Cardiff: Avalon.

Felstead, A. (1996) 'Identifying gender inequalities in the distribution of vocational qualifications in the UK', *Gender, Work and Organization*, vol 3, no 1, pp 38-51.

FEU (Further Education Unit) (1993) *Paying their way: The experiences of adult learners in vocational education and training in FE colleges*, London: FEU.

Fevre, R. (1989) *Wales is closed*, Nottingham: Spokesman.

Fevre, R., Gorard, S. and Rees, G. (2000) 'Necessary and unnecessary learning: the acquisition of knowledge and skills in and outside employment in South Wales in the twentieth century', in F. Coffield (ed) *The necessity of informal learning*, Bristol: The Policy Press.

Fevre, R., Rees, G. and Gorard, S. (1999) 'Some sociological alternatives to Human Capital Theory', *Journal of Education and Work*, vol 12, no 2, pp 117-40.

Field, J. (1998) 'Understanding participation in lifelong learning in Northern Ireland: schooling, networks and the labour market', Presentation at BERA Annual Conference, Belfast.

Field, J. (2000) *Lifelong learning and the new educational order*, Stoke-on-Trent: Trentham.

Finegold, D. and Soskice, D. (1988) 'The failure of British training: analysis and prescription', *Oxford Review of Economic Policy*, vol 4, no 3, pp 21-53.

Fordham, P., Poulton, G. and Randle, L. (1983) 'Non-formal work: a new kind of provision', in M. Tight (ed) *Education for adults Volume II*, London: Croom Helm, pp 243-54.

Francis, H. (1976) 'The origins of the South Wales Miners' library', *History Workshop Journal*, vol 2, p 183.

Frazer, L. and Ward, K. (1988) *Education for everyday living*, Leicester: NIACE.

Frow, E. and Frow, R. (1990) 'The spark of independent working-class education: Lancashire 1909-1930', in B. Simon (ed) *The search for enlightenment: The working class and adult education in the twentieth century*, London: Lawrence and Wishart.

Fryer, R. (1990) 'The challenge to working-class education', in B. Simon (ed) *The search for enlightenment: The working class and adult education in the twentieth century*, London: Lawrence and Wishart.

Fryer, R. (1997) *Learning for the twenty-first century*, London: DfEE.

Fryer, R. (1999) 'Practical implications of the Learning Age in Wales', Speech given to the Wales Digital College Network Conference, Cardiff, January.

Furlong, J. (1991) 'Disaffected pupils: the sociological perspective', *British Journal of Sociology of Education*, vol 12, no 3, pp 293-307.

Furter, P. (1977) *The planner and lifelong education*, Paris: UNESCO.

Future Skills Wales (1998) *Technical report*, London: MORI.

Gallie, D. (1988) *Employment in Britain*, Oxford: Basil Blackwell.

Gallie, D. (1994) 'Methodological appendix: the social change and economic life initiative', in D. Gallie, C. Marsh and C. Vogler (eds) *Social change and the experience of unemployment*, Oxford: Oxford University Press.

Gambetta, D. (1987) *Were they pushed or did they jump*, Cambridge: Cambridge University Press.

Gann, N. (1999) *Targets for tomorrows' schools: A guide to whole school target-setting for governors and headteachers*, London: Falmer.

Garner, C., Main, B. and Raffe, D. (1988) 'A tale of four cities: social and spatial inequalities in the youth labour market', in D. Raffe (ed) *Education and the youth labour market*, London: Falmer.

Garner, L. and Imeson, R. (1996) 'More bricks in the wall: the ending of the Older Students' Allowance and the new "16 Hour Rule". Has the cost of higher education for mature students finally got too high?', *Journal of Access Studies*, no 11, pp 97-110.

Gerber, T. and Hout, M. (1995) 'Educational stratification in Russia during the Soviet period', *American Journal of Sociology*, no 101, pp 611-60.

Gershuny, J. and Marsh, C. (1994) 'Unemployment in work histories', in D. Gallie, C. Marsh and C. Vogler (eds) *Social change and the experience of unemployment*, Oxford: Oxford University Press.

Girod, R. (1990) *Problems of sociology in education*, Paris: UNESCO.

Gleeson, D., Glover, D., Gough, G., Johnson, M. and Pye, D. (1996) 'Reflections on Youth Training: towards a new model of experience?', *British Educational Research Journal*, vol 22, no 5, pp 597-613.

Gorard, S. (1997a) *The region of study*, Working Paper 1, Patterns of Participation in Adult Education and Training, Cardiff: School of Education, Cardiff University.

Gorard, S. (1997b) *School choice in an established Market*, Aldershot: Ashgate.

Gorard, S. (1997c) *Initial educational trajectories*, Working Paper 8, Patterns of Participation in Adult Education and Training, Cardiff: School of Education, Cardiff University.

Gorard, S. (1998a) 'Four errors ... and a conspiracy? The effectiveness of schools in Wales', *Oxford Review of Education*, vol 24, no 4, pp 459-72.

Gorard, S. (2000a) 'Adult participation in learning and the economic imperative: a critique of policy in Wales', *Studies in the Education of Adults*, vol 32, no 2, pp 181-94.

Gorard, S. (2000b) '"Underachievement" is still an ugly word: reconsidering the relative effectiveness of schools in England and Wales', *Journal of Education Policy*, vol 15, no 5, pp 559-73.

Gorard, S. (2000c) *Education and social justice*, Cardiff: University of Wales Press.

Gorard, S. (2000d) 'Robbing Peter to pay Paul: resolving the contradiction of lifelong learning', in R. Edwards, J. Clarke and N. Millar (eds) *Supporting lifelong learning*, Milton Keynes: Open University.

Gorard, S. (2001a) 'International comparisons of school effectiveness: a second component of the "crisis account"?', *Comparative Education*, vol 37, no 3, pp 279-96.

Gorard, S. (2001b) *Quantitative methods in educational research: The role of numbers made easy*, London: Continuum.

Gorard, S., Fevre, R., Rees, G. and Furlong, J. (1997c) *Space, mobility and the education of minority groups in Wales: The survey results*, Working Paper 10, Patterns of Participation in Adult Education and Training, Cardiff: School of Education, Cardiff University.

Gorard, S., Fevre, R. and Rees, G. (1999d) 'The apparent decline of informal learning', *Oxford Review of Education*, vol 25, no 4, pp 437-54.

Gorard, S., Rees, G., Furlong, J. and Fevre, R. (1997a) *Outline methodology of the study*, Working Paper 2, Patterns of Participation in Adult Education and Training, Cardiff: School of Education, University of Wales, Cardiff.

Gorard, S., Rees, G., Fevre, R. and Furlong, J. (1997b) *A brief history of education and training in Wales 1900-1996*, Working Paper 4, Cardiff: School of Education, University of Wales, Cardiff.

Gorard, S., Rees, G., Fevre, R. and Furlong, J. (1998a) 'Society is not built by education alone: alternative routes to a learning society', *Research in Post-Compulsory Education*, vol 3, no 1, pp 25-37.

Gorard, S., Rees, G., Fevre, R. and Furlong, J. (1998b) 'Learning trajectories: travelling towards a learning society?', *International Journal of Lifelong Education*, vol 17, no 6, pp 400-10.

Gorard, S., Rees, G., Fevre, R. and Furlong, J. (1998c) 'The two components of a new learning society', *Journal of Vocational Education and Training*, vol 50, no 1, pp 5-19.

Gorard, S., Rees, G., Fevre, R., Renold, E. and Furlong, J. (1998d) 'A gendered appraisal of the transition to a learning society in the UK', in R. Benn (ed) *Research, teaching and learning: Making connections in the education of adults*, Leeds: Standing Conference on University Teaching and Research in the Education of Adults.

Gorard, S., Rees, G. and Fevre, R. (1999a) 'Two dimensions of time: the changing social context of lifelong learning', *Studies in the Education of Adults*, vol 31, no 1, pp 35-48.

Gorard, S., Rees, G. and Fevre, R. (1999c) 'Patterns of participation in lifelong learning: do families make a difference?', *British Educational Research Journal*, vol 25, no 4, pp 517-32.

Gorard, S., Rees, G., Fevre, R. and Welland, T. (2001a) 'Lifelong learning trajectories: some voices of those in transit', *International Journal of Lifelong Education*, vol 20, no 2, pp 169-87.

Gorard, S., Rees, G. and Salisbury, J. (2001b) 'The differential attainment of boys and girls at school: investigating the patterns and their determinants', *British Educational Research Journal*, vol 27, no 2, pp 125-39.

Gorard, S., Rees, G. and Selwyn, N. (2002b) 'Work-place learning and the "conveyor belt effect": an assessment of the impact of National Targets for Lifelong Learning', *Oxford Review of Education*, vol 28, no 1, pp 75-89.

Gorard, S., Salisbury, J. and Rees, G. (1999b) 'Reappraising the apparent underachievement of boys at school', *Gender and Education*, vol 11, no 4, pp 441-54.

Gorard, S. and Selwyn, N. (1999) 'Switching on the learning society? Questioning the role of technology in widening participation in lifelong learning', *Journal of Education Policy*, vol 14, no 5, pp 523-34.

Gorard, S. and Selwyn, N. (2001) *101 key ideas in Information Technology*, London: Hodder and Stoughton.

Gorard, S., Selwyn, N. and Rees, G. (2002a) 'Privileging the visible: examining the National Targets for Education and Training', *British Educational Research Journal*, vol 28, no 3.

Gorard, S., Selwyn, N. and Williams, S. (2000a) 'Could try harder!: problems facing technological solutions to non-participation in adult learning', *British Educational Research Journal* , vol 26, no 4, pp 507-21.

Gorard, S. and Taylor, C. (2001) *A review of the statistics on student hardship in Wales*, Report to the National Assembly Working Party on Student Hardship.

Granovetter, M. and Swedberg, R. (eds) (1992) *The sociology of economic life*, Boulder, CO: Westview Press.

Green, F. (1994) 'The determinants of training of male and female employees, and some measures of discrimination', in R. McNabb and K. Whitfield (eds) *The market for training*, Aldershot: Avebury.

Green, F. and Ashton, D. (1992) *Educational provision, educational attainment and the needs of industry*, Report Series No 5, London: National Institute for Economic and Social Research.

Greenhalgh, C. and Mavrotas, G. (1994) 'Workforce training in the Thatcher era – market forces and market failures', in R. McNabb and K. Whitfield (eds) *The market for training*, Aldershot: Avebury.

Greenhalgh, C. and Stewart, M. (1987) 'The effects and determinants of training', *Oxford Bulletin of Economics and Statistics*, vol 49, no 2, pp 171-90.

Gwent Training and Enterprise Council Ltd (1996) *Economic and Labour Market Assessment 1995/96*, Newport: Gwent TEC.

Gwent Training and Enterprise Council Ltd (1997) *Economic and Labour Market Assessment 1996/97 Final Report*, Newport: Gwent TEC.

Halsey, A., Heath, A. and Ridge, J. (1980) *Origins and destinations: Family, class, and education in modern Britain*, Oxford: Clarendon Press.

Hand, A., Gambles, J. and Cooper, E. (1994) *Individual commitment to learning. Individuals decision-making about lifelong learning*, London: Employment Department.

Hanson, J. (1968) *Profile of a Welsh town*, Swansea: J.I. Hanson.

Harrison, R. (1993) 'Disaffection and access', in J. Calder (ed) *Disaffection and diversity — Overcoming barriers to adult learning*, London: Falmer.

Haskel, J. and Martin, C. (1993) *The causes of skill shortage in Britain*, Oxford Economic Papers No 45.

Hesketh, A. (1998) *Graduate employment and training in the new millennium*, Cambridge: Hobsons.

Hodkinson, P. and Bloomer, M. (2001) 'Dropping out of further education: complex causes and simplistic policy assumptions', *Research Papers in Education*, vol 16, no 2, pp 117-40.

Hodkinson, P., Sparkes, A. and Hodkinson, H. (1996) *Triumphs and tears: Young people, markets and the transition from school to work*, London: David Fulton.

Holden, C. (1999) 'Globalisation, social exclusion and labour's new work ethic', *Critical Social Policy*, vol 19, no 4, pp 529-38.

Holden, R. and Hamblett, J. (2001) 'The "Learning Society", and small and medium-sized enterprises: empowering the individual?', *Journal of Vocational Education and Training*, vol 53, no 1, pp 121-37.

Hopper, E. and Osborn, M. (1975) *Adult students. Education, selection and social control*, London: Francis Pinter.

Howell, R. (1988) *A history of Gwent*, Llandysul: Gomer Press.

Humphrys, G. (1972) *Industrial Britain. South Wales*, Newton Abbot: David and Charles.

Husen, T. (1986) *The learning society revisited*, Oxford: Pergamon Press.

IFF (Industrial Facts and Forecasting) (1994) *Skill needs in Britain*, London: IFF.

Istance, D. and Rees, G. (1994) 'Education and training in Wales: problems and paradoxes revisited', *Contemporary Wales*, no 7, pp 7-27.

Istance, D. and Rees, G. (1995) *Lifelong learning in Wales: a programme for prosperity*, NIACE Cymru policy discussion paper, Leicester: NIACE.

Jahoda, M., Lazarfeld, P. and Zeisel, H. (1972) *Marienthal: The sociography of an unemployed community*, London: Tavistock.

Jarvis, P. (1983) *Adult and continuing education*, Beckenham: Croom Helm.

Jarvis, P. (1985) *The sociology of adult and continuing education*, London: Routledge.

Jarvis, P. (1993) *Adult education and the state*, London: Routledge.

Jenkins, E. (1974) *Neath and district. A symposium*, Neath: Elias Jenkins.

Johnson, R. (1993) 'Really useful knowledge, 1790-1850', in M. Thorpe, R. Edwards and A. Hanson (eds) *Culture and processes of adult learning*, London: Routledge.

Jones, G. (1982) *Controls and conflicts in Welsh secondary education 1889-1944*, Cardiff: University of Wales Press.

Jones, G. (1996) *Wales 2010 three years on*, Cardiff: Institute of Welsh Affairs.

Jones, S. (1991) *The history of Port Talbot*, Port Talbot: Goldleaf.

Keep, E. (1993) 'Missing presumed skilled – training policy in the UK', in R. Edwards, S. Sieminski and D. Zeldin (eds) *Adult learners, education and training*, London: Routledge.

Keep, E. (1997) 'There's no such thing as society.... Some problems with an individual approach to creating a learning society', Paper presented to 2nd coordinating meeting of the ESRC Learning Society Programme, Bristol.

Keep, E. (2000) 'Learning organisations, lifelong learning and the mystery of the vanishing employers', Global Internet Colloquium on Lifelong Learning, Milton Keynes: Open University.

Kelly, T. (1992) *A history of adult education in Great Britain*, Liverpool: Liverpool University Press.

Kennedy, H. (1997) *Learning works: Widening participation in further education*, Coventry: Further Education Funding Council.

Knowles, M. (1990) *The adult learner: A neglected species*, Houston: Gulf.

Lazar, D. (1996) 'Competing economic ideologies in South Africa's economic debate', *British Journal of Sociology*, vol 47, no 4, pp 599-626.

Leadbeater, C. (1999) *Living on thin air: The new economy*, London: Viking.

Levitas, R. (1996) 'The concept of social exclusion and the new Durkheimian hegemony', *Critical Social Policy*, vol 16, no 1, pp 5-20.

Lewis, R. (1993) *Leaders and teachers. Adult education and the challenge of labour in South Wales 1906-1940*, Cardiff: University of Wales Press.

Livingstone, D. (1998) *The education-jobs gap*, Toronto, Canada: Garamond Press.

Lovering, J. (1990) 'A perfunctory sort of post-Fordism: economic restructuring and labour market segmentation in Britain in the 1980s', *Work, Employment and Society*, Special Issue, pp 9-28.

Low, G. (2000) 'Older students ignored say MPs', *Times Educational Supplement FE Focus*, 21 April, p 1.

Lowe, J. (1970) *Adult education in England and Wales: A critical survey*, London: Michael Joseph.

Lundvall, B. and Johnson, B. (1994) 'The learning economy', *Journal of Industrial Studies*, vol 1, no 2, pp 23-42.

MacKay, T. (1999) 'Education and the disadvantaged: is there any justice?', *The Psychologist*, vol 12, no 7, pp 344-9.

Maguire, M., Maguire, S. and Felstead, A. (1993) *Factors influencing individual commitment to lifelong learning*, Research Series No 20, Sheffield: Employment Department.

Main, B. and Shelly, M. (1990) 'The effectiveness of the Youth Training Scheme as a manpower policy', *Economica*, no 57, pp 495-514.

Mansell, W. (2000) 'Lifelong learning for all is "Utopian"', *Times Educational Supplement FE Focus*, 3 March, p 1.

Marginson, S. (1993) *Education and public policy in Australia*, Cambridge: Cambridge University Press.

Marsh, C. and Blackburn, R.M. (1992) 'Class differences in access to higher education in Britain', in R. Burrows and C. Marsh (eds) *Consumption and class: Divisions and change*, London: Macmillan.

Marshall, G., Swift, A. and Roberts, S. (1997) *Against the odds? Social class and social justice in industrial societies*, Oxford: Oxford University Press.

Martinelli, A. and Smelser, N. (1990) 'Economy and society: overviews in economic sociology', *Current Sociology*, vol 38, no 2/3.

McGavin, H. (2000a) 'Lifelong learning drive is "insulting"', *Times Educational Supplement FE Focus*, 29 September, p 35.

McGavin, H. (2000b) 'Executives should "sweat over skills"', *Times Educational Supplement FE Focus*, 7 April, p I.

McGivney, V. (1990) *Education's for other people: Access to education for non-participant adults*, Leicester: NIACE.

McGivney, V. (1992) *Motivating unemployed adults to undertake education and training*, Leicester: NIACE.

McGivney, V. (1993) 'Participation and non-participation: a review of the literature', in R. Edwards, S. Sieminski and D. Zeldin (eds) *Adult learners, education and training*, London: Routledge.

McGivney, V. (1996) *Staying or leaving the course*, Leicester: NIACE.

McIlroy, J. (1990) 'The demise of the National Council of Labour colleges', in B. Simon (ed) *The search for enlightenment: The working class and adult education in the twentieth century*, London: Lawrence and Wishart.

McNabb, R. and Whitfield, K. (1994) *The market for training*, Aldershot: Avebury.

McNair, S. (1996) 'Learner autonomy in as changing world', in R. Edwards, A. Hanson and P. Raggatt (eds) *Boundaries of adult learning*, London: Routledge.

Mezirow, J. (1990) *Fostering critical reflection in adulthood*, San Francisco, CA: Jossey-Bass.

Mid Glamorgan Training and Enterprise Council (1996) *Mid Glamorgan Labour Market Assessment 1995-96*, Bridgend: Mid Glamorgan TEC.

NACETT (1994) *Review of the National Targets for Education and Training: Proposals for consultation*, London: NACETT.

Nash, G., Davies, T. and Thomas, B. (1995) *Workmen's halls and institutes*, Cardiff: National Museum of Wales.

Nash, I. (1999) 'Job training fails to hit spot', *Times Educational Supplement FE Focus*, 12 February, p 31.

National Assembly of Wales (2001) *Cymru Arlein – Online for a better Wales*, Cardiff: National Assembly for Wales.

National Skills Agenda (2001) *Opportunity and skills in the knowledge-driven economy*, Nottingham: DfEE Publications.

Neill, M. (1995) 'Computers, thinking, and schools in the "New World Economic Order"', in J. Brook and I. Boal (eds) *Resisting the virtual life: The culture and politics of information*, San Francisco, CA: City Lights.

New Opportunities Fund (2000) *Lifelong learning: Wales*, London: New Opportunities Fund.

NIACE (National Institute of Adult Continuing Education) (1994) *Widening participation: Routes to a learning society*, NIACE Policy Discussion Paper, Leicester: NIACE.

NIACE (2000) *The learning divide revisited*, Leicester: NIACE.

OECD (Organisation of Economic Co-operation and Development) (1996) *Education and training: Learning and work in a society in flux*, Paris: OECD.

OPCS (Office for Population Censuses and Surveys) (1993) *1991 Census. Report for Wales. Part one*, London: HMSO.

Park, A. (1994) *Individual commitment to lifelong learning: Individuals' attitudes. Report on the quantitative survey*, London: Employment Department.

Penn, R., Martin, A. and Scattergood, H. (1990) *Employment trajectories of Asian migrants in Rochdale: An integrated analysis*, ESRC Social Change and Economic Life Initiative, Working Paper 14.

Pettigrew, A., Hendry, C. and Sparrow, P. (1989) *Training in Britain. A study of funding, activity and attitudes. Employers' perspectives on human resources*, London: HMSO.

Piatt, W. (2001) 'Bribe students to study', *New Statesman*, 2 April, p 34.

Polanyi, K. (1957) *The great transformation*, Boston, MA: Beacon Press.

Pope, R. (1997) *Building Jerusalem*, Cardiff: University of Wales Press.

Port Talbot (1996) *Port Talbot official street atlas*, Streetezee Town Plans Ltd.

Preece, J. (2000) 'Challenging the discourses of inclusion and exclusion with off limits curricula', in R. Edwards, J. Clarke and N. Miller (eds) *Supporting lifelong learning*, Milton Keynes: Open University.

Pyke, N. (1996) 'Dearing champions the young no-hopers', *Times Educational Supplement*, 29 March, p 1.

Ranson, S. (1992) 'Towards the learning society', *Educational Management and Administration*, vol 20, no 2, pp 68-79.

Rees, G. (1997) 'Making a learning society: education and work in industrial South Wales', *Welsh Journal of Education*, vol 6, no 2, pp 4-16.

Rees, G., Fielder, S. and Rees, T. (1992) 'Employees' access to training opportunities: shaping the social structure of labour markets', Paper to Seminar on Training and Recruitment, Royal Society of Arts.

Rees, G. and Rees, T. (1980) 'Educational inequality in Wales: some problems and paradoxes', in G. Rees and T. Rees (eds) *Poverty and social inequality in Wales*, London: Croom Helm.

Rees, G. and Rees, T. (1983) 'Migration, industrial restructuring and class relations: an analysis of South Wales', in G. Williams (ed) *Crisis of economy and ideology. Essays on Welsh society 1840-1980*, BSA Sociology of Wales Study Group.

Rees, G. and Thomas, M. (1991) 'From coalminers to entrepreneurs? A case study in the sociology of re-industralisation', in M. Cross and G. Payne (eds) *Work and the enterprise culture*, London: Falmer.

Rees, G. and Thomas, M. (1994) 'Inward investment, labour market adjustment and skills development: recent experience in South Wales', *Local Economy*, vol 9, pp 48-61.

Rees, G., Fevre, R., Furlong, J. and Gorard, S. (1997) 'History, place and the learning society: towards a sociology of lifelong learning', *Journal of Education Policy*, vol 12, no 6, pp 485-97.

Rees, G., Gorard, S., Fevre, R. and Furlong, J. (2000) 'Participating in the learning society: history, place and biography', in F. Coffield (ed) *Differing visions of a Learning Society: Research findings Volume Two*, Bristol: The Policy Press, pp 171-92.

Rees, G., Williamson, H. and Istance, D. (1996) '"Status Zero": jobless school-leavers in South Wales', *Research Papers in Education*, vol 11, no 2, pp 219-35.

Rees, T. and Bartlett, W. (1996) 'A market in adult guidance? Trends in the UK, Germany and France', Paper presented at the ESRC Learning Society Programme Seminar, University of Bristol, 17 September, mimeo.

Reynolds, D. (1990) 'The great Welsh education debate', *History of Education*, vol 19, no 3, p 251-64.

Reynolds, D. (1995) 'Creating an educational system for Wales', *The Welsh Journal of Education*, vol 4, no 2, pp 4-21.

Roberts, C. (1983) 'The sociology of education and Wales', in G. Williams (ed) *Crisis of economy and ideology. Essays on Welsh society 1840-1980*, BSA Sociology of Wales Study Group.

Roberts, K. and Parsell, G. (1990) *Young people's routes into UK labour markets in the late 1980s*, ESRC 16-19 Initiative Occasional Papers 27, London: City University.

Roberts, K., Parsell, G. and Connolly, M. (1991) 'Young people's transitions in the labour market', in M. Cross and G. Payne, *Work and the enterprise culture*, London: Falmer.

Robins, K. and Webster, F. (1999) *Times of the technoculture: From the information society to the virtual life*, London: Routledge.

Robinson, P. (1995) 'Do the NET Targets make sense?', *Training Tomorrow*, vol 9, no 6, pp 19-20.

Sargant, N. (1996) 'Learning and leisure', in R. Edwards, A. Hanson and P. Raggatt (eds) *Boundaries of adult learning*, London: Routledge.

Sargant, N., Field, J., Francis, H., Schuller, T. and Tuckett, A. (1997) *The learning divide: A study of participation in adult learning in the UK*, Leicester: NIACE.

Schratz, M. (1996) 'Learning biographies in adult education: a comparative study', *Research in Post-Compulsory Education*, vol 1, no 1, pp 19-33.

Schuller, T. and Field, J. (1999) 'Is there a divergence between initial and continuing education in Scotland and Northern Ireland?', *Scottish Journal of Adult Continuing Education*, vol 5, no 2, pp 61-76.

Schultz, T. (1961) 'Investment in human capital', *American Economic Review*, LI, vol 1, pp 1-17.

Scottish Office (1991) *Access and opportunity: A strategy for education and training*, Edinburgh: HMSO.

Selwyn, N. and Gorard, S. (2002) *The information age: Technology, learning and exclusion in Wales*, Cardiff: University of Wales Press.

Selwyn, N., Gorard, S. and Williams, S. (2001) 'The role of the "technical fix" in UK lifelong education policy', *International Journal of Lifelong Education*, vol 20, no 4, pp 1-17.

Sennett, R. and Cobb, J. (1972) *The hidden injuries of class*, New York, NY: Norton.

Shackleton, J. and Walsh, S. (1997) 'What determines who obtains National Vocational Qualifications?', *Education Economics*, vol 5, no 1, pp 41-53.

Simon, B. (1990) 'The struggle for hegemony 1920-1926', in B. Simon (ed) *The search for enlightenment: The working class and adult education in the twentieth century*, London: Lawrence and Wishart, pp 15-70.

Skills Task Force (2000) *Tackling the adult skills gap: Upskilling adults and the role of workplace learning*, Sudbury: DfEE.

Smelser, N. and Swedberg, R. (eds) (1994) *The handbook of economic sociology*, Princeton, NJ: Princeton University Press.

Smithers, A. and Robinson, P. (1991) *Beyond compulsory schooling – A numerical picture*, London: Council for Industry and Higher Education.

Spielhofer, T. (1996) 'Attitudes of local employers towards young people and their previous education', Paper presented at British Educational Research Association Annual Conference, Lancaster.

Squires, G. (1993) 'Education for adults', in M. Thorpe, R. Edwards and A. Hanson (eds) *Culture and processes of adult learning*, London: Routledge.

Stasz, C. (1997) 'Do employers need the skills they want? Evidence from technical work', *Journal of Education and Work*, vol 10, no 3, pp 205-23.

Strain, M. (1998) 'Towards an economy of lifelong learning: reconceptualising relations between learning and life', *British Journal of Educational Studies*, vol 46, no 3, pp 264-77.

Strauss, A. (1962) 'Transformations of identity', in A. Rose (ed) *Human behaviour and social processes: An interactionist approach*, London: Routledge and Kegan Paul.

Sutherland, P. (1997) 'The implications of research on approaches to learning for the teaching of adults', in P. Sutherland (ed) *Adult learning: A reader*, London: Kogan Page, pp 192-200.

Tan, H. and Peterson, C. (1992) 'Postschool training of British and American youth', in D. Finegold, L. McFarland and W. Richardson, *Something borrowed, something blue? A study of the Thatcher government's appropriation of American education and training policy PART 1*, Wallingford: Triangle, pp 83-105.

Taylor, S. and Spencer, L. (1994) *Individual commitment to lifelong learning: Individual's attitudes. Report on the qualitative phase*, London: Employment Department.

TES (1998a) 'Huge drop in number of adults doing work-based training', *Times Educational Supplement,* 25 August, p 34.

TES (1998b) 'PGCE student, 53, denied loan', *Times Educational Supplement,* 18 September, p 5.

TES (1998c) 'Skills can save us, says Blunkett', *Times Educational Supplement,* 18 September, p 27.

THES (1997) 'Worthless without that piece of paper at the end', *Times Higher Education Supplement,* 16 May, p 8.

Thomas, W. (2001) 'The decision to return to full-time education', *Education Economics,* vol 19, no 1, pp 37-52.

Thring, A. (1998) 'Training is for dogs', *Education Today,* vol 48, no 3, pp 54-8.

Tight, M. (1996) *Key concepts in adult education and training,* London: Routledge.

Tight, M. (1998a) 'Education, education, education! The vision of lifelong learning in the Kennedy, Dearing and Fryer reports', *Oxford Review of Education,* vol 24, no 4, pp 473-86.

Tight, M. (1998b) 'Lifelong learning: opportunity or compulsion?', *British Journal of Educational Studies,* vol 46, no 3, pp 251-63.

Titmus, C. (1994) 'The scope and characteristics of educational provision for adults', in J. Calder (ed) *Disaffection and diversity. Overcoming barriers to adult learning,* London: Falmer.

Tremlett, N., Park, A. and Dundon-Smith, D. (1995) *Individual commitment to learning. Further findings from the Individuals Survey,* London: Employment Department.

Tuckett, A. (1997) 'An election shopping list for lifelong learning', *Times Educational Supplement,* 14 March, p 32.

Tuckett, A. (1999) 'Spring may be a difficult step', *Times Educational Supplement,* 2 April, p 24.

Tuckett, A. and Sargant, N. (1999) *Marking time: The NIACE survey on adult participation in learning 1999,* Leicester: NIACE.

Tuijnman, A. (1991) 'Lifelong education: a test of the accumulation hypothesis', *International Journal of Lifelong Learning*, no 10, pp 275-85.

Tymms, P. and Stout, J. (1999) 'Target-setting', *Education Journal*, no 37, pp 28-9.

van Herten, L. and Gunning-Schepers, L. (2000) 'Targets as a tool in health policy: Part One, lessons learned', *Health Policy*, vol 53, no 1, pp 1-11.

Wales 2000 (1996) Issue 7, published with the *Western Mail*, July.

Wales Digital College (1998) *The University for Industry and Wales: A partnership challenge*, Cardiff: Wales Digital College.

Wales, C., Nadi, A. and Stazer, R. (1993) 'Emphasizing critical thinking and problem-solving', in L. Curry, J. Wergin and Associates (eds) *Educating professionals*, San Francisco, CA: Josey-Bass, pp 178-211.

Weil, S. (1986) 'Non-traditional learners within traditional higher education institutions: discovery and disappointment', *Studies in Higher Education*, vol 11, no 3, pp 219-35.

Wells, A. (2001) 'Basic skills 25 years on', *Adults Learning*, vol 12, no 10, pp 9-11.

Welsh Department (1937) *Education in Wales: Memorandum No 5. Report on adult education in Wales 1936*, Cardiff: Board of Education.

Welsh Office (1993) *National Targets: The way forward 1994/95*, Cardiff: Welsh Office.

Welsh Office (1995a) *1994/95 Welsh Training and Education Survey*, Cardiff: Welsh Office.

Welsh Office (1995b) *Statistics of education and training in Wales: Schools, No 2*, Cardiff: HMSO.

Welsh Office (1995c) *A bright future: The way forward*, Cardiff: HMSO.

Welsh Office (1996) *Digest of Welsh Local Area Statistics 1996*, Cardiff: HMSO.

Welsh Office (1997) *A bright future: Beating the previous best*, Cardiff: HMSO.

Welsh Office (1998) *Learning is for everyone*, London: The Stationery Office.

West Wales Training and Enterprise Council (1996) *West Wales Annual Labour Market Assessment 1995/96*, Swansea: West Wales TEC.

Whitfield, K. and Bourlakis, C. (1991) 'An empirical analysis of YTS, employment and earnings', *Journal of Economic Studies*, vol 18, no 1, pp 42-56.

Williams, J. (1983) 'The economic structure of Wales since 1850', in G. Williams (ed) *Crisis of economy and ideology. Essays on Welsh society 1840-1980*, BSA Sociology of Wales Study Group.

Yang, B. (1998) 'Longitudinal study of participation in adult education: a theoretical formulation and empirical investigation', *International Journal of Lifelong Learning*, vol 17, no 4, pp 247-59.

Yeomans, D. (1996) *Constructing vocational education: From TVEI to GNVQ*, Leeds: School of Education, University of Leeds.

Young, S. (1996) 'Disability and class still bar to success', *Times Educational Supplement*, 26 April, p 8.

Zhou, X., Moen, P. and Tuma, N. (1998) 'Educational stratification in urban China', *Sociology of Education*, no 71, pp 199-222.

Zukin, S. and DiMaggio, P. (eds) (1990) *Structures of capital: The social organization of the economy*, Cambridge: Cambridge University Press.

Appendix: The research sites

The complex patterns of social and economic change in industrial South Wales have not, of course, affected all localities within the region uniformly. The collapse of employment in the staple industries, for example, has impacted most severely on those parts of the region where those industries were formerly concentrated. New job opportunities have tended to develop away from the centres of industrial decline; for example, recent manufacturing investment has tended to focus on the M4 corridor, away from the coalfield itself. Accordingly, each local area in South Wales has a history of social and economic development that is specific to its characteristic location within the broader patterns of regional change. Moreover, this characteristic local history has important implications for the nature of local learning opportunities and how these are understood by residents.

In what follows, therefore, we provide outline accounts of the local patterns of development in three areas within South Wales, where we conducted our primary data collection for our principal empirical study. At one level, therefore, these accounts provide insights into the places where our research was mainly concentrated. At another, however, they illustrate the significance of local context for people's participation in adult education and training and the extent to which differentiation between localities is a key element in understanding people's learning biographies.

Bridgend

Bridgend was originally a market and agricultural town. It grew to service the iron and coal industries to the north in the 19th century, becoming a focal point for transport networks (Boddy et al, 1990). Work began on an ordnance factory here in 1938, which grew to employ 34,000 people, mostly women, at its peak during the war of 1939-45. Much of this factory has now been converted to Bridgend Industrial Estate, where over 75 firms operated by 1950, employing over 3,000 people. By 1967, this estate had extended to 200 acres.

At the same time, in the north part of the current travel-to-work-area, the coal industry declined as rapidly as it had grown. In the mid-1920s, there were 409 local collieries, employing 40,000 men; but by the 1970s there were only seven working collieries employing 6,000.

Its population, unlike the two other research sites, has increased since 1981, partly due to in-migration but mostly because of a relatively high birth rate coupled with a low death rate, the highest and lowest respectively in South Wales (Welsh Office, 1996). Bridgend is very unusual in this respect. It also shows a slight decrease in unemployment, which is reasonably common, coupled with a low rate of long-term unemployment that is not. Its workforce has a relatively high proportion of female and part-time employees. It is the site of several multinational companies and overseas investments, including Japanese firms such as Sony, and North American firms such as: Acco UK Ltd, Align-Rite Ltd, Biomet Ltd, Carters (J and A) Ltd, Ford Motor Co. Ltd, Harman-Motive Ltd, and Jamont UK Ltd ('Wales 2000', 1996). In fact, 5,200 people are employed in 17 overseas plants in the study area. These newer jobs have tended to be filled by women (Boddy et al, 1990).

The proportion of residents with qualifications beyond A level is relatively high for South Wales and rose from 7% in 1981 to 9% in 1991, with an average 14 A level points per candidate in 1995 (Welsh Office, 1996). In 1995, 37% of the relevant year groups gained five or more GCSEs grade C, but a relatively large 11% did not gain even one Certificate of Education or GCSE grade G.

The occupational profile of the area is also changing, with skilled manual jobs being replaced by associate professional ones. Only 5.4% of the population reported being able to speak, read or write any Welsh, perhaps because in one year alone 8% of the inhabitants has moved home, a quarter of them from outside the area.

The expanding town of Bridgend is represented in the fieldwork for this study by three electoral districts that have been chosen to represent the range of social, especially educational, conditions of the site. The populations of the three districts are similar, between 5,224 and 5,755 in 1991. In general, the district with the most highly qualified workforce also has the most stable population, but a larger number of residents who have moved from outside the region, and a larger proportion of residents from recent ethnic minority backgrounds. It has larger houses, less industry on site and the residents are in more professional occupations. The opposite conclusions can be drawn about the districts with the least qualified workforce, and these conclusions hold for all three research sites.

Coity Higher is a suburban district in south-central Bridgend, with some large semi-detached houses and a few shops. A clear majority of the residents are professionals or associate professionals and 34% of the workforce have a higher educational qualification such as degree or diploma. Coity is also the only district in which a substantial proportion of inhabitants moved there from outside the UK in the year preceding the census. The Newcastle district is based on a housing estate and has a mixture of modern and council owned property and older semi-detached houses. It is in central and west-central Bridgend. The most common occupational classification of residents is associate professional, but there are also a large number of skilled manual workers and nearly 28% are educated to degree level or equivalent. It has the lowest economic activity rate for both men and women of the three districts in the study. St Bride's Minor is in the north, on the outskirts of Bridgend town. It is therefore much less densely populated. The housing is a mixture of new developments and semi-rural. It has a high rate of economic activity, but also a high rate of male unemployment and only 11% of the workforce are educated to above A level standard.

Neath-Port Talbot

The new Unitary Authority of Neath-Port Talbot is centred on two neighbouring conurbations. Since it also includes the Lliw valley and surrounding areas, the overall population density is low. The population is not reproducing itself, dropping in the years 1981-92 (Welsh Office, 1996), partly due to out-migration from the area. The economic activity rates are low, even for South Wales. A high proportion of the jobs available are in manufacturing, with a low proportion of service jobs that are otherwise the most common form of employment in West Wales (West Wales TEC, 1996). Consequently, there is a low proportion of female and part-time employees in Neath-Port Talbot. It is also the area in our study with the highest proportion of Welsh language speakers, 10.6% able to speak, read or write some Welsh.

Neath-Port Talbot has fewer overseas investors than the other sites, relying until recently on nationalised industries. The North American firms locally tend to be smaller concerns than those in Bridgend: Borg Warner Automotive Ltd, Texturing Technology Ltd, and TRW Steering Systems Ltd ('Wales 2000', 1996). In all, 3,950 individuals are employed in 15 overseas plants.

The proportion of residents with qualifications above A level equivalent is low but rose slowly from 5% in 1981 to 6% in 1991, with 13 A level points per candidate. In 1995, 33% of the relevant year group gained five GCSEs grade C, while 9% gained no qualifications at all. In the Annual Labour Market Survey a particularly large number of firms in this site reported problems of literacy and numeracy among potential employees. It has the lowest proportion of students continuing to full-time education after 16 in the area, but in 1996 it had the largest numbers on Youth Training or training credits (West Wales TEC, 1996).

The town of Neath, unsuccessfully proposed as a site for a university in the 1850s (Eaton, 1987), has grown and shrunk dramatically this century. Its earliest industrial development was for the reduction of imported copper ores and later for lead. Iron, coal, tinplate, and oil-refining also played a part. The Metal Box Company settled locally in 1935 to use the tinplate, and the British Aluminium Company arrived in 1938. Its population grew from 14,000 in 1901 to 32,000 in 1951, but by 1971 it had fallen again to 29,000 (Jenkins, 1974). It continues to fall partly as a result of economic decline and partly as a result of structural changes in the form of clearance of the central town area. It has been the site of Neath Tertiary College since 1982.

The town of Port Talbot, a concentration of industry and population on a narrow strip of coastal plain (Port Talbot, 1996) has an even more uneven history. It grew from 1860 onwards due to industries such as tinplate works, the docks and also small tobacco producers, which replaced the more common cattle and sheep farming (Jones, 1991). As well as producing new development, Port Talbot became a magnet for industries inland from places like Cwmavon that were rebuilt at the dockside. It also drew the coal trade from Porthcawl, which has since become a seaside resort. However, some depression was caused by protectionist policies in the US at the turn of the century, and it is important not to overestimate the size of town at that stage. In 1901 fewer than 100 men worked in iron and steel, and fewer than 800 in tinplate, with perhaps the same again in mining. The population was only 7,552 which is only half that of Neath at the time. A boom came in the Great War when there was an increased demand for munitions, particularly from the 1901 Port Talbot and 1916 Margam Steelworks. The decline in demand and the depression after the war, despite having MacDonald, the local MP, as Prime Minister, led to the closing of the Steel Works in 1931 (opening again in 1934) as well as local collieries. There was 43% male unemployment, and all building stopped until another war created another surge in demand. By 1921 the population of the recently established borough combining Port Talbot, Margam, Sandfields and Cwmavon was 40,027. In 1952 the Steel Company of Wales, one of the first integrated steel works in Britain, opened on Margam Moors. By 1965 it employed 18,000 people and offered 30 apprenticeships per year (Fevre, 1989), but the local population was still only 52,000 that may be indicative of the draining effect of the depression. The docks ceased to export coal in 1962 and the old docks closed in 1971. A new Tidal Harbour exporting only iron and steel opened in 1970, which has the deepest berthing facility in the Bristol Channel, and is dedicated to the import of raw material for the steel works at Port Talbot and Llanwern. The building of the M4 motorway and the position of Port Talbot on the InterCity line between London and Swansea opened land communications. It briefly became so prosperous that the steelworks became renowned as 'Treasure Island' (Jones, 1991). BP Chemicals opened a plant there in 1963, and the Steel Company of Wales was nationalised and then privatised again. Its employees then fell from 18,000 to 4,000 and Treasure Island became 'Giro City' (Fevre, 1989).

The three electoral districts chosen to encapsulate the range of social conditions in the established manufacturing site of Neath-Port Talbot are not as close in population size as in the other two sites. The largest district had 6,975 residents and the smallest had 4,455 in 1991, and as with the other sites, there are slightly more women than men. Cimla is a relatively leafy suburb of the town of Neath with large semi-detached houses and off-street parking. The population is relatively stable, showing few house moves from 1990 to 1991, with a high rate of economic activity, especially for women. The population is relatively well-educated for this site, with 19% of the workforce educated beyond A level and a high proportion of non-manual and professional occupations. Unemployment is low. Bryn and Cwmavon are two separate communities in a valley to the north outside Port Talbot. They are effectively large villages on hillsides and the valley floor with a range of styles and age of housing, acting as residential commuter areas for Port Talbot. Sixteen per cent of the workforce have higher educational qualifications, most being in skilled or associate professional occupations.

Sandfields West is a large council housing estate on the sand dunes by Aberafan Beach, very close to the industry in Port Talbot. Originally designed for the workforce of the local steelworks, it has very few shops and little variety of housing. Developed from prefabricated housing placed there during

1939-45, it is an 'instant community' with a slightly forlorn air. The population is relatively stable, as assessed by moves between 1990-91. Very few of the residents are of recent minority ethnic origin. They have a low rate of economic activity, and only 5% of the workforce have qualifications beyond A level. Most of those in work have manual or unskilled occupations. There is high male unemployment, and a significant number of the residents are on government schemes.

Blaenau Gwent

The new Unitary Authority of Blaenau Gwent is the smallest of our three sites, based on two valleys running north of Newport, 'where the valleys meet the mountains of Gwent'. It is the site of the proposed first new urban village in Wales, at Victoria where the Festival of Wales was held (Blaenau Gwent, 1996). It has a low birth rate and high population death rate, one of the lowest and highest respectively in South Wales (Welsh Office, 1996). The population is therefore falling heavily, and the situation is not helped by the out-migration of many young people. It is still the most densely populated of the three sites, but has the fewest roads. Three of the electoral wards — Nantyglo, Tredegar and Cwm — are among the most highly deprived in Wales (Gwent TEC, 1997). The area has very low civilian activity rates, especially for women, and long-term unemployment is high.

Although it does have some overseas investment, including Japanese, German and US in an industrial base of over 260 companies of whom 75% are new to the area (Blaenau Gwent, 1996), this is concentrated in Ebbw Vale town, with all of the local North American companies located there: Aeromotive UK Ltd, ITT Automotive UK Ltd, and Sears Manufacturing Company Europe ('Wales 2000', 1996). These companies are generally in industrial estates and business parks.

Blaenau Gwent has a poor record in terms of educational outcomes at all levels (Welsh Office, 1996), and although the proportion of the population qualified beyond A level rose from 4% in 1981 to 5% in 1991, 5% is still one of the lowest in Wales, with an average 12 A level points per candidate. 28.5% of the relevant year group gained five GCSEs grade C. The population is uniform with very few Welsh language speakers (1.2% can speak, read or write some Welsh), and almost no residents of recent minority ethnic origin. Seven per cent of residents had a different address in 1990-91, of whom less than 2% moved from outside the district.

The three electoral divisions chosen to encapsulate the variety of social and educational conditions in the depressed coalfield site of Blaenau Gwent are somewhat varied in size, ranging from Llanhilleth with a population of 5,372 to Cwm with 3,760. Beaufort is in the north of the authority, almost outside the valleys and near the heads of the valleys road just south of the Brecon Beacons and Black Mountains. It is rural in nature with scattered housing and small villages with the addition of recent industrial and business parks. While most of the occupations in Beaufort are classified as manual, just as they are in all of Blaenau Gwent, few of these jobs are unskilled or even part-skilled. In addition, Beaufort has many more professionals than the other two districts and 7% of those economically active are educated to degree level. Even so, only 50% of the adult population is in a full-time job.

Cwm is directly in the middle of the valley, a traditional mining village with one long terraced street on the floor of the valley. Of those economically active, 4% are educated to degree level. Cwm has the lowest unemployment of the three districts, and most of those employed are in manual occupations. Llanhilleth is another mining village, near the Newport end of the valley, with more varied housing than Cwm, spread in tiers up the side of the valley. Of those economically active, 1% are educated to degree level, the lowest figure of all nine districts taking part in the survey. The district has a low rate of economic activity, and most of those in jobs have occupations that are manual, many of them unskilled or part-skilled. In all three districts the major industrial classification for woman's jobs is 'other services', for men it is still mining-related in Cwm and Beaufort, but metal-related in Llanhilleth.

Index